AF560023

TEACHING METHODS AND CHILD DEVELOPMENT

TEACHING METHODS AND CHILD DEVELOPMENT

SURESH DUTT

ANMOL PUBLICATIONS PVT. LTD.
NEW DELHI - 110 002 (INDIA)

ANMOL PUBLICATIONS PVT. LTD.
4374/4B, Ansari Road, Daryaganj
New Delhi - 110 002
Ph.: 23261597, 23278000
Visit us at: www.anmolpublications.com

Teaching Methods and Child Development

ISBN 81-7488-784-9

PRINTED IN INDIA

Published by J.L. Kumar for Anmol Publications Pvt. Ltd., New Delhi - 110 002 and Printed at Mehra Offset Press, Delhi.

Contents

Preface

Wordsworthian saying 'Child is the father of man' will ever remain relevant. Making of a nation depends on the sound development of children. For formation of civilized, cultured and happy society, we have to educate and train our children properly. As such 'Child Psychology' is the basis which is to be thoroughly researched and understood.

Amidst plenty of literature available on child psychology, the present work is unique which embodies latest research and developments in the field.

Volumewise organization of the work is: The Child and Personality Development; Moral Values in Child Development; Understanding Children; Behaviour Modification and Child Development; Teacher and the Child Development; Experiments in Teaching for Child Development; Curriculum and Child Development; and Teaching Methods and Child Development.

This encyclopaedia will prove a veritable mine of information for students, researchers, academics in the field of psychology and education. Besides this, administrators, policy planners, psychologists, and psychiatrists will also find this most useful and informative.

S. D.

1

Teachers Need for Psychology

What is a teacher's most important qualification? A sound answer is that there are numerous qualifications that a person must have to be an effective teacher; it is useless to ask that any one of them be defined as the all-important one. To asset that one qualification is more needed by teachers than any other is no more logical than to insist that the foundation of a house is more important than the walls or the floors. A house, to be any kind of a house, has them all—and other important parts, too.

But, to follow the analogy a step further, there can be no argument about the essential function that a firm foundation serves—whether it be houses or the abilities of teachers we are talking about. Among the qualifications that may be considered foundational is the teacher's understanding of the behavior of children and youth and the way in which their behavior is related to their growth, development, and learning. When a teacher has real depth of understanding of human behavior and development, the sound instructional methods he has learned will more effectively be put to use. Then, also, his counseling of pupils will have a good chance of being helpful. In his many informal relationships with boys and girls he will then be much more likely to say and do the things that develop their self-respect and self-confidence and that instill in them a *love of learning.*

PSYCHOLOGY'S RELATION TO THE UNDERSTANDING OF HUMAN BEHAVIOR AND DEVELOPMENT

How does a teacher acquire an understanding of human behavior and development? The answer is not simple. Certainly some people have had the kinds of experiences with boys and girls that lead to a liking for youngsters. This is unquestionably an important prerequisite to the development of perceptiveness into the meanings of what they do and what they say.

Then, too, some persons are of such a disposition that they interrelate well with other people—especially with younger individuals. Their own personality traits invite freedom of response—self-revealing responses—on the part of those with whom they associate.

Desirable and important as such traits are they will be greatly strengthened when the teacher combines with them a sound, functioning knowledge of the forces that work within and upon a human being—that direct and shape his pattern of behavior. Such is the kind of knowledge that this book is about.

The purpose behind the writing of this book is to present the concepts and principles that psychology and other closely related sciences have to offer as tools for the deepening and organizing of our understanding of human behavior in general and of human individuals in particular. The purpose—stated a bit differently—is to relate psychology to *teaching* and especially to the very important matter of the teacher's need for insight into the behavior of children and youth.

There is a central theme that runs throughout this book. It is that *persons* are a chief concern of teachers and that helping them to understand themselves and to live well with themselves and others is an important prerequisite to the maturing of the potentialities that are in them. Basically this is a book in psychology. More particularly, it is a book in the psychology of human growth and development.

But what is psychology? That is, what actually is its subject matter? Also, just where, in the total domain of psychology, should we expect to locate this present kind of study? It seems altogether proper to try to clarify our thinking in these regards as a first step in getting under way with the topics of this book.

PSYCHOLOGY DEFINED AS THE STUDY OF BEHAVIOR

Psychology has frequently and correctly been defined as the study of behavior. One writer comments that the psychologist "takes it for granted…that you know he is talking about human and animal behavior, not the behavior of stars or machines or atoms." He then adds, "The person Entrained in psychology is usually surprised at the word 'behavior'" and surmises that instead of 'behavior' most persons would expect 'mind' or 'thought' or 'feeling' to be specified as the subject matter of psychology. (Morgan, 1956)

Morgan, who was just quoted, states in support of his definition that it *is* behavior which we observe when we set out to study another person. "We know very well," he says, "that there are events going on within a person—events that can be called 'thoughts,' 'feelings,' or more generally, 'mental abilities.' We can and do make them from the fairly trustworthy inferences about those events, but we always make them from the way a person behaves. It is what he says, does, and writes that we as scientists can observe and record. Hence it is only behavior that we can study."

This emphasis on behavior should remove one misconception about the subject matter of psychology. It is the notion that psychology is a body of abstract laws and principles which have little if any connection with a student's immediate and personal interest in people and what they do. Psychology is not about data and principles and laws as ends in themselves. Psychology *does* make use of carefully gathered data and the principles that these data suggest, but the significance of the data and principles is in the light they throw on behavior. The student who keeps this explanation in mind as he proceeds with the study of psychology may avoid needless experiences of "losing sight of the forest because of the trees."

A world about what is not meant by behavior, as here used, may be helpful. It is not to be equated with what sometimes is meant by 'good' or 'bad' conduct, or behaving in a conforming or nonconforming way. These are, for psychology, *instances* of behavior. They are by no means the whole of behavior or the whole of what psychology is about. This explanation is made in the present context because occasionally someone in this manner restricts the meaning of 'behavior', with the result that he and others have quite different ideas about what they are trying to discuss.

There is probably no term that could be used to describe the subject matter of psychology that would be wholly free from objections, and this goes for the word 'behavior.' But the term does have the merit of designating something to which we have access, namely, the responses that individuals make. When one tries to understand another person, he will be likely to make some headway only if he is thoughtfully attentive to the things that the person says and does and deliberately lets actions 'speak' for themselves.

We have defined one of the terms that make up the title of this book, namely, psychology. Now we may examine three other terms. While is the meaning of the terms 'growth' and 'development'? And what special significance is there in the use of the word 'human' in the title of the book?

MEANING OF HUMAN GROWTH AND DEVELOPMENT

First, let us see how the world *human* fits into our discussion. There is a reason for using 'human' in the discussions that follow, instead of 'child' or 'adolescent'. The authors wish to take into account as far as possible in this book the entire school-age span of years, plus considerable preschool and even prenatal 'biography'. And they feel also that much of what the various chapters contain will be applicable to behavior beyond the usual school-age years. Especially are they interested in emphasizing that behavior and development are continuous and that no individual can be thought about advantageously without clear regard for the relationship between present and past experience—and even future experience.

In passing it may be noted that the word 'human' suggests what has earlier been indicated: that our interest is in the behavior of man rather than that of the lower animals. This is substantially correct, simply because we believe that it is the behavior of persons that teachers most need to understand; we should, therefore, try to build our concepts around that point of reference.

It would, nevertheless, be an unfortunate thing if we were to fail to recognise the very important role that studies of lower animals have in solving the problems of psychology. Much that we understand about man's behavior is the result of the laboratory findings with the not always so lowly white rate or the chimpanzee or some other experimental subject, more manageable than man. These kinds of studies constitute what is called comparative psychology.

Growth and Development

Many of the problems studied in psychology relate closely to the facts about growth and development. Indeed, it is difficult to investigate, interpret, and explain human behavior without viewing it in the context of growth and development—without considering it as something emergent, dynamic, and changing. There is always, in the experience of the individual whose behavior we want to understand, an inescapable reference to changes taking place in him, some of which he ties deliberately to bring about and some of which occur as part of an unfolding natural plan.

The very existence of an organism depends upon change. Old cells are constantly being replaced by new cells; tissues grow and become strengthened as the organism exercises them to meet the increasing demands of life; the fluids of the body and their important constituents are continuously replenished: these and other changes are necessary to an organism's survival.

Development is more than Change. An individual may be considered changed when, for example, he loses a finger or has a few front teeth extracted and replaced by some the dentist supplies. But no matter how extensive the changes in a person may be they do not necessarily add up to development. Development means a progressive sequence of changes in the organism—a sequence characterized by orderliness and coherent design.

There is still more to development. An adequate description of the development of an organism emphasizes the *close relationship between changes in structure and changes in function:* The important corollary to the fact that a young robin is growing feathers on its wings is the increasing imminence of the little creature's first flight. Flight is the function of wings. The corollary to the human baby's cumulative strength and length of feet and legs—as well as his improving coordination—is his gradual approach to a level of function that legs serve, namely walking.

Thus it is with every aspect of an organism's structural growth: emergence of related functions is the natural counterpart. And there is another side to the coin. Just as increase in growth is accompanied by new and improved functions, so also, conversely, is decline in growth accompanied by decline in functions.

A definite feature of development is, therefore, the orderly unfolding of the increasingly complex systems of the organism. Growth processes are not capricious; they are lawful and the more we learn about them the more predictable they reveal themselves to be. This is the fact that gives incentive and hope to the researcher's study of the various aspects of human growth and development. And it is the fact that underscores the importance of a close working relationship between those who teach and those who apply their efforts to scientific investigation of growth, development, and behavior.

The term 'development' has now been defined. But what does 'growth' mean? Does growth have a meaning different from development, or are the two synonymous and quite properly to be used interchangeably? The answer: growth and development do mean different things.

Growth is the gradual increase in magnitude of a living thing or any of its parts; or an increase in the magnitude or scope of something the organism does. The emphasis in this definition is on *increase in magnitude:* Examples of growth are an individual's increase in height or weight; the lengthening of his bodily extremities; the *enlargement* of the organs of his body; the gains (*i.e. growth*) made by him in vocabulary or in arithmetic—these latter representing functions.

Development is more comprehensive than growth. As we consider what was said about development, we may conclude—and correctly so—that development includes growth.

Again, let us make explicit a point that belongs to the central theme of this book. It is that for the teacher these kinds of knowledge (about growth and development) are essential because he must not only know as much as he can about the varying needs of the individual that accompany growth changes but also about *the impact these changes have on the individual's concept of himself.*

AREAS OF STUDY IN PSYCHOLOGY

Psychology has already been defined in this chapter as a study of behavior. This statement may be amplified to the student's advantage by some discussion of the kinds of behavioral phenomena that are studied in psychology.

Often what a person sees as he examines the chapter titles of psychology books are certain key words, such as perception, motivation, emotion, learning, intelligence, and personality.

These words are the names of behavioral phenomena about which psychology has much to teach but about which there is still a great deal that has eluded the best efforts of researchers. Frequently when the psychologist uses these key terms, he is designating what to him are psychological *problems* or problem areas—his explanations do not fully cover all the facts that pertain to the phenomena.

Let us now take a brief bird's-eye view of some of the problems and related topics that are of vital concern to psychology. Certain of these will be dealt with at chapter length later in this book.

Heredity

How much of what one sees in behavior is attributable to gene-controlled inheritance? When and how does heredity begin to collaborate with environment—with the physical-social surroundings of the individual? To what extent does biological inheritance set limits on human growth and development that are not to be transcended by virtue of the kinds of *nurturing* the individual gets?

Such are the kinds of questions for which psychologists as well as biologists have been trying for years to get satisfactory answers. Evidence will be presented in numerous later discussions indicating the extent to which research has given the answers to questions about heredity.

Perception: One's Observation of One's World and One's Self

Every individual has his own special view of his world and himself. When we consider to what extent that which a person does is dependent upon "the way he sees things," we can appreciate the importance that psychologists attach to perception. Does each person have sensations of a given situation that are the same as those of another person? Or does each individual have a

the relation of both to the make-up of different societies. There are, then, the questions of how the agencies of society (the family, the school, and the peer groups, for example) influence and help shape the behavior pattern (shall we say the "life style") of the individual.

Growth-related Tasks. Individuals *work at* their experiences, especially at the business of growing up—something which does not end with one's twenty-first birthday. There is the aspect of task and everlasting challenge in much of the sweep of one's living with parents, peers, and other people. There is the very real task of learning to live with one's own body and all else that makes up one's own person. There is the element of task in learning to communicate satisfactorily with other persons. Learning the role of male or female has its task implications; so does choosing a mate, and determining one's choice of life work. And, perhaps above all else, there is the 'necessity' of growing into the sort of person that is suggested, sometimes faintly, sometimes more clearly, at each step of one's experience.

These are some of the concerns of psychologists and teachers. They are matters that in one form or another we all think about and talk about. Psychologists try systematically to investigate them and to give some consistency to the explanation of them.

There is also another approach to the understanding of what psychology is. That is to examine the applications that are made of psychology to practical work with people.

APPLICATIONS OF PSYCHOLOGY

Psychology is put to work in many places. Business, industry, government, the military agencies: these and many others make use of the methods and knowledge of psychology. But for the purposes of this book, it would seem desirable to give attention largely to the applications of psychology in situations more or less closely related to the school.

Psychological Diagnosis and Therapy

One thing that many psychologists do is to furnish consultation services. This may be done in any one of several different ways. Clinical psychologists, for example, work with persons whose behavior deviates from normal. They are not to be confused with psychiatrists, who are medically trained and medically licensed. Clinical psychologists must be well informed about the conditions that motivate behavior and those that 'structure' personality. They must be skilled in the use of methods of analyzing human traits and, especially, in the circumstances that lead to malconditions of personality. They must be expertly trained in methods of counseling clients in order that their interpretations may help the latter to better mental health. Here, in the work of clinical psychologists, we see the application of psychology to the important task of repairing personalities that have been damaged. Increasingly the knowledge that has proved its worth in this connection is being put to use in the *prevention* of personality disorders. This is an especially important development as it pertains to the beginnings of emotional disturbances in children.

Applications to work with Exceptional Children

Many children as well as adults have physical handicaps, mental handicaps, or both. Some of the work of school psychologists is with the problems of handicapped youngsters. School psychologists have played leading roles in the development of methods for determining the learning potentialities of children who are blind, deaf, mentally retarded, or suffering from cerebral palsy or other handicaps. And psychologists, through extensive researches on the learning and adjustment problems of handicapped children, have provided the knowledge for extensive improvements in instructional methods and materials for their schooling. Today, thanks to effective use of these kinds of knowledge, there are thousands of handicapped boys and girls who are learning in school how to become useful, happy citizens rather than unhappy burdens on their relatives and society in general.

The Gifted. The foregoing paragraph relates the work of psychologists to the study of handicapped children and the improvement of their lot in life. There is another category of exceptional children and youth whose education and guidance has been greatly influenced in recent years by the work of psychologists: those who are unusually gifted in their learning aptitudes and talents. We as citizens of a great nation have taken much pride in our virtually unlimited natural resources, but we have been tardy in the recognition that the greatest resource of all is the talents of our youth. Psychology has been of inestimable value in the discovery and development of these talents.

Psychology has, for one thing, raised basic questions about the nature of giftedness and has—particularly during the past thirty years in this country—corrected numerous erroneous ideas to the effect that the very bright and the gifted were likely in other respects to be queer or below average in development. The reader will find in Chapter 10 some of the evidence of the contributions of psychology to better understanding of superior intelligence.

Psychology has also provided the methods to locate and study giftedness. The development of tests of mental ability opened the way to the identification of individuals of high academic promise; development and standardization of numerous other tests has greatly improved the chances of early discovery of a wide variety of special abilities and talents.

In addition—as in the case of handicapped children—psychologists have worked closely with school administrators and teachers in planning better educational programs for the gifted. They have also provided expert help in arranging experiments and other studies to prove the values of this or that kind of educational program for the gifted.

Alliance with Instruction and Guidance for all Children

Not all children with whom psychologists work are either handicapped or unusually gifted. As a matter of fact, the largest share of the services of psychologists is devoted directly or indirectly to normal children and youth.

Most students—not just those in the categories mentioned above—have taken tests of learning ability ("I.Q." tests they are called by the man on the street), and perhaps they have also had the benefit of various measurements of their specialized abilities and interests and accompanying interviews with consultants trained in counseling psychology.

As a consequence of these tests and conferences their programs of schooling were tailored more closely to their abilities and interests; perhaps also they were helped to get a clearer view of their vocational objectives.

Even more extensively, psychology reaches into the school and college classrooms where learning, in all its many aspects, takes place. Researches by educational psychologists, which have included carefully controlled experiments on various aspects of learning and personal development, have supplied many valuable suggestions for curricular and instructional improvement.

Closely allied with the nation's teaching force are more than seven hundred school psychologists, approximately five hundred educational psychologists, nearly a thousand counseling and guidance psychologists, and over six hundred developmental psychologists. These are accredited psychologists.

Many other men and women who are not known primarily as psychologists but who have extensive training in psychology perform roles which overlap with those of the psychologists and result, through collaboration of effort, in the penetration of psychology into almost every activity of the school or college.

OBJECTIVES OF PSYCHOLOGY FOR TEACHERS

The preceding discussion provides the basis for examining the objectives to be attained by the prospective teacher through the study of psychology.

In a monograph entitled *Educational Psychology in Teacher Education,* Rivlin has listed five of these objectives. The present writers believe that Rivlin's statement serves as an exceptionally useful body of criteria by which the prospective teacher may judge his progress in the study of psychology.

1. Educational psychology should develop the student's interest in people, both children and adults, and help him to understand them. The student "should learn why people behave as they do" and how their behavior patterns may be modified. He should try to improve his insight into his own adjustment. He should not only like children but through his increased knowledge of growth and development he should gain increasing respect for them as individuals.

2. Educational psychology should have a favorable effect on the attitudes, behavior, and psychological understanding of students in both personal and professional relationships. This means, for one thing, that educational psychology should develop in the student "a point of view that sees pupils as personalities as well as learners, that regards educational procedures and values as susceptible of objective study and evaluation, and that interprets teaching as being more than a bag of tricks." As the prospective teacher studies the basic patterns and the individual variations of human growth he should become aware of the unique world of each individual child and be "better able to determine the kind of educational environment needed for optimum development of the children with whom he will be in daily contact."

3. Educational psychology should help the prospective teacher to make use of the body of knowledge that it

derived from research studies in this field. The student, in gaining this objective, will come to understand "the fundamental facts about human growth and development, learning, personality and adjustment, measurement, and evaluation, and the techniques and methods of educational psychology." Lest these facts remain abstract bits of information it is important that the student gain an understanding of the principles and the theories which make the facts explicable.

4. Increased ability to learn is the fourth objective set forth for the student of educational psychology. The principles that relate to the improvement of learning can be studied advantageously by the student as he applies them to himself as well as to pupils with whom he may work.

   One aspect of this objective is the development on the part of the student of the habit of reading professional books and articles in the field. Rivlin emphasizes the far-reaching importance of the student's acquisition of self-direction in his study.

   This is something which the student should get from all his school and college work, but something which in any case it would be most incongruous for him not to acquire from a course in educational psychology.

5. Finally, there is the objective of appreciation and understanding of research in education. The point is made that "teachers cannot be satisfied to have educational questions decided merely by debate or emotional appeal."

   While not many teachers will ever assume major responsibility for the planning of researches and the direction of them, increasingly they are becoming participants in important experiments and investigations, and in all cases they have the right and the obligation to become, as Rivlin says, "intelligent consumers of educational research." (Rivlin, 1953)

THE NEXT STEP

We have now examined the meaning and something of the scope of psychology. We have noted the debt that teaching owes to psychology and especially to developmental psychology. And we have found a central theme which we can expect to help us achieve a sense of direction and clear purpose as we proceed to other chapters. The theme, reiterated, is that *persons* are a major concern of teachers; that helping them to understand themselves and to grow in their abilities to get along well with themselves and others is basic to their attainment of a mature personality.

Let us now sample some basic ideas concerning the study of human behavior and development as our next step? The authors suggest that as we do this, we think of the next chapter as essentially an extension of the present one.

2

Modes of Learning

The great amount of academic learning required of individuals living in modern, civilized societies has already been suggested. To accomplish their learning goals, Americans devote 20 to 30 per cent of their lifetimes to full–time education, and many of them continue throughout their lives to spend part of their time in further study. All this effort, however, appears to fall short of satisfying our need for knowledge and skill. Each of us is reminded almost daily that he could function more effectively and with greater joy in his work, recreation, and social activities if he knew more or had more skill. In addition to our individually sensed need for more personal effectiveness, we have, as a nation, become acutely aware of our need for more and better–trained personnel in many strategically important occupations. Indeed, it has been said that one of the ten top scientific events of the last year was the awakening in America of "the necessity of better and more widespread training of scientists." The question is: How can we meet these needs more fully?

There are several approaches to our goal of achieving greater knowledge and skill. One way is to improve the efficiency of our learning efforts. This approach, fortunately, has been a major concern of the science of educational psychology for the past half century.

The importance of the work which educational psychologists have done was amply demonstrated during the emergency period of World War II. When the war came, America suddenly found herself without adequate preparation. The situation required the rapid training of tremendous numbers of men and women for new military and civilian–defense occupations. In accomplishing this great task, psychologists contributed very significantly. On the basis of a survey of their activities, Wolfe says that "the important stock in trade of the psychologist working on military training problems consisted of his knowledge of the principles of learning. The judicious application of these principles helped speed the training of a victorious army and navy."

There is still, of course, much to be learned about how to learn efficiently, but a comprehensive survey of this area of educational psychology yields many practical suggestions—many more, in fact, than most teachers usually apply.

As will be recalled from our discussion in previous Chapter, the teacher has a twofold goal in applying the principles of learning: guiding pupils in their mastery of specific concepts and skills; and teaching them *how* to learn and to solve problems efficiently. Without effective teacher guidance in learning how to learn after the early grades, students do not make significant improvement in study skills from all their practice in studying. With appropriate teacher guidance, however, students who are learning the concepts and skills of any subject–matter area may acquire more effective learning methods also.

In testing this assumption, Leggitt studied the effects of teacher–guided practice in the application of certain study skills, in reading, interpretation of graphs and tables, summarizing, and outlining. During an 18–week semester of a course in American government, 42 pairs of ninth grade students served as experimental and control groups. The effectiveness of teacher guidance is indicated in Figure 2.1. As the graph shows, the group given guided practice improved steadily in study skills. The nonguided group made no appreciable improvement.

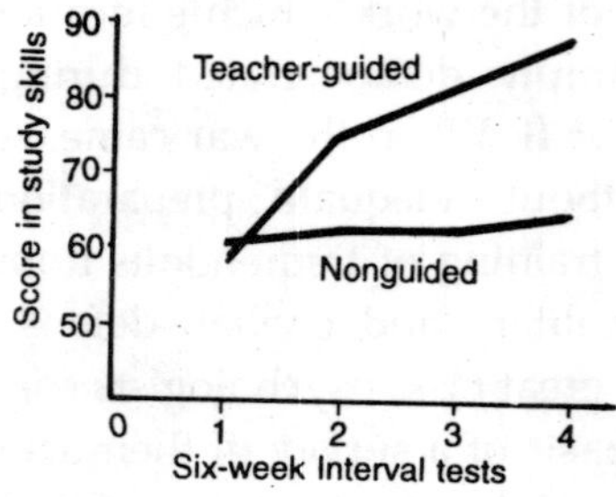

__Figure 2.1__ Teacher Guidance in Study Skills Results in Improvement as ninth grade students study American government. (Adapted from Dorothy Leggitt, Sch. Rev., 1934, Vol. 42, p. 684.)

Whether the general teaching procedure is systematic teacher direction or teacher guidance of pupils' self–discovery learning, good teachers in every subject try to facilitate effective mastery of specific concepts and skills and at the same time try to guide pupils in becoming more efficient learners. An understanding of the following general principles of efficient learning and appropriate application of them should aid teachers in accomplishing these goals.

ACTIVE "SELF–RECITING" LEARNING

Effective learning is not a process of absorption, of passive reception of impressions—it is more a process of active striving and searching, of creative construction of integrated response patterns to meet problem situations. Gates first demonstrated this principle in an historically important experiment on memorizing, the general results of which have been confirmed in several areas of learning. As they memorized short biographies, different groups of children from grades 3 to 8 were directed to use self–recitation for different proportions of the total time allotted. One group spent the entire practice period reading and rereading a biography. Five other comparable groups spent, respectively, the last 20, 40, 60, 80, and 90 per cent of the time in self–recitation—that is, in actively trying to recite a selection without reading from the copy, but glancing at it only when necessary to prompt themselves. The relative effectiveness of each amount of self–recitation is shown in Figure 2.2. The number of ideas recalled for each condition is expressed as a percentage of the average number recalled for all conditions.

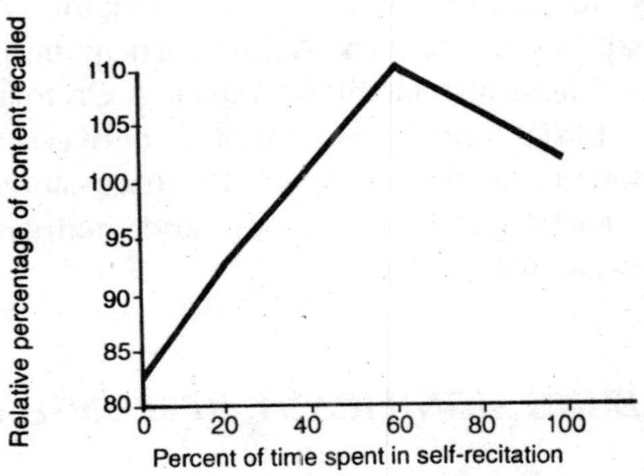

Figure 2.2 *Self-recitation Facilitates Memorizing. (Adapted fromA.I. Gates, Arch. Psychol., 1917, vol. 6, no. 40, p.41.)*

As the figure reveals, spending any proportion of the study time in active self–recitation is superior to devoting all of it to passive reading and rereading. The appropriate proportion of time to spend in self–recitation will, of course, vary with the nature of the content and the mode of attack employed in reading it. For Gates's particular selections, the optimum proportion proved to be about 60 per cent. For longer passages, greater proportions of time will probably be required for reading [55]. It is possible (and desirable) to use the equivalent of self–recitation in the reading itself. If the student employs a question–raising and self–answering mode of attack in studying science, social studies, or literature, little extra time as such may be needed for self–recitation.

Active self–recitation is a general principle of efficient learning. Forlano has reported that self–reciting methods improve efficiency of learning spelling, English vocabulary, and arithmetic combinations. In teaching handwriting, Hertzberg found that a copying method, which required the equivalent of active self–recitation, produced 40 per cent greater gains than did any of four different tracing methods which demanded of the children little or no initiative or active conceptualization of the task [30]. Several studies show that such applications of the principle of self–recitation as outlining, summarizing, and reading to answer questions improve understanding and retention of prose content in social studies and science. Active participation in class discussions of problems also facilitates learning. On this factor, Carpenter and Fort found correlations between frequency of pupil–volunteered contributions to discussions and achievement—in social studies, English, and mathematics—ranging from. 43 to .84, for grades 4 to 11.

VISUALIZING SIGNIFICANT, RESPONSE–GUIDING CUES

Self–constructed mental maps or conceptualized schema guide the learner in executing anticipated action patterns. According to cognitive learning theory, the more readily the individual can identify the response–guiding cues, the more quickly he should be able to learn appropriate responses to them. Two experiments indicate that children are able to solve experimentally contrived discrimination problems more effectively when the guiding cues are presented distinctly than when they are either embedded in a total configuration or require discrimination between remembered cues.

Outlines, diagrams, pictures, and motion–picture films are some of the media employed by teachers for making relevant features of problem situations more identifiable. As an illustration of these procedures, both Hall and Erickson have suggested that teachers use chalk of different colors to identify more sharply the significant features of problem–solving demonstrations. And Hanna has indicated that a graphical analysis—which brings out the relevant components of a problem—is superior to a verbal analysis, for teaching fourth and seventh grade pupils arithmetic problem solving. His "graphical dependencies" method is illustrated by a diagrammed representation of the problem: "Sam had 12 marbles. He found 3 more and then gave 6 to George. How many did Sam have left?

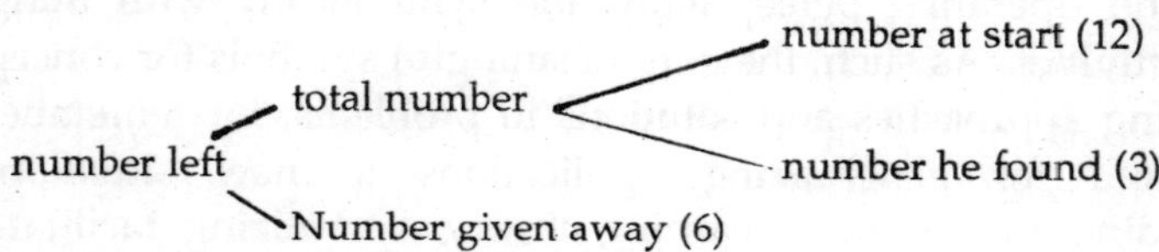

When a complex, sequential pattern of action is to learned, slow–motion films are often helpful in identifying the significant features of the response to be imitated. For example, when films demonstrating engine–lathe operation were carefully integrated with other modes of instruction on this process, adults given this supplementary visual guidance mastered the skill rather quickly. Other adults, whose instruction was confined to the "conventional lecture–demonstration method," required more time [70]. In teaching 13 equated pairs of tenth grade boys the high jump, Priebe and Burton compared the results of giving explanations and demonstrations only with the results obtained from using these same procedures *plus* slow–motion films of the performances of champion jumpers and of the boys themselves—as they progressed in acquisition of the skill. Good form, defects, and specific coordinations were visualized and analyzed in slow motion and sometimes in stopped frames. In order to maximize their usefulness, the films were run, discussed, and then rerun. Over a six–week period, weekly tests revealed superior progress for the group whose instruction was supplemented by the films.

VERBAL CONCEPTUALIZING AND GENERALIZING

In the experiments described above, the films themselves were accompanied by verbal explanations. Such explanations often enhance the effectiveness of demonstrations. For example, Thompson found that demonstration *plus* teacher–guided verbalization of the steps in assembling a mechanical puzzle reduced the number of trials required for mastering it to half the number required when silent demonstrations only were employed [66]. Words are the human being's most useful tool for designating, discriminating, differentiating, classifying, organizing, generalizing, and operating perceptually and symbolically with things and activities. As such, they are meaningful symbols for conceptualizing approaches and solutions to problems, for remembering, and for generalizing applications to new situations. According to cognitive learning theory, verbalizing facilitates learning because words are effective tools in the cognitive map making which guides performance.

Words in Motor Learning: The caller for square dancing is not superfluous: his rhythmic verbalizations guide the dancers through the intricate patterns of the dance. Several experiments indicate that both self-guided verbalizations facilitate discovering and memorizing solutions to perceptual motor problems. Both Warden and Husband directed blindfolded students learn multiple-U high-relief finger mazes, such as the one diagrammed. Upon reaching the criterion of mastery—3 out of 4 trials without error—each subject was asked about his method. The procedure most frequently employed was to verbalize the discovered pattern as a guide to memorizing it, that is, to say to oneself, "Two turns right, two left, one right," and so on. Some subjects, however, constructed visual images of the unseen pattern. Still others said they developed motor-kinesthetic "feelings" for the pattern. In both studies, verbalizing the pattern proved to be the best approach—it required fewer trials and less time to master the mazes than either of the other two procedures. Moreover, when the students in Warden's study were asked to draw the maze as they

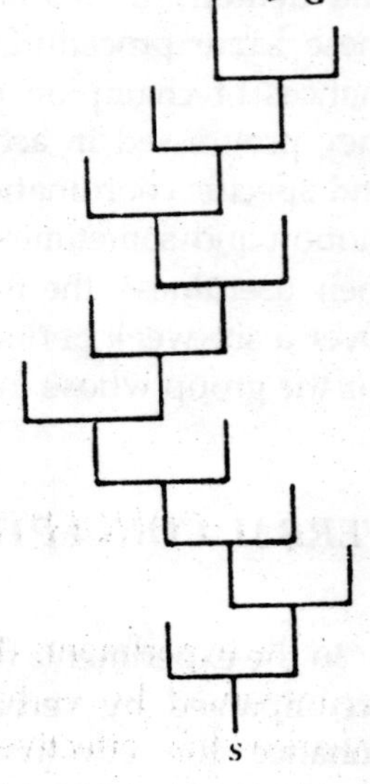

had imaginatively constructed it, the verbalizers were much the most accurate. Apparently, verbalizing a task aids students in creating a more accurate cognitive guide for learning it. Teacher direction to verbalize such procedures is also effective. The general suggestion to "verbalize what [you are] thinking and doing" aided fourth grade pupils in mastering a complicated design problem which required them to arrange the several parts of a design in layers in a particular order. More explicit verbal instructions to college students on how to learn a maze and how to solve a disk–transfer problem also facilitated mastery.

Labeling in Remembering: Two investigations indicate that naming objects they see helps children to remember them and to deal with them more effectively in problem situations. In one experiment, Pyles hid a toy always under the same one of five different nonsense–shaped molds (randomly arranged in each different trial), and directed comparable groups of two to seven–year–old children to discover and remember in subsequent trials which mold the toy was hidden under. Using counterbalanced orders of groups and conditions to control possible differential practice effects, she varied the extent and kind of verbalization. For condition A, the children were told: "One of these shapes has a toy under it; see if you can find the shape which has the toy." For condition B, the directions were the same, except that when the toy was found, the mold was given an unfamiliar name, such as *Mobie*, and the children were directed to repeat the name. (The names of the other molds were *Kolo, Tito, Gamie, Bokie:*) For condition C, the directions were similar to those for B, except that the identifying words were already familiar (*cat, dog, rabbit, bear, monkey*). For conditions B and C, in which the objects to be discriminated were named, fewer trials were required to reach the criterion of mastery—four successive correct choices—than for condition A where labeling was not employed. In their experiment, Kurtz and Hovland found that when a group of elementary school children both encircled *and* read aloud the names of 16 familiar objects, they remembered more of them a week later than did a comparable group who had merely encircled them.

Words Mediate Generalizations. Most of the studies already reviewed could be interpreted to indicate that verbalizing facilitates learning either by designating sharper discriminations or by mediating generalizations. As an example of how a word mediates a generalization, consider the common meaning of the word "balance" in several applications such as balanced scales, equation, diet, account, or art composition. The word "balance" connotes the same general kind of operation to achieve equilibrium of components or forces in each of these different situations. Having learned the concept in one situation, the word for it mediates generalizations to other situations. Two studies demonstrate especially well the function of verbalization in generalizing.

Using as subjects 59 preschool children divided into experimental and control groups, Shepard first trained both groups to press a button at the signal of a red light and not to press it for a blue light, reinforcing them by saying "Right" and "Wrong" for correct and incorrect responses, respectively. Then, after testing both groups for generalizing—in a test to be described—the investigator trained the experimental group to call red, red-orange, orange, and yellow lights Mo, and to call the blue light *Lee.* To determine the effect of the verbal training given only to the experimental group, she tested both groups on generalization test both *before* and *after* the verbal training. The generalization test consisted of a presentation of *all* the lights with the request to press the button at the appropriate signals. Would the experimental group of children, who had been trained to press the button only for a red light, now generalize the response and press the button for all lights call *Mo*? The average number of generalized responses of the two groups both before and after verbal training are graphed in Figure 2.3.

As the graph shows, *after* the verbal training, the experimental group made more generalized responses to light other than red which also had been called *Mo.* That this increase in generalizing was caused by the verbal training is further indicated by the fact that the control group—without the intervening verbal training—did not generalize responses except for the very similar red-orange light.

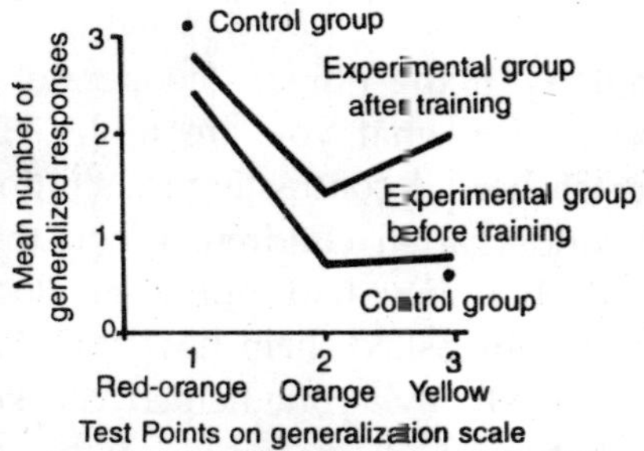

***Figure* 2.3** *Preschool Children, Trained to Press a Button to Red Lights Only, Generalize the Response—after Verbal Training—and Tend to Press the Button to All Lights Called "Mo." (From Winifred O. Shepard, Child Development., 1956 Vo., 27, p. 314)*

In another study it has shown that children who have already in their vocabulary appropriate terms for labeling concepts—such as the term "triangle" for varied triangular figures—discover such concepts in new situations more readily than do students who lack names for the concepts.

Factors Affecting Effective Verbalizing. Whether verbalizing facilitates learning or not depends upon several factors: the student's understanding of the words employed, the degree of clarity or distinctiveness with which the words discriminate between concepts, the learner's maturity and proficiency in verbalizing, and the extent of teacher guidance or of the learner's resourcefulness in labeling.

Meaningfulness. It will be recalled the Pyles found that both nonsense terms and familiar names aided children in discovering under which nonsense-shaped mold a toy had been hidden. Familiar names, however, were helpful than nonsense. In concept-guided sorting. Carey and Goss also found familiar names more helpful than nonsense labels. The limitation of meaningless terms becomes more apparent, however, in more complex situations.

Sometimes school children's verbalizations are unrelated to meaningful, concrete experience, consequently, they reflect only a superficial understanding of the concepts discussed. As an illustration, we have Hughes's report of some eighth grade students' definitions of the phrase "cooperate with others." It means, they said: "Do what you are told." "Don't whisper." "Agree with the teacher." A contrasting illustration was provided by a group of kindergarten children. When their teacher was teacher observed that they had put their floor blocks away quickly and neatly, she asked them how they had done such a good job. They replied: "Everyone helped. Stacked them right—big ones on the bottom. Nobody got in a fight. It didn't take too long. We weren't forever putting away blocks." Such a verbalization of their concrete experience in discovering how to work together efficiently probably enhanced their understanding of the process. The components of the task became both more clearly differentiated and better integrated into an organized pattern. When a process is thus clearly conceptualized, it is more likely to be remembered and applied in other situations as a generalized pattern of effective teamwork.

Distinctiveness. Dietze found for preschool children that distinctively different labels (such as *jod, daf, and meep*) are more effective verbal guides in discriminating and classifying forms than similar or rhyming labels (such as *beem, meem,* and *peem*).

Maturity. The factor of individual differences—in maturity and in proficiency of verbalizing—has been found related to effectiveness of verbalizing in learning both abstract concepts and in arithmetic problem solving. Other aspects of this factor were taken up in Chapter 3 when we discussed the role of maturation in terms of readiness for learning.

Guidance. Children learn to employ verbalization both from teacher guidance and from self-guided experience. Norcross and Spiker showed that the effect of guidance in naming specific stimuli is extended to naming other stimuli, with consequent facilitation in learning discriminations. Pyles noted that 13 children, without any guidance, discovered the usefulness of verbalizing in finding under which hold a toy was hidden. Spontaneously calling the nonsenseshaped molds "the cup", "Old Mother Shop", "the slide", "the smoothed one", and so on, these resourceful children required only 11.9 trials to master the problem, while the uninstructed group as a whole required 47.1 trials.

Summarizing our review, we find that appropriate verbalization helps students to structure and solve problems, memorize and retain concepts, and apply the generalized products of learning to related situations. Words, as labels, classify similar things and events and thus facilitate generalized responses to them. Words also function in designating discriminated differences, and thus they guide appropriately differentiated responses in innumberable situations. As symbols for things and events experienced in the past, the present, and imaginatively anticipated in the future, words make possible complicated, integrated responses to stimulus situations extended in time and place. They—with other less precise and differentiated symbols—make it possible to reason, to substitute imagined provisional trials for more awkward or impossible overt action. And because they also function in communication between individuals, they contribute to cooperative problem solving.

Meaningfulness of Content and Approach

Social studies, science, literature, mathematics, and other areas of the school curriculum are sometimes approached as a collection of isolated facts to be memorized. Such a procedure, however, is needlessly inefficient. Original mastery retention, and generalized applications are all more efficient when such concepts are studied as organized, interrelated systems of ideas, and when the learner searches for or creates generalized principles of wide-scope application.

Meaningful Content. Several experiments have shown that meaningfulness of content is a determinant of efficient learning. Lyon-acting as his own subject—memorized in one reading per day 200 units each of four kinds of material, varying in meaning. Meaningless nonsense syllables required 93 minutes; almost as meaningless digits required 85 minutes; meaningful prose required only 24 minutes; and both meaningful and otherwise well- structured poetry was memorized in only 10 minutes.

A more precise illustration of the close relationship of meaningfulness of content to efficiency of learning has been demonstrated by Noble in a series of experiments. He first constructed a scale of words ranked in order of meaningfulness—determined by the average number of response associations which could be made to each word in one minute. Lowest in the scale is the artificial word *gogey* which produced only 99 association. A word of medium meaningfulness, *rostrum* elicited 2.73 associations. *Kitchen*, the most meaningful in his scale of 96 words, stimulated his subjects to respond with an average of 9.61 associations. From this scale of words, Noble constructed three 12-word lists—containing, respectively, words of low, medium, and high degrees of meaningfulness. The rates of acquisition and the total number of trails required by 72 college students to memorize each of the three lists—by the serial anticipation method—are shown in Figure 2.4.

As is clearly shown in the figure and in other data, efficiency of learning is closely related to the meaningfulness of the mate-

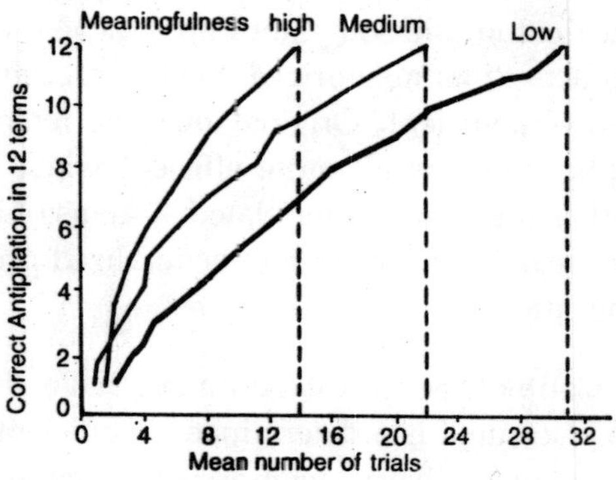

Figure 2.4 Rate of Learning and Total Trials, Required for Mustery Vary for Lists of Words of Low, Medium, and High Degree of Meaningfulness. (After C.E. Noble, J. Exp. Psychol., 1952, Vol. 43, p. 440.)

rial learned. In this instance, the progress curve is steepest for the most meaningful material; it requires less than half as many repetitions for mastery than does the least meaningful list.

Meaningful Approach. Efficiency of learning also varies with the meaningfulness of the approach. For example, one may establish—with sufficient repetitions—any number of arbitrary associations between the nonsense word bep and each of the following groups of words; club, picnic, reaches, beet; potato, careful, pasture, raised; and crawls turnip, pleasant, closet. Reed found that directing college students to search for meaningful concepts governing these and other similar paired associations aided them in learning the associations. In this instance, the common feature connection bep with each group of four words is that each group contains the name of a vegetable. Once this concept is discovered, it can be applied—without further specific practice—in associating bep with other word groups containing names of vegetables.

This type of generalization—which meaningful material and meaningful approaches make possible—is probably the "secret" of efficient learning. Such learning takes advantage of the learner's background of prior learning. In Reed's experiment, only individuals who had already learned the concept of vegetables as a class of things could, of course, identify the common feature connecting bep with the word groups including beet, potato, and turnip. Another economy which a meaningful approach to learning affords is that multiple-element tasks can often be reduced to multiple applications of a single general principle. In this case, bep—as a generalized concept—designated any group of words containing a vegetable name. These advantages of a meaningful approach to learning, as we shall see in the next chapter, are also explainable as products of transfer of learning.

Experiments with school content also indicate the advantage of a meaningful approach to learning. In teaching third grade children borrowing in subtraction, Brownell and Moser compared meaningful and "mechanical" procedures. Using the following example to illustrate a meaningful approach, the teacher explained: "I can't take 8 from 5, so I borrow 10 from 6 tens. I cross out 6 and write a little 5 to show that I borrowed a 10. I write a little 1 in front of 5 to show I now have 15 instead of 5." The comparable mechanical explanation was this: "I can't take 8 from 5, so I think 5 as 15. Then I think 8 from 15 is 7, and I write 7. Since I thought of 5 as 15, I must think 6 as 5. Then I think 2 from 5 is 3 and write 3." When the children were tested to measure their accuracy, their retention (after a six-week period), their ability to transfer the approach to untaught three-digit numbers (such as 539–242), and their rated degree of understanding, it was found that those children taught meaningfully surpassed those taught mechanically. Furthermore, this experiment suggest that relatively meaningless procedures frustrate the individual's natural need to understand. Children taught mechanically indicate this frustration by asking such questions as: "But where did you get the 1 to make the 5 a 15...?"

$$\begin{array}{r} 6\ \ 5 \\ -2\ \ 8 \\ \hline 3\ \ 7 \end{array}$$

In memorizing passages of prose or poetry, it is often effective to read the selection thouhgtfully, thinking of the central meaning and constructively organizing the component ideas around it. For example, Cofer found that college students who were learning folk tales required fewer trails to reach comparable levels of mastery when they reproduced ideas in organized sequences than when they attempted to reproduce the tales verbatim.

School learning also affords many practical illustrations of the advantages of a meaningful approach. In the previous chapters we have cited several examples of how children—working with concrete and semiconcrete materials—discovered, generalized, and effectively applied concepts in self-discovery projects. Reading for meaning provides context as a very effective cue in identifying unfamiliar words. Spelling a word such as "appointment" is facilitated by identifying the familiar root, the recognized suffix, and by generalizing from experience with other instances of doubled consonants, as in "appear" or "apply." First grade children are aided in learning manuscript writing by noticing that all

26 letters in the alphabet are represented by simple circles and straight or curved lines. Geometry is mastered more effectively by trying to understand and apply creatively its system of theorems than by attempting verbatim memorization of them. And social studies, science, mathematics, and other such subjects are comprehended more effectively as systems of interrelated functional concepts than as collections of isolated facts. Without the integration of basic ideas or principles, collections of facts are useless. For example, students who study mathematics as a collection of rules and techniques are often confused in deciding which rule or technique to apply in a particular problem. The problem 7/8–2/3=? was given to one such student. He decided to use the rule: Invert the divisor and multiply.

A Preliminary Overview

The separate parts of an integrated activity or learning project take on meaning as their interrelationships in the whole are perceived. Just a map-guided exploration of a new city yields more understanding than street-by-street meanderings, so an initially projected comprehensive outline of a topic in social studies or science contributes to efficient mastery of the subtopics.

There are many illustration of the application of this principle. The high school band or orchestra conductor, for example, may give his students an overview of a new piece by playing a recording of it. Then, before working on troublesome parts, the ensemble will play through the entire piece. In memorizing a poem, a speech, or a musical composition, the first step should be complete reading a self-reciting review. The unifying pattern or thread of meaning in the piece as a whole provides generalized cues for remembering the parts or segments. In learning a complex motor skill such as swimming, we should initially practice the skill as a whole before concentrating on such aspects as kicking, arm movements, or breathing. The comprehensive grasp of the skill makes the practice on the minor features more meaningful and therefore more effective. Knapp and Dixon found that among groups of college students who were learning to juggle three paddle-tennis balls, those who began practice with first one, then two, and finally three balls mastered the skill less quickly than those whose tried to juggle all three from the beginning. Those who used only one or two balls failed to attain the speed and to grasp the complexity of performance demanded in three-ball juggling.

Another experiment suggests the effectiveness of an overview in problem-solving learning. Hildreth presented three jigsaw picture puzzles (of a train, a stem shovel, and a ferryboat) to 100 children, aged seven to ten, who were subdivided into groups for two different modes of presentation. The picture puzzle to be assembled was presented to one group without explanation or prior opportunity to see it. A preliminary overview was given to the other group. As an aid in organizing the parts, the teacher, prior to the assembly task, showed the latter group the completed picture puzzle and named and pointed out its various features. A comparison of the results of the two procedures revealed that "puzzle solving proved easier and quicker" when preceded by a preliminary overview. The educational implication is that "school problem solving will be more successful to the extent that the pupils can be given an overview of the whole, some knowledge of the central meaning of the problem, and some meaningful clues to aid solution."

Whole Versus Part Methods of Memorizing. The whole approach has the advantage of giving grater meaning to a skill or concept to be learned, but there are materials on which part-by-part memorizations is more efficient for some individuals. If the selection is long, it is sometimes effective to memorize small, meaningful segments separately after a preliminary study of the whole. Relatively immediate, clear knowledge of progress as subgoals are attained is better motivation than the long-deferred or more vague evidence of progress which is characteristic of the whole method. Moreover, memorization by the whole method often entails overpractice on some parts (usually the beginning and end of a piece are learned first), whereas in the part method, the amount of practice can be adjusted economically to the needs of each part. Notwithstanding these merits of the part method, the whole method is generally more efficient for mature individuals, for children of superior intelligence, and for individuals who have learned to employ it skillfully. Hovland writes, in his summary of the literature, that "the best advice seems to be learn by using the largest units are meaningful and within the individual's capacity."

Often a combination of whole and part methods is effective. Given the task of memorizing a five-verse poem, for example, the individual might first achieve an overview and general understanding by thoughtfully reading the entire poem. Then, employing the principle of self-recitation, he might verbalize the main ideas or think through the poem in his own words. After a second reading, he would try to recite it verbatim. This attempt would reveal the verse on which the learner experiences most difficulty. He would then, studying it separately, master this most difficult verse. Then, returning to restudy of the whole, he would repeat the whole-to-part sequence. This alternation between whole and part methods takes advantage of the meaningfulness of the whole, of the enhanced motivation in clear knowledge of progress, and of the economy of adjusting the amount of practice to the needs of each verse. It also employs the principles of self-recitation and perception of the effects.

Organization

Organization—as a factor facilitating learning—is another variation of the more general principle of meaningfulness. The thousands of facts and skills which students learn in school can be mastered more efficiently if appropriate techniques and principles are utilized for grouping and classifying them, if they are integrated into expanding developmental systems, and if inductive generalizations can be drawn from them.

Classification. Even from the study of relatively few facts, we can often achieve, through appropriate classification, both meaning-enhancing generalizations and criteria for making fine discriminations. To try to understand, for example, the world of hundreds of thousands of different animals as an unclassified collection would be an impossible undertaking. However, from experience with relatively few animals and Linnaeus's scheme for classifying them, many children achieve functional understanding of the great variety of animal life. To illustrate: one may never have heard of a dingo, but if he knows that the genus-species name is *Canis dingo,* he immediately infers that it is a doglike animal, since it belongs to the same genus as *Canis familiaris.* Or, one may temporarily confuse the porcupine with the common European hedgehog—both having spiny coverings. However, in Linaeus's classification, they are discriminated. The porcupine, with its well-developed incisors for eating foliage and bark, belongs to the order *rodentia.* The insect-eating hedgehog belongs to the order *insectivora.*

Many other schemes for classifying concepts and skills provide similar economies in learning. Sentences may be analyzed into subjects and predicates, into parts of speech, and other structural components. There are the times tables—or better, a single 10-by-10 or 12-by-12 table or products—in multiplication. In spelling, we may classify many words according to certain common features; we may observe, for example, that back, lack, sack, and tack are similar, except for the initial consonant. Such multiple-element bodies of facts can be taught more efficiently if they are organized logically or grouped to bring out common features or principles than if presented as heterogeneously mixed lists.

Prentice and Asch have demonstrated experimentally the effectiveness of "logical organization" as a factor facilitating learning and recall of associated abstract concepts. To 32 college students they presented, for associating together, two different series of 16 related and 16 unrelated pairs of figures. In the related pairs, the second member of a pair is an identity, completion, common part, missing part, or a continuation of the first. Four minutes after the memorization presentations, the first member of each pair in both series was again presented. In these test presentations, the subjects were asked, upon seeing the first member of each pair, to recall and to draw the second member.

The average number of correct reproduction of both logically associated and nonassociated forms.

Fitting or logical organization greatly facilities such learning. In two presentations of each series, over three times as many logical associations as unrelated associations were learned.

Sequential Integration. Organization can also contribute to efficiency of learning the sequences of topics which comprise many school curricula, such as the series of topics in social studies, science, or mathematics.

When each new topic in a sequence is related to or developed as an extension of the organized accumulation or meaningful integration of preceding topics, the efficiency of learning is increased. Such facilitation is more probable when concepts learned are functionally classified or catalogued and hierarchically organized as broad general concepts subconcepts, and specific illustrations. Then the related new concepts reactivate and mobilize "relevant subsuming concepts in the individual's existing cognitive structure" and enhance the meaning of them.

Inductive Generalizations. In studying a sequence of topics, retention and extension of meaning are also facilitated by searching the accumulating facts or data for organizing principles. Guilford exposed sequences of digits through an aperture and directed students to memorize such sequences as the following: 8-7-9-6-10-5-11-4-12-3-13-2-14-1-15 and 7-12-1-5-11-14-2-8-6-10-3-9-4. Discovering that the first sequence could be conceptualized as a progression of arithmetic differences alternating in sign, or simply as two alternating series, one ascending and the other descending.

Guilford's subjects quickly memorized it. For some subjects, the pattern emerged in the first trial; other subjects required several trials or a hint to look for some schema before a helpful pattern of organization occurred. The second series—determined by no particular system—was memorized with greater difficulty.

Proceeding from the Familiar and Concrete to the new and Abstract

As we have already observed, verbalized concepts or cognitive guides to skilled performances often facilitate learning. But the verbalizations are effective only when they are based on adequate concrete experience. Therefore, concrete experience—actual or recalled—should be the first step in approaching an understanding of abstract concepts. This concrete experience is provided—as the illustrations which follow show—by visual and manipulatable materials in the classroom, by laboratory activities, by excursions into the community, and by drawing on the composite of children's background of experience.

For example, ample visual and manipulatory experience with appropriate objects facilitates understanding such abstract processes as adding, subtracting, multiplying, dividing, and the applications of these processes in problem solving. To provide such experience in the classroom, arithmetic corners include such materials as boxes, play money, jars of different sorts of beans, rulers, paper of various colors, boxes of small sticks, elastic- tied bundles of sticks or tickets, an abacus and other counting and computing devices. Fernald describes a child's concrete approach to a problem which at an abstract level was too difficult for him: "If there are three brothers and their father gives them each two cents, how much do they have altogether?" Taking up a box of pennies and finding two kinds of beans, he placed on his desk a big red bean for the father, three white beans to represent the sons. Then he gave each white bean two pennies. After counting the pennies he announced his answer: "Six." As children acquire understanding and confidence, they learn to express and to solve such problems abstractly—in this instance, as $2 \times 3 = 6$.

The teacher-guided recall of out-of-classroom experiences of children can also be utilized to enrich the meaning of many abstract concepts in science and social studies. The composite extent of such classroom experiences is surprising. Often an analogy can be a bridge for stepping from the already familiar to the new and puzzling. For example, a child orchestra encountered difficulty in learning the rhythm of a dotted quarter followed by an eighth note. When their teacher called attention to the same notation pattern in the familiar songs "America" and "America, the Beautiful," they readily achieved the rhythm in the new instrumental piece.

Job Analyses Learning Tasks

There are usually several approaches to complex tasks, but often they are not equally efficient. Glancing back and forth, for example, from copy to typewriter results in less efficient typewriting than keeping one's eyes continuously on the copy. And employing all 10 fingers systematically with either of these procedures is more efficient than using the forefingers only. Without teacher or pupil analyses to determine the most efficient mode of attack in learning skills, varied techniques—less effective than potentially possible—are often acquired.

Variations In Efficiency Of Self-discovered Approaches. For adding such columns of digits as that below,

$$\begin{array}{c}7\\6\\9\\3\\\underline{5}\end{array}$$

the most efficient procedure is to think the cumulative sums consecutively: 13, 22, 25, 30. Mature elementary education students, however, sometimes rearrange the numbers into easier combinations to avoid higher-decade additions. For example, one prospective teacher said: "I added 7 and 3; then I added 5, making 15. Next I added 5 instead of 6. This made 20. Finally, I added 10 to 20, because the other 1 from 6, when added to 9, made 10. The 10 added to 20 made 30."

Flourney observed many similarly inefficient procedures in 48 third grade children whom she directed to think out loud as they solved problems. One child, adding 28 + 6, said: "I took 2 from 6 and then added it to 28. Then I had 30. I added 4 more to 30.

Then I had 34." In adding such single-and two-digit numbers, 23 of these children added the units and carried to the tens column. In higher-decade columns addition, 11 of them counted, but they did not do so in noncolumn addition. And 4 skipped around to find easier combinations. For the same type of problem, 11 of the children employed a variety of procedures. All of these procedures are satisfactory, of course, as initial approaches. But, as the children progress in understanding and confidence, they should be directed or led to discover more efficient procedures. Otherwise immature procedures may persist.

Left-handers—abandoned by their right–handed teachers to instruct themselves in handwriting, sewing, and other manual skills—discover and acquire a variety of awkward modes of attack. In writing, for example, left–handed individuals often twist the wrist into a cramped position above the line being written so that they can see and avoid smearing what they are writing. One child found he could accomplish these purposes by writing backwards, from right to left. He wroten for go.

Systematic Teacher Direction for Learning Efficiently: On the basis of a job analysis of the task, Cole proposes the following adaptations as guides for learning efficient left–handed writing.

1. The position of the paper should be such that the lower edge is at right angles to the arm being used—just the opposite of the position for the right–handed child.

2. The pencil or pen should be grasped at least 1 to 1 1/2 inch from the point. This will avoid the child's covering or smearing with his fingers what he has just written.

3. The hand should slide along on the ends of the two smallest fingers, far enough below the line being written to miss the longest loops.

4. "Any slant between vertical and 45 degrees to the left of the base line is entirely satisfactory." The usual right slant from the base line would require of the left–handed child too great a proportion of push rather than pull movements,

and the latter are easier to execute without pricking the paper.

5. As a further aid to avoid pricking the paper, the point of the pen should have a rounded nib.
6. As with the right–handed pupil, either an arm movement or wrist–and–hand movement may be used.
7. "The proportions of the letters are, of course, the same no matter which hand is used," except that the slant is reversed or vertical.

Improvements in study methods: Such job analyses to discover efficient modes of attack are applicable to all learning tasks. Guides to secondary school and college students on how to study are general applications of this principle. The results of self–inventories of study skills, such as those presented in Figure 2.5, can aid the student both in directing his attention to needed improvements in study skills and in evaluating his progress in learning them.

The percentile ranks of the college student represented in Figure 2.5 are based on his self–ratings—before and after a

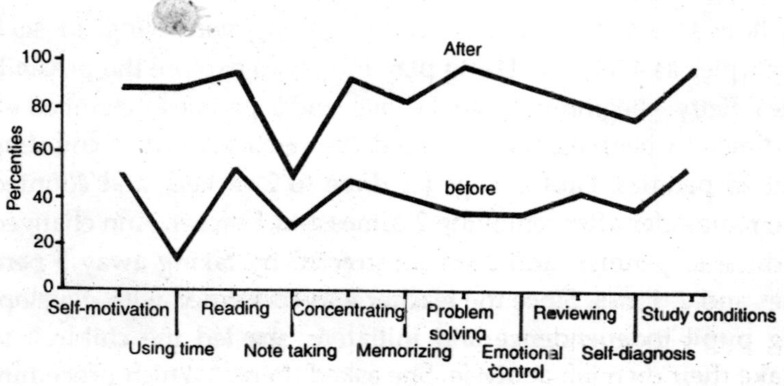

Figure 2.5 *College Student's Profile of Study Indicating Status Before and After Guided Effort to Improve Studying Procedures.*

semester of guided effort to improve his study skills—on such items as the following:

Do you try to improve the efficiency of your reading by converting the topical headings of the text into questions and then reading the passage to answer them for yourself?

Do you make good use of notes, by trying to make a question–outline or a topical outline of class notes, and by re–writing in outline form those parts which you could not outline during a class discussion or lecture?

Do you review and prepare for examinations effectively, by working out individual illustrations of general principles?

A threefold approach to improving the study skills of students produced significant improvement; the threefold approach included individual diagnosis, knowledge of effective methods, and specific applications by each student to his own study tasks.

Guidance toward more efficient modes of attack in learning can be systematic (as in the handwriting illustration) or it can accomplished by teacher guidance of pupils' self–discovery experiences.

The latter procedure is illustrated in children's self–discovery of how to substract in problems requiring borrowing, in such examples as 42c—25c. Using play money to explore the possibilities. Betty—beginning with 4 dimes and 2 pennies—changed all 4 dimes to pennies, then counted the remainder after counting out 25 pennies. Paul changed 1 dime to 2 nickels, and counted the remainder after removing 2 dimes and 1 nickel. Ann changed 1 dime to pennies, and then substracted by taking away 5 pennies and 2 dimes. Since the teacher was concerned with developing pupil independence and initiative, she led the children to make their own job analysis. She asked them: "Which procedure demonstrated by the three children is most efficient, both when the money is manipulated and also when the problem is expressed in writing?"

THE DEVELOPMENTAL ATTAINMENT OF EFFICIENT MODES OF ATTACK

High levels of efficiency are often finally attained even though the initial approach or intermediate stages are not efficient from the points of view of time and motion. Sometimes auxiliary aspects of performance—ultimately superfluous—are very helpful in the initial stages of learning a complex performance. And when they are no longer needed, they are dropped, either voluntarily or at the teacher's suggestion that the task can be performed more efficiently by eliminating them.

As initial self–discovery processes, a child might add 2 + 5 by making two and five marks (// + /////) and then counting them. Knowing the double 3 + 3 = 6, he may add 3 + 4 by thinking 3 + 3 and 1 more = 7. He may solve the problem 33 - 17 by representing 33 as three bunches of 10 sticks each and 3 single sticks, and then by removing one bunch and 7 sticks of another.

These and other aids often make learning easier, more meaningful, and independent. As the child grows in understanding and confidence, such crutches are abandoned in favor of more efficient modes of attack.

Despite our observation that children voluntarily give up many of these immature habits, some teachers object to the use of crutches on the assumption that practice of the ultimately unnecessary processes tends to fix them as permanent habits. Brownell, however, has demonstrated that most children readily give up such crutches when they are no longer needed.

He found that third grade children who used the crutch illustrated to guide them through the ancillary process of borrowing in subtraction achieved greater understanding and accuracy.

$$\begin{array}{r} 8\ 6\ 1 \\ \underline{5\ 4\ 9} \\ 3\ 1\ 2 \end{array}$$

During 15 days of instruction and for the end–of–instruction test on the sixteenth day, the children were directed to use the crutch to remind themselves that, in borrowing a ten, the 6 tens in the minuend (in this particular example) have been reduced to 5 and that the one unit has been increased to eleven. After the end–test, they were encouraged to perform the operations more efficiently without using the crutch. As is revealed in Figure 2.6, their use of the crutch declined rapidly. In a post–test on the

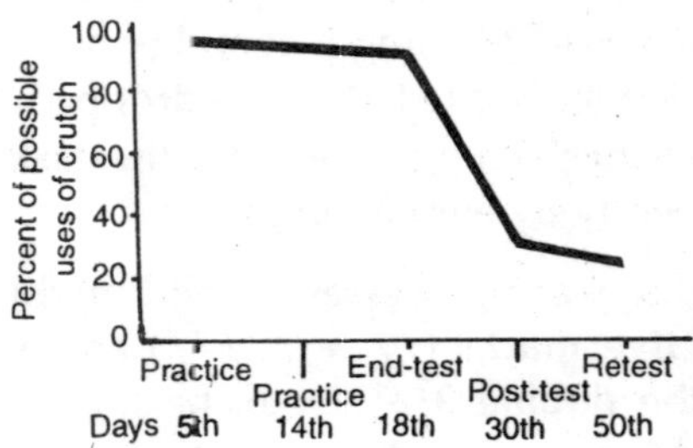

Figure 2.6 Crutches, When no Longer Needed, are Abandoned for Satisfying Short Cuts, as is Indicated by Decreasing use of a Crutch for Borrowing in Subtraction. (From W. A. Brownell and H.E. Moser, Duke Univ. Res. Studies in Ed., No. 8, Duke Univ. Press Durham, N.C., 1949)

thirtieth day and on the delayed–retention test on the fiftieth day, there were many instances in which the children could have used the crutch. However, Brownell found that on both tests, they used it in only 29 and 22 per cent of these instances, respectively. Even during the instructions period—when its use was advised—some pupils voluntarily began to abandon it. Children returned to the crutch, however, when it was needed—after a lapse of time in use of the skill or with difficult problems, and when it could be employed in learning the new process of long division.

As was demonstrated in the preceding chapter, practice does not bind us to habits. Thorndike has shown how initially frequent responses are abandoned when responses providing greater motive satisfaction are discovered. Subject C, asked to write word completions for the beginning syllable *el–*, wrote *evate, ephant, ephant, evate, ephant, ephant, ephant, f, f, f, f, f, f, f, f:* Despite the initial frequency advantage for *elephant*, it was finally abandoned for *elf:* The general tendency of Thorndike's subjects was to abandon longer completions for shorter ones, because they are easier.

Generalizing from these results, we may conclude that when a crutch or learning aid clarifies or simplifies the initial approach to a learning task, it should be used without fear that it will become habitual and thus encumber the ultimate mode of attack with unnecessary processes. Inefficient processes are, however, sometimes continued beyond the stage of their effective use because they are comfortable and they permit us to delay exerting the additional effort it would require to master a more efficient procedure. Insecure and unconfident children continue with the old procedures because they fear the possibility of failing in a new learning venture. In all such instances, it is motive satisfaction, however—not repetition—which binds individuals to familiar habits.

SUMMARY

One way in which we can help our children and youth achieve greater knowledge and skill is to teach them how to learn more efficiently. As they learn specific concepts and skills in every area of the curriculum, they can, with appropriate guidance, also become more proficient as learners. In such guidance, both systematic teacher direction and teacher guidance of pupils' self–discovery experiences are effective. Our review of some of the scientifically established factors affecting the efficiency of learning suggests the following generalized principles teacher guidance:

1. Leading an individual passively through a verbal or motor performance is an inefficient way of helping him to learn it. An active, self–reciting procedure results in more effective mastery and retention of the organized sequences of concepts and skills in many areas of the curriculum.

2. Outlines, diagrams, pictures, and slow–motion films—which aid in visually identifying the relevant features of problem situations and solutions—facilitate the pupil's attempts to structure approaches and execute appropriate patterns of response.
3. When the verbalization is based on adequate concrete experience, appropriate verbal conceptualizing of learning tasks aids in structuring and solving problems, in memorizing and retaining discovered solutions, and in applying generalizations. Words—as symbols for things and events—facilitate discriminating, generalizing, and reasoning.
4. Meaningfulness—both of content and approach—is a general determinant of efficient learning.
5. One way to make learning more meaningful—and therefore more efficient—is to take a comprehensive overview before attempting to master the subparts and details.
6. Organisation—as classifications, as integrated developmental sequences, and as generalizations—also facilitates learning by providing a more meaningful approach.
7. Proceeding from the familiar and concrete to the new and abstract is another meaningful approach which enhances understanding and increases the efficiency of learning, especially when complex concepts are involved.
8. The student without teacher guidance does not always discover the most efficient modes of attack. Therefore, systematic direction or guidance in making job analyses of learning performances often result in the attainment of higher levels of proficiency.
9. The student may ultimately attain high levels of proficiency, even though he does not from the outset use the most efficient approach. When crutches aid the immature learner in the initial stages of comprehending and executing complex performances, they should be utilized. When they are no longer needed, children give them up for more efficient procedures.

Perhaps a student's most important asset in developing efficient modes of attack in learning is the ability to generalize. Since generalizing is so essential a factor in learning, we have already discussed it in several preceding chapters. The development of generalized modes of problem solving was introduced as an important educational objective in previous Chapter. Since the learner utilizes his past experiences, simplifies multiple–element tasks, and anticipates future problems by generalizing, it was defined as an essential condition of learning in this Chapter. Its significant roles in structuring approaches to problems, in the trial–and–check process of learning, and in meaningful and other efficient modes of attack in learning were brought out. In the next chapter, we shall summarize, extend, and systematize our understanding of the role of generalizing in learning.

3

Relation of Learning to Teaching

In previous chapters we have described several more or less systematic outlooks in psychology, each of which includes a theory of learning. We have seen how much in contrast are the chief tenets of the two major families of learning theory—the one leading to teaching which is highly mechanistic and the other leading to teaching with emphasis upon reflection and creativity.

This chapter focuses upon principles of learning which are not usually clearly attached to either S-R associationism or the Gestalt-field outlook. They are widely stated in textbooks of educational psychology, irrespective of the over-all orientation of psychologists. Although we shall see that the manner in which these principles are interpreted and used is influenced by whether one is an exponent of associationism or of field psychology, in the main they lead to somewhat similar classroom results.

The principles to be presented in this chapter are close to classroom practice in the sense that they provide rather specific directives to teachers. In this respect, the present chapter is a bridge between the relatively abstract theory of preceding chapters on learning and the largely "how-to-do-it" emphasis of Part IV, which follows.

Before moving into an elaboration of these widely accepted principles of learning, we should make it clear that most psychologists, and particularly those with the widest reputation, are interested as much as ever in "system building," i.e., constructing a body of theory which is cohesive and internally consistent and within which all elements, even minor ones, harmonize with the central premises. Examples of such persons on the side of field psychology are John Dewey, Boyd H. Bode, E. C. Tolman, Ernest E. Bayles, H. F. Wright, Arthur Combs, Donald Snygg, Carl Rogers, Nathaniel Cantor, Gardner Murphy, Kurt Lewin, R. G. Barker, and R. Lippitt. On the side of associationism are Edward L. Thorndike, John B. Watson, E. R. Guthrie, P. Sandiford, A. I. Gates, C. L. Hull, K. W. Spence, B. F. Skinner, and D. O. Hebb.

These persons, like prominent figures in all the other social and natural sciences, recognize that scientific progress has thrived on systematization, such as the theory of relativity in physics. Nevertheless,most scientists recognize a different level of principle—what we might call "working principle" because of its immediate applicability in practice. The chief condition which a working principle must meet is that it not be in consistent with the major system to which its practitioners are committed. However, it may be equally consistent with more than one competing system.

The principles to be described have been selected from a wide range of literature. They are not presented as an inclusive listing of "working principles" of learning; they represent but a sampling of some of the useful statements which can be made.

HOW MAY WE IMPROVE MOTIVATION?

When a person develops a state of tension resulting from unsatisfied need, we say that he is motivated. Motivation may spring from a variety of needs, ranging from those which are largely physiological in origin to those which are primarily psychological, such as a conflict in religious belief. The person's aim becomes the reduction of tension, which can occur only as the need is satisfied or partially satisfied.

Obviously, motivation plays a central role in learning. Students who are motivated work purposefully and energetically. They display few if any "discipline" problems. A teacher who can keep his students well motivated has won more than half the battle.

The Role of Personal Involvement

Where possible, through the medium of a democratic classroom climate, a teacher's task is to help induce personal involvement. Because of the interactive character of the most productive classroom situations, both students and teacher eventually test their attitudes, values, beliefs, skills, or knowledge. Specific techniques for doing this are described in further Chapter.

After saying this, we would be unrealistic if we failed to concede that such a step is easier to describe than to achieve in practice. In virtually every school subject, a few students will appear well motivated; likewise, a few will appear to have no motivation toward learning and in spite of a teacher's best efforts will remain that way. Another group will respond more or less well to the teacher's efforts to produce motivation. It is among this middle group that teachers feel their greatest sense of accomplishment or frustration.

Extrinsic vs. Intrinsic Motivation

We have dealt with this subject elsewhere and present here only a brief review. Intrinsic motivation is that which arises when the resolution of tension is to be found in mastering the learning task itself; the material learned provides its own reward. A boy who studies the construction of model airplanes diligently so he can make a model is experiencing intrinsic motivation. Extrinsic motivation occurs when a person pursues a learning task, but for reasons which lie outside of it. If a boy studies model airplanes because he thinks it will please his father, an ex-pilot, rather than because of a personal interest in model planes, he is moved by extrinsic motivation. After making the distinction, it is necessary to point out that in most learning situations motivation cannot be dichotomized so neatly. It is a function of the total situation and hinges on some blend of personal concern for the work itself and concern for extrinsic factors. As a practicable working principle, motivation is probably always a function of an interactive situation.

Obviously, both emphases on motivation work in the sense that they both lead to learning. However, educational psychologists condemn extrinsic motivation as undesirable because, since the material learned does not in itself serve any purpose of the learner, he tends to forget it as soon as his extrinsic purpose is met. In addition to poor retention of material learned, extrinsic motivation usually leads to careless, inaccurate learning. The learning task is hurried through as quickly as possible so that the reward may be obtained. If Johnny tries for a B in arithmetic because his father promises him a one-dollar reward, Johnny is not likely to care how he gets the B—copying someone else's answers is as good a way as any. This appears to be the working out of Thorndike's law of effect and is incompatible not only with the tenets of field psychology but with what is usually recognized in the literature as the best of modern school practice.

In spite of the undesirability, on psychological grounds,of an emphasis on extrinsic motivation, in some situations many teachers feel they have no choice but to employ it. When this is the situation, teachers may be undecided as to whether to use rewards or punishments. A number of studies—in the Thorndike tradition—have been conducted in an attempt to determine whether it is more effective to praise students for what they learn or blame them for what they do not learn. After reviewing these studies, Stephens decides that the evidence is so conflicting that no definite conclusion can be drawn. The only conclusion which seems warranted is that either praise or blame is usually more effective in promoting learning than a policy of ignoring the achievement or lack of achievement of students.

The role of Success

Although occasional failure, including in some cases even punished failure, is not inimical to the progress of learning, fairly regular success is a *must.* As Pressey and his associates put it, "Learning feeds on success." Unless motivation is extraordinarily high, a continuous succession of failures discourages students to the point where frustration blocks further effort.

However, too much can be made of the role of success. An uninterrupted series of successes may be as bad for the cause of learning as an uninterrupted series of failures. In further Chapter we suggest that it is healthful to let students make a certain number of mistakes—provided they are the kinds of mistakes one can learn by.

Related to the question of success vs. failure as a contributor to motivation is the question of whether students should be kept informed at all times of progress. The answer seems to be that a knowledge of progress spurs them on to additional effort, although this would not be the case if the goal were easy and a student found he was on the verge of success with extra time left.

Demotivation Caused by 'Pat' Answers

We experience our strongest motivation in situations which are puzzling. If we completely solve the problem facing us, all sense of tension disappears; we cease to be interested because there is nothing to be interested in. Some misled teachers feel that each unit of work, or each class period, should end with a full resolution of whatever issue was under study. They sometimes feel that it is better for a teacher to tell students the "right answers" than to let them leave the class 'unsatisfied.' No policy could be more effectively calculated to destroy sustained motivation. A truly skilled teacher will see to it that each day students leave class with unanswered questions. Even an entire semester's work should not "wrap up" a subject "for keeps."

Tests as Sources of Motivation

Some teachers feel that in order to keep students working it is necessary to give them frequent tests, both announced and unannounced. We are talking here of tests used for purposes of motivation, not for remedial purposes. Stephens surveys a number of relevant studies and draws a different conclusion. At the college level, the research evidence suggests that tests given once or twice a term produce just as much motivation as frequent tests. In high school the results differ, in that tests spaced about two weeks apart seem efficacious. *Daily tests produce less motivation than no tests at all.* Further, the studies indicate that students learn less in courses in which they are given surprise tests than in courses where test dates and coverage are announced ahead of time.

Of course, tests employed as motivating devices function primarily as extrinsic motivation. A student's primary goal in such a situation is not to learn the subject content for its own sake but to pass the test. Generally speaking, frequent and widespread use of tests for other than remedial reasons indicates commitment to a mechanistic psychology.

Self-Imposed Goals vs. Teacher-Imposed Goals

It is a well-known fact among psychologists that when a person develops goals which he sees as personal to himself, although perhaps involving others whom he cares about, he tends to set ambitious goals. The tendency actually is for most students to set goals that are difficult to the point of being unrealistic—students who have great difficulty with mathematics sometimes choose engineering as their career.

In most school subjects it is not feasible for students to operate as free agents in setting their goals in the course. However, an experienced teacher has a pretty good idea of what an average student can achieve and it makes for better motivation to discuss the objectives of the course with students. Through such discussion, students and teacher both may come to feel more personal involvement in the course objectives.

HOW MAY WE MAKE LEARNING MORE EFFICIENT?

In this book, improving the efficiency of learning means establishing situations in which maximum change of insight may occur in a given time. Although insightful learning may proceed very rapidly, it seldom can be hurried. Some of the most efficient possible learning situations appear on the surface as unnecessarily—even hopelessly—time consuming.

Readiness and Learning

A young person is ready to learn something when he has achieved sufficient physiological maturation and experiential background so that he not only can learn but wants to. For example, it is physiologically impossible for a child of 3 months to learn to walk. For all except an occasional prodigy, it appears impossible for a child of 2 to learn to read; not only is his neuromuscular system insufficiently developed, but he doesn't want to read. A youth of 12 is not normally ready to study subjects such as calculus, advanced economic theory, or Shakespeare. His lack of readiness is probably more attributable to absence of suitable experimental background than to inadequate development of physiological structures, although until a person is fully matured physically it is usually difficult to say to what extent incomplete development of physical structure is a hampering agent, particularly in the case of primarily "intellectual" learning tasks. There is evidence to suggest that certain school subjects can be taught successfully much earlier than was once supposed—algebra is a case in point.

Much of the research on readiness has pertained to the teaching of reading and arithmetic. When is a youngster old enough to learn to read or to do long division? Although specific figures are frequently given, e.g., a child is often said to be ready to read at the age of 6.5 years, they can be highly misleading. There is great individual variation among children. Some are ready to read at the age of 3; others might as well wait until they are 8.

Serious problems may result from taking data on readiness literally, particularly when virtually all formal education is *mass* education in most countries. It is a matter of administrative convenience to require all children to begin school at about the same age. If Mary, who is ready to read at 3, has been taught by her parents to read, and is reading at, say, a fourth-grade level when she enters the first grade, she is bound to find the school's reading program insufferably dull. She may become a highly bored and frustrated child and so will frustrate teachers and parents. If Johnny is incapable of learning to read at 6 1/2, when we normally begin reading in this country, he may face a year or two of failure and eventually develop a mind-set against reading which will make it difficult for him to learn to read at any age.

Similar problems occur at all age levels. Some persons are never ready for certain learning tasks which are assigned regularly in school. For example, one of the authors was required to take a succession of physical education activity courses while a freshman and sophomore in college. He was *never* ready, in the sense that a combination of poor coordination, poor vision, lack of previous experience, and negative mind-set made it impossible for him to achieve, even at the minimum standards set by the instructors. Fortunately, in physical education classes, a C is usually conferred for regular attendance and harmless conduct.

Our definition of readiness presents the same problem as our definition of intelligence; it is impossible to isolate those factors which are innate and those which are a product of learning. We can only assume that when a person is ready for a new learning, it is because he has developed his ability and interest to the point that he sees the new learning as the next step for him to make.

We do not even have conclusive data on the possible degree to which strong motivation may speed physiological maturing. An average youngster may achieve the necessary coordination to perform a particular physical task at the age, say, of 12; but those who are especially interested in learning the task, and who begin trying it at an earlier age, may significantly accelerate the development of coordination.

Studies indicate that there is nothing to be gained by starting youngsters on a particular learning task earlier than readiness normally permits. Whether readiness for a particular task hinges primarily on genetically controlled maturtion or primarily on experience and desire, most children, if started at a task much earlier than it is normally learned in our culture, do not learn it well, if at all. They tend to flounder, making gains which are offset by retrogressions. The one who is started later on the same task may learn so much more rapidly that he quickly catches up with the child started earlier. This apparent fact should not be taken as a denial of the point made earlier: a number of subjects now normally reserved to high school or college could be taught effectively in elementary school if there were good social reasons for doing so. We have mentioned certain aspects of higher mathematics in this connection; foreign language is another example. There are social reasons, however, for keeping the elementary curriculum sufficiently uncluttered to be able to focus on fundamental language and arithmetic skills.

The Role of Practice

Although some learning is of an "Aha!" character, i.e., the learner gets the point in a flash and does not forget it, other learning requires lengthy practice. If a teacher is to help students make the most efficient use of practice he must remember several important principles concerning its use.

First, repetition *per se* does not teach. Thorndike's original "law of exercise" suggested that animals—and humans—learn an act merely by repeating it enough times. In the 1930s Thorndike himself decided that such a notion had no experimental support and retracted his earlier statement. When we use the term *practice* we refer to trials which have an experimental character, trials in which the action is varied, even though slightly, each time the learner asks himself, "What did I do wrong?" or "How can I do it better?" Pressey, Robinson, and Horrocks cite a study in which the conclusion was drawn that "...repetition that occurs in acquiring skill is not repetition of one set of identical elements, but the gradual development of structural features. Instead of doing the same thing over and over, the learner progresses to more advanced stages of performance."

Old-fashioned teachers who kept Johnny after school until he could write 100 times on the blackboard "It is wrong for boys to spill ink on little girls' hair" undoubtedly taught Johnny something but assuredly not that it is wrong to spill ink on little girls' hair.

Practice may be *massed or distributed.* Massed practice means long practice periods. Disturbed practice means a succession of shorter practice periods with rest or other forms of activity spaced between. Virtually all of the research evidence seems to show spaced practice to be more efficacious than massed practice. With massed practice both fatigue and boredomy reduce attention and cause practice to turn into mere repetition.

In many instances, spacing actually speeds up the learning process. It is fairly common for persons to reach a plateau—a dead end—in learning, and to re-establish progress after a waiting period. One of the authors knows a person who learned to swim "wrong." He never mastered the popular crawl stroke. He began learning this stroke in his 40s but was handicapped by poor coordination—he inhaled when his face was under water and exhaled when it was out. After a summer of near drowning, he again attempted, the following June, the crawl stroke. Surprisingly, in the first trial he did much better. Although gains were slow that summer, the following year, after a winter's rest, he did better still.

Although not usually so interpreted, the experimentation on practice lends more support to the insight theory of learning than to any of the S-R associationistic interpretations of the learning process. The fact that practice, to be effective, must be experimental, that is, accompanied by a questioning attitude, supports the notion that the role of practice is not to strengthen neural connections but to contribute to the development of an insight. We perfect our thought patterns by trying them out experimentally.

One qualification needs to be made in connection with distributed practice as well as distributed study of any sort. Too much has been written about attention span. Some writes state with great specificity, in terms of number of minutes, what the attention span of a person of a given age is. Attention span refers to the length of time which a person can pursue a learning task without having his attention falter seriously. Attention span is obviously a function of the level of motivation, and it is misleading to say, as some psychologists have said, that the attention span of children increases with age. *It increases with motivation.*

We have seen small children work as persistently and diligently at a task as any adult would be likely to do. The difference between childhood and adulthood appears to be that adults are better able to subordinate short-run pleasures in the interest of longer-range pleasures; adults find it easier to "live for the future." Hence, they can more easily develop long-range motivation for a short-range learning task which requires massed practice—like learning a foreign language quickly.

Fatigue does not interfere seriously with learning provided sufficient motivation is present. This statement is true only within limits, for exhaustion can become so intense that even the highest level of motivation flags. Conversely, in the absence of motivation, a rather simple learning task can produce marked feelings of ennui.

Part vs. Whole Learning

This issue dates back to the 1920s, when connectionism was first being challenged by the Gestalt outlook. The standard connectionist approach had been "piecemeal" learning: one begins with individual elements and learns them one by one, eventually assembling them into a whole. It would be wrong to imply that the connectionists originated an atomistic approach to teaching; such an approach dates back much farther than Thorndike. However, associationist thinking in psychology did provide a rationale for the atomistic approach by giving it theoretical support.

The Gestaltists insisted that we learn best when we begin with the largest unit we can comprehend. In studying a poem, for example, instead of beginning with a word-by-word or line-by-line analysis, students should read the entire poem through rather quickly and try to size up its over-all meaning. Once this is done, a Gestaltist would have no objection to an analytical approach; when a person has gained some "feel" for the entire poem, analysis plays a different role: each part is studied with respect to how it fits into the total picture.

The part vs. whole issue has plagued teachers of reading for almost half a century. Should a child learn to read by learning first the alphabet, then how to pronounce syllables, then words, then finally sentences, paragraphs, and themes? Or should he begin with simple themes and strive as rapidly as possible to envision word groups and later entire sentences or paragraphs as units? Under the latter approach (sight reading) students get a feel for pattern and, so the argument runs, learn to read more rapidly and fluently.

As Pressey points out, the experimental evidence to date favors conclusively neither one view nor the other. Most educational psychologists today, even those with an associationist orientation, argue in favor of the 'whole' method for all types of material susceptible to such an approach. Yet, as Pressey points out, the relative superiority of one method or the other may hinge largely on the learner's "motivation,...patience, and the extent to which he perceives the learning situation as being important and fulfilling a need." Pressey also suggests that intellectual capacity is a significant factor, in that persons with higher than average IQ tend to learn better by wholes. The amount and quality of prior practice also enters the picture: practice in either approach seems to increase one's efficiency in utilizing that approach. Finally, some learning materials lend themselves better to part learning, some to whole learning.

It is the observation of the authors that people who begin a learning task by the "part method" tend at some point in its achievement to move to the "whole method." When this transition is made, progress is likely to accelerate rapidly. A good example of what happens may be found in the learning of typing.

The old-fashioned way of teaching typing was first to teach students the location of the letters on the keyboard and how to stroke each letter at will. The next step was to teach them to type syllables. Next came words, then phrases, then sentences. This was the "part method" with a vengeance.

Students can learn to type this way. However, they usually hit a plateau, a period of no progress in spite of diligent practice. Rather suddenly—often it comes with a rush in a matter of a few days—a student finds that he is no longer "spelling out" words on the typewriter. In fact, he is typing entire phrases or sentences without attention to individual letters or words. He had moved to "patterntyping." He has suddenly gained a feel for a stroking pattern appropriate to phrases, sentences, or groups of sentences. Now typing speed and accuracy tend to soar.

When a typist can no longer recall where individual letters are on the keyboard he has moved to a fundamentally different approach and apparently the only one whereby a high level of skill can be achieved.

One of the authors does all of his writing (except signing checks) on a typewriter. The only way he can visualize where a particular letter is on the keyboard is to arrange his hands in typing position and stroke a word containing the letter, meanwhile *watching to see where his finger lands* when the letter in question is struck.

Sometimes stroking a single word is difficult without stroking a phrase or sentence which contains it.

HOW MAY WE IMPROVE RETENTION?

Most of the studies of retention have been made by connectionists and have been based on a learner's ability to reproduce at some later date a response which he could once make. Studies of recall have included both sensorimotor and verbal responses. In previous Chapter we suggested that much of what is learned in school is quickly forgotten. Pressey has summed up a number of studies of recall of verbal responses—the so-called "fact learning" which is so commonly emphasized in schools. He concludes that "At the end of a course, students remember about three- fourths of the facts covered. One year following the conclusion of a course, students remember about one-half the facts covered. Two years following the conclusion of a course, students remember about one-fourth the facts covered." These studies do not take us beyond two years after the learning occurred. There is every reason to suppose that the process of forgetting continues until, for most types of "fact courses," virtually all is lost. There is no research as yet which furnishes a basis for contradicting the opinion of Wrightstone, paraphrased on previous Chapter, to the effect that many school courses might as well not be taken at all if their value is to be judged from any long-range results which we can measure. On the hopeful side, we know with little question that learning can be quite permanent; formal education is not necessarily doomed forever to be largely wasted.

Meaning and Retention

Material which is meaningful to students is remembered much better than material which is not. Defining meaning is not easy, and since this problem is dwelt on at length in further Chapter, we will say here only that meaningful material is confined to *relations* between facts (generalizations, rules, principles) for which students see some use. Solitary facts are on essentially the same level of meaninglessness as nonsense syllables, and approximately the same forgetting curves apply to both.

Making learning meaningful is a matter of selecting the right content—it must be reducible to principles—and helping students see its applicability in situations which they are concerned about. However, as McDonald points out, the learning of any kind of organizing principles contributes to retention.

Results of learning meaningful material are apparent enough. Cronbach cites a study in which tests requiring the application of major generalizations to new problems were administered at the beginning of a course in zoology, at the end, and a year later. The respective scores were 35, 65 and 65. There was no loss of material learned. In another study, where zoology students were asked to draw conclusions, i.e., infer principles, from experiments not previously studied, the respective scores were 30, 57, and 64. Students did even better after an interval of a year!

Stephens sums up the situation very nicely when he says, "If the material is sufficiently meaningful, there may be no forgetting whatever. An important governing principle, like the idea of the conservation of energy, may so help us organize the rest of our ideas that it stays with us for life. Content that is not so brilliantly structured but which still has much meaning will be remembered in proportion to its meaning. Nonsense material is headed for extinction before the last syllable is uttered."

Possibly the whole point is that material which can be learned insightfully, particularly on the level of *generalized insight*, becomes a permanent part of one's personality structure. All school learning could be of this nature if teachers understood well enough the basic psychological principles involved.

The Role of Purpose in Forgetting

It is pleasant to be able to forget some things. Any rounded study of retention would have to include study of the extent to which our wishes govern memory. We do not automatically remember new events of experience according to the length or spacing of practice sessions or any other mechanical formula. We do a reasonably good job of remembering what we really want to remember and forgetting what we prefer to forget.

One professor we know makes no attempt to remember his automobile license number. "I have no reason to," he says, "because I have the number on a tag attached to my key chain. It is easier to refer to the tag than to try to keep the number in mind."

Some experiences are so painful that our mental health benefits by either forgetting them or restructuring them in memory so that what we recall does not resemble closely what actually happened. On the other hand, some experiences are so pleasurable that we not only remember them in detail but in memory embellish them. The fish we caught on our Canadian trip of 1951 become larger and more plentiful every year.

With respect to learning in school, where controversial content is concerned, we tend to forget that with which we do not agree and to remember that with which we do. A frequently cited study was conducted by J.M. Levine and Gardner Murphy, in the early 1940s. Students were grouped according to whether they were procommunist or anticommunist in attitude (at that time a student could be safely procommunist). Both groups of students were given both pro- and anticommunist reading references. In a later memory check, the anticommunist students remembered the anticommunist arguments much better than they did the procommunist arguments, and vice versa.

Purposive forgetting and remembering are examples of psychological homeostasis. Through them we preserve our self-organization in a reasonably adequate state. We employ forgetting and remembering to heal psychological wounds, to shore up self- respect, and to make better sense generally out of our psychological world.

The final point of the foregoing sentence perhaps deserves a little elaboration. In further Chapter we discussed the Gestalt "law of Pragmanz" and related laws—all having to do with perception. It will be recalled that, according to these principles, when a person perceives fragmentary, incomplete, or unsymmetrical objects he tends to see them as more complete, perfect, and balanced than they actually are. Probably every time we recall an experience we have a repetition of perception, in the sense that we reinterpret what we recall in the interest of making a more pleasing pattern out of it. Virtually all texts in educational psychology cite experimental evidence to support this view. One of the better treatments is on pp. 188–191 in the text by Frederick J. McDonald, cited earlier. Perhaps the main lesson to be had from this research is that forgetting is an active and not a passive process, just as is any learning which has promise of retention.

The Role of Overlearning

A person can learn something well enough to make a perfect score on a test given immediately after the learning; he can then continue practice on the same material for an indefinite time, or at least until boredom poses an insurmountable barrier. It has been found that such overlearning does contribute to retention. Hence, most books in educational psychology list overlearning as a means of improving retention.

It should be noted, however, that, when the material to be learned is sufficiently meaningful, overlearning never necessary. Overlearning is an antidote for attempts to teach relatively meaningless content.

Nevertheless, when a person is faced with a learning task such as acquiring the vocabulary of a foreign language, overlearning may be the sensible course to pursue. Overlearning is measured in terms of the percentage of additional practice spent after initial mastery. According to one study, reported by Stephens, 50 per cent of overlearning produced a gain in retention after an elapsed time of 28 days of approximately 25 per cent; 100 per cent of overlearning contributed only slightly more gain than this, possibly because boredom interfered with its effectiveness. Other studies do not produce the same percentages, but all seem to agree that overlearning contributes to retention.

Spaced Review vs. Cramming

Apparently retention is higher if study periods are spaced methodically over the course of an entire semester than if a student waits until a day or two before the final examination and "burns the midnight oil." Results on the final may be equally good; some students learn to cram quite effectively. But long-range results from cramming are likely to be meager—although tempered, of course, by the interplay of the other factors we mention.

The issue of spaced review vs. cramming is not the same as the issue of distributed vs. massed practice. Studies on the relative effect on retention of distributed and massed practice are inconclusive. The issue is in what temporal relationship to the initial learning should review occur—whether it be distributed or massed. The answer seems to be suggested by the nature of a typical forgetting curve, as shown in Fig. 3.1. Since the rate of forgetting is much more rapid relatively soon after the initial learning, we may hypothesize that review periods should follow immediately after the initial learning and not be delayed. McDonald cites experimental evidence to suggest that spaced but frequent reviews immediately following initial learning, followed by widely spaced "brush-ups" during the period of desired retention, represent the most effective approach.

Readers should remember that when we say 'review' we are not referring to repetition; rather, we mean practice with an experimental cast, as described earlier. Review is even more effective if it seeks to go beyond the initial learning by tying it in with new learning or interpreting it on a more sophisticated level. Readers should also remember that the forgetting curve reproduced in Fig. 3.1 and the present discussion of the role of practice in improving attention apply primarily to either complicated sensorimotor learning or verbal learning which is relatively low in meaningfulness and intrinsic motivation. Learning of the most desirable kind produces a rather flat forgetting curve and does not have to be practiced to be remembered.

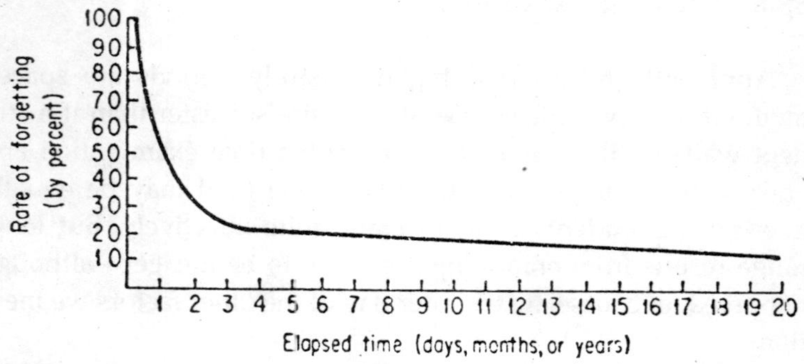

Figure 3.1 A Typical Forgetting Curve

Effects of Intervening Events

A great deal of writing is available on the general subject of the effect on recall of previously assimilated new items of learning, and conversely, the effect on recall of new learnings of what was learned previously. When a second set of learnings intrudes upon a first set, and prevents or distorts the recall of the first set, we say that *retroactive inhibition* has occurred. When a first set of learning intrudes upon a second set, and prevents or distorts the recall of the second set, we say that *proactive inhibition* has occurred. Since there is a strong tendency for any two sets of related learnings to mingle with and to influence each other in reciprocal fashion, some writers prefer not to make the above distinction but rather to use the term *interactive inhibition.*

Students who read the present book frequently report that, by the time they have completed the first three chapters, so many different points of view about key issues in psychology have been presented that they "can't remember any of it." They then go on to say that they could remember well enough through the first three or four positions, but after that, with the addition of still others, they "can't even remember the first ones." This would seem to be a clear example of interactive inhibition. (Fortunately, several years of experience using the manuscript of this book prior to publication demonstrated that most students could learn, by the end of a semester, to recall all of the major positions treated and to distinguish them sharply from one another. This suggests that sometimes a suitable antidole for interactive inhibition is simply more study.)

HOW IS LEARNING TRANSFERRED FROM SITUATION TO SITUATION?

Transfer of learning involves the ability to utilize in new situations that which one has previously learned. The assumption underlying our entire public education system is that the knowledge gained when certain learnings are required in schools not only will be available in the future but also will be applied to some degree in the solution of new problems as they arise in further school and life situations. Society supports education only because it assumes that learning in school facilitates learning and thinking in situations outside school.

The basic problem of transfer is: How can we teach for maximum effective transfer of learning? Problems subordinate to the principal one are: (1) How does a person's current learning assist in meeting future learning situations? (2) How does what youngsters learn in school affect what they learn and what they do outside school? (3) Does it have as much effect as it should, and how can it be made more effectual?

More specifically, will an individual carry over the arithmetical abilities he learned in a classroom to the problems he actually meets in business or in tasks about the house? Will a student of algebra automatically apply his algebraic knowledge to the solution of problems in physics? Will a knowledge of health practices insure that a boy will acquire good health habits? Does practice in memorizing, reasoning, persevering, and willing improve the mental process in general? Can one improve his perception, retention, and imagination in all fields by practice in one? If so, what kind of task should he practice?

Since many problems of life cannot be specifically foreseen, schools must give students general preparation to cope with them. Consequently, the critical question of teachers in regard to transfer is not whether it takes place but what conditions enhance the greatest amount of transfer.

The Theory of General Transfer

Prior to the sixteenth century, general transfer of training through mental discipline was widely accepted in education circles. Transfer supposedly was automatic; when a child's mind had been adequately disciplined, it would function more effectively in any learning, willing, or thinking situation. The idea was that faculties of the mind lie dormant until they are exercised. Such faculties as memory, will, reason, and perseverance are the "muscles of the mind"; like physiological muscles they are strengthened through exercise. Not long ago a colleague of one of the authors, a professor of history, said, "I know that students forget in a few years most of what they learn in their history courses. But this doesn't really concern me much. The main value of history is in the disciplining effect it has on students. That effect will remain with them as long as they live."

The doctrine of mental discipline gave transfer its first highly systematic development. Certain subjects such as Latin and geometry supposedly were endowed with unusual transfer qualities. Since, in mental discipline theory, transfer is assumed to be automatic, once a faculty has been developed it goes into operation whenever its use is appropriate.

The theory of mental discipline has been discredited to the point that school subjects no longer can be justified in terms of improving students' minds through exercise. Evidently there is transfer of *learning* but not the general transfer implied in mental discipline. Methods of solving arithmetic problems can be transferred to solution of problems in algebra. The learning of Latin may, and often does, facilitate the learning of English grammar.

However, if experimental research is to be trusted, transfer is not automatic and it is not a matter of disciplining minds.

Herbartian apperception, S-R associationisms, and Gestalt-field theories of learning, while disagreeing on many things, all harmonize in their opposition to mental discipline. Their strongest weapon has been systematic research which tests the results of mental discipline through measurement of just how much memorization strengthens a "memory faculty." Studies developed at the turn of the twentieth century by James, Thorndike, and Woodworth experimentally refuted validity of a mental discipline theory of transfer. Of course, even today mental discipline may be, and often is, defended through philosophic reasoning divorced from research.

Transfer by Identical Elements

S-R associationists attempted to replace the mental discipline theory of transfer with the theory of transfer by *identical elements.* The identical elements theory was developed by Thorndike, who contended that what is learned in one situation is usable in another only to the degree that there are identical elements in the two situations. Identity may be in content, method, procedures, or aims.

Thorndike assumed that, if an S is connected with an R and that same S-R connection is applicable in another situation, it will operate, automatically and mechanistically. A S may be a single stimulus or a group of stimuli, and similarly an R may be a response or a group of responses. Although study of Latin did not discipline faculties of a generalized mind, it supposedly did contribute to transfer to the degree that there are identical elements in Latin and English vocabularies; the 'port' of Latin *porto* transfers to the 'port' of English *transport.* Consequently, in accordance with identical elements, if Latin is taught at all, emphasis should be upon roots or segments which are identical with those in English.

If one tries to base a school program on this conception of transfer his only choice is to incorporate in the curriculum as many learning tasks as possible which, when reproduced outside of school, will contribute to the effectiveness of living. An entire generation of curriculum makers did, in fact, adopt this approach. They studied American community life much as an efficiency expert would conduct time-and motion studies in a factory. They then tried to list specific verbal and motor responses which are needed in daily life and to teach these without more than minor modification in school.

This approach to education poses many difficulties, not the least of which is that there are so many kinds of situations in life to be coped with that a school could not possibly teach them all, even in the 12 or 13 years of required attendance. Curriculums became hopelessly cluttered, and in most schools the results of this cluttering remain today. If only identical elements transfer, the work of the school becomes virtually hopeless.

Under such a situation, someone must decide for each school which among the hundreds of thousands of possible learnings that might be justified are important enough to be taught. Who is to make this decision? Almost everyone will claim the right—legislators, businessmen, labor leaders, patriotic organizations, unpatriotic organizations, parents, school boards, school administrators, and occasionally even a teacher who has the courage to express an opinion.

Pedro T. Orata has concentrated his professional study upon transfer of learning. In 1941 he said, "The evidence which tends to disprove Thorndike's theory of identical elements continues to cumulate... He continued, "Not a simple succession of elements is transferred, but rather an attitude of response or a way of seeing the same kind of solution for different problems. Whereas senseless learning does not transfer, meaningful learning does. The process of learning for transfer becomes one of organization and reorganization of experience."

Orata also lists some conclusions that have developed from his studies. He notes that transfer is found in approximately 80 per cent of studies, it is not an automatic process which may be taken for granted, and the amount of transfer is influenced by many factors. Factors centered in the learner are age, mental ability, personality, stability attained by a learned pattern, knowledge of direction, attitude toward the learning situation, efficient use of past experience, accuracy of learning, and acceptance of methods, procedures, principles, sentiments, and ideals. Factors centered in the learning situation are meaningfulness of the learning situation, suitable organization of subject matter presentation, and provision for continuous reconstruction of experience.

Identical elements theory affirms that transfer occurs, but apparently does not explain how. Psychic atomism and mechanism are inadequate to explain transfer of learning. Some critics of identical elements theory interpret it as really a fragmented faculty psychology—elements in learning may be construed as small faculties.

Transfer of Generalizations

Almost all of the studies of transfer have shown that at least some transfer does occur, although not of a kind so general as to support the notions of the mental disciplinarians. The question which we now debate is, What is the mechanism of transfer? There is no longer any doubt that transfer is possible, but to take fullest advantage of it we must know just how it operates.

As early as 1905, Charles H. Judd, an American educator, asserted that not only does transfer occur if you let it, but the medium of transfer is the *sensed relationships between the elements of a situation.* A statement of relationships is a *generalization.* It may also be called a *principle, rule,* or *law.* Judd's experiment has become something of a classic; it is described in most textbooks which treat the problem of transfer. He selected two groups of boys comparable in those variables which seemed relevant. One (the experimental) group was instructed in the principle of the refraction of light. The other (control) group was not. Both groups of boys were then asked to hit underwater objects with darts. (At the beginning of the experiment, none of the boys had any skill in throwing darts.)

Both groups of boys were instructed to hit targets placed 12 inches under water. The boys who had had theoretical training in the principles of refraction did as poorly at this task as the control group: they had to learn to throw darts before their theoretical training could help. Once this was accomplished, the target was moved to a position four inches under water. Immediately, the experimental group showed a conspicuous superiority over the control group. Their understanding of the nature of refraction had given them cues as to where to aim the darts in order to hit underwater objects which are not where they appear to be. Judd's experiment and his interpretation of it is related in detail in his various books.

Judd's findings antedated similar findings by the Gestalt psychologists, Kohler, Koffka, Wheeler, Perkins, and other Gestaltists (see further Chapter for an account of the work of these men) all insisted that what animals and human beings tend to learn in any meaningful learning situation is *relationships.* Statements of such relation are *theories* (or as previously stated, generalizations, principles, rules, or laws), which, as Judd said, are "...a kind of summary of many experiences. It [theory] makes possible the proper interrelating and interpreting of a whole body of varied experience."

Since accumulated experimentation has shown that attempts to base transfer on identical elements leads to more problems that it solves, and since the generalization theory of Judd and the Gestaltists seems highly productive as a basis for transfer, virtually all educational psychologists today seem to prefer the generalization theory.

More recent research supports Judd's position. In 1957 Kittell measured the relative effects of three amounts of direction to sixth-grade learners in their discovery of established principles on transfer to differing situations and on retention of learned principles. He concluded that "Evidence from this experiment in conjunction with that of similar experiments indicates that furnishing learners with information in the form of underlying principles promotes transfer and retention of learned principles and may provide the background enabling future discovery of new principles."

However, Judd and most other investigators of the generalization hypothesis stop short of a fully adequate statement of the conditions of transfer. It is increasingly apparent that the achievement of a generalization by a student does not in itself guarantee transfer. Even Cronbach's recent statement stops just short of mentioning that for transfer to occur students must be motivated toward that end. He points out that to facilitate transfer students need to learn general principles, that these principles must be clearly understood, that students must be shown places in which the principles can apply, and that they must be given opportunity to recognize the applicability of the principles in increasingly varied and complex situation. This is excellent as far as it goes, but it still leaves out one ingredient which seems indispensable—the motivation of students. A more refined and practicable statement of the conditions of transfer, and one which divorces transfer fully from a mechanistic orientation, is to be found in the recent writings of Ernest E. Bayles. Bayles tells us that "*Any given item of training will transfer if and when—and only if and when—(1) opportunity offers, (2) a trained individual sees or senses it as an opportunity,* and (3) *he is disposed to take advantage of the opportunity.*" In this statement, we take it that "item of training" may be defined as "an insight susceptible to generalized application."

One may operate on habit, and transfer may occur with little or no reflection. Or transfer may occur in a highly reflective situation. In either case transfer is not automatic. A habit is a skillfully executed application of a principle in a situation wherein application of that principle apparently will help a person achieve a goal. Even habits are not blind, automatic behaviors. Rather, they are precise adjustments to situations which call for them. They are products of tested insights which are used in new situations.

Transfer of learning occurs because of perceptual similarities between two situations. When it occurs it is in the form of generalizations, concepts, or insights which are developed in one learning situation and are usable in others. For learning to be most useful in future situations it is essential that insights that are gained be generalized. But even then we cannot safely assert that transfer of generalizations takes place automatically. For transfer to occur, a learner should not only generalize but understand how the generalization can be used, and he should have a desire to use it.

McConnell says, "the consciousness that one is acquiring meanings and abilities which are widely applicable in learning and living is what creates a frame of mind favorably to transfer.... Important as it is, however, this attitude is not enough. One must make an aggressive attempt to interpret new problems in the light of previous experience, and to bring to bear upon the novel situation those understandings and abilities which are relevant and serviceable."

Gertrude Hendrix' new clue to transfer of training is that "...it is the intermediate flash of unverbalized awareness that actually counts for the transfer power...." She found that the way a person learns a generalization affects the probability of his recognition of an opportunity to use it. In method I (a conventional method) a generalization was first stated, then illustrated, then applied to new problems. In method II, the generalization was not stated but "drawn out of" the learners by asking questions; teaching was for unverbalized awareness.

In teaching for unverbalized awareness the stage was set in such a way that as soon as the generalization dawned the learner would begin to apply it. Students were asked to find the sum of the first two odd numbers, the sum of the first three odd numbers, the sum of the first four odd numbers, etc. As soon as the subject knew the relationship between these sums and the number of odd numbers to be added, he started to gasp a little, or smile, or grew tense. That is, he showed in some way that something had happened to him. (The answer: the sum of the first *n* odd numbers is n^2, Furthermore, he began to give succeeding answers rapidly, getting them by the sort cut rather than by the laborious process of adding; he revealed possession of the generalization by transfer behavior based on that generalization.

In method III, students were taught as in method II except that subjects were asked to state the rule they had discovered. Arrival at a correct verbalization (method III) took about wide as long as discovery of a generalization on an unverbalized level (method II). In every case included in two experiments, the highest transfer effects were achieved in the group taught by the unverbalized awareness procedure. The lowest transfer effects came from the group taught by the method in which the generalization was stated first, then illustrated, then applied to new problems. Groups who learned by conscious generalization showed up somewhere between the other two groups. Hypotheses emerging from the data are as follows:

1. For generation of transfer power, the unverbalized awareness method of learning a generalization is better than a method in which an authoritative statement of the generalization comes first.
2. Verbalizing a generalization immediately after discovery does not increase transfer power.
3. Verbalizing a generalization immediately after discovery may actually decrease transfer power.

Crucial Points in Regard to Transfer

Transfer of learning may be summarized in six crucial points:

1. Opportunity for transfer may occur in many situations. It is not inherent in any subject but is possible from any field of knowledge.
2. Transfer is not dependent upon exercise with disciplinary subjects.

3. Transfer is dependent upon methods of teaching and learning which use lifelike situations. It is facilitated by teaching for large generalizations which have transfer value.
4. Transfer is not automatic; opportunities for transfer must be recognized, and the person concerned must want to use them.
5. Transfer varies according to difficulty of generalization of subject matter and intellectual ability of individuals.
6. Insights need not be put into words for their transfer to occur.

HOW MAY PRINCIPLES OF LEARNING BE APPLIED IN THE TEACHING OF A SCHOOL SUBJECT?

In this section there is an example of teaching which illustrates a good many of the principles stated earlier in the chapter. It makes no attempt to incorporate all of them.

Further explanation of the rationale of this section is needed. In our opinion, list of the empirically based principles of learning now included in textbooks of educational psychology harmonize with the Gestalt-field family of learning theories. Although most writers of books in this field try to steer an eclectic course, choosing equally from the experiments of connectionists and field psychologists and refraining from expressing any preference, the research itself, if viewed objectively, appears to reflect, in the main, Gestalt-field assumptions. This is the case, in many instances, whether or not the researchers concede these assumptions. For example, the whole point of most discussions on motivation is that purpose be brought into the picture; yet purpose has been the forte of Gestalt-field psychology and has been played down by all varieties of associationism. As time goes on, we realize more and more that most examples of readiness are just as much a function of experience and purpose as of maturation. The new conceptions of practice seem to imply field theory rather than associationism. Present tendencies with respect to the part vs. whole issue likewise seem to favor the Gestaltists. The studies of retention, which emphasize *meaning* and *motivation* as the primary bases for retention, are wholly on the side of the Gestalt-field position. The "generalization" position with respect to transfer likewise is most consistent with the Gestalt-field point of view.

One difficulty with studies of learning in the past is that the results obtained depended largely on how closely learning was supervised. If learners (whether pigeons or human beings) are highly restricted, one gets the results which Skinner gets. If learners are allowed a considerable amount of freedom they appear to learn insightfully. The results of learning experiments depend more than most experimenters realize on the design of the experiment, rather than on the actual morphology of the learning process. (This was pointed out in further further Chapter).

Another relevant comment is that almost all associations have moved steadily over the years in the direction of a Gestalt-field position. such movement has often taken the form of adoption of an eclectic position following the original espousal of a connectionist or behaviouristic point of view. The evolution in Thorndike's own thought is a striking example of this kind of development. In the 1930s, toward the end of his influential career, Thorndike began expounding the concept of *belongingness.* Although he stated this concept ambiguously, and the word itself was poorly chosen, it appears that he meant something like the Gestalt "law of Pragnanz." His suggestion was that we perceive, and learn, something with more ease if it forms a sensible pattern. Sandiford illustrates this by suggesting that a number sequence of 2, 4, 8, 16, etc., has more "belongingness" than 1, 3, 4, 2, 5, 11, 13, 15.

But let us get on with the main task of the section. Our illustration of the teaching of a subject insightfully is taken from the subject of arithmetic, specifically the teaching of the multiplication combinations involving the 9's. We use the 9's because these combinations are generally considered the most difficult. Furthermore, we use arithmetic because most teachers feel that, however one might teach other subjects, arithmetic must be taught by rote.

Let us assume that we are in a fourth-grade class and are ready to attack the 9's. We already have learned the 2's, 3's, 5's, 10's, and 11's, and we have learned them in such way as to have developed insight into the relationships involved in these tables. We can anticipate a kind of dialogue between students and teacher, which might go somewhat as follows:

The teacher reminds students of the tables they know already and has them review these tables until it is clear that they know them well. The review process might appear on the surface as drill in the old-fashioned sense, but there is a fundamental difference. The teacher makes certain that students understand the relationships involved, i.e., relationships of the same general type as those they are about to learn in connection with the 9's. After the review, the teacher suggests that the class advance to the 9's. (Some students are likely to protest that the 9's are more difficult than any of the others.)

The teacher begins writing the tables on the blackboard, at the same time asking members of the class to supply answers which they already will have learned from their study of the other tables. A "side trip" may be necessary to help students grasp the insight that the product of 9×2 is the same as that of 2×9. What appears on the blackboard is something like this:

$9 \times 1 = 09$	$9 \times 7 =$
$9 \times 2 = 18$	$9 \times 8 =$
$9 \times 3 = 27$	$9 \times 9 =$
$9 \times 4 =$	$9 \times 10 = 90$
$9 \times 5 = 45$	$9 \times 11 = 99$
$9 \times 6 =$	$9 \times 12 =$

To this point, the answers supplied are based on students' prior learning of the 2's, 3's, 5's, 10's and 11's. Let us now envisage the following dialogue:

Teacher: How do we know the answers to 9×1, 9×2, and 9×3?

Class: Because we know the 1's, 2's, and 3's.

Teacher: and what about 9 × 5, 9 × 10, and 9 × 11?

Class: We know these because we know the 5's, 10's, and 11's.

Teacher: The ones that are left are the hard ones, aren't they? What is the answer to 9 × 7, Jimmie? Tell me without looking at the tables in your book. (Within instruction procedure, when the teacher addresses Jimmie or any other pupil, he anticipates that at least most members of the class are thinking along with the student spokesman.)

Jimmie probably will say nothing but will stare at the teacher, baffled. The teacher may then ask various other members of the class the answer to 9 × 6, 9 × 8, and 9 × 4. After the class begins to demonstrate a certain amount of bafflement (perhaps approaching the point of mild frustration), the teacher may entice them in this manner: "Would you like to gain enough understanding of the rest of the 9's so that after today you will know the answers to all of them?" The class is likely to respond in the affirmative with considerable enthusiasm.

Teacher: All right, let's work at this thing together. June, go to the board and write the 10's up to 10 × 5 right beside the 9's. (The class now will have before it the following combination.)

10 × 1 = 10	9 × 1 = 09
10 × 2 = 20	9 × 2 = 18
10 × 3 = 30	9 × 3 = 27
10 × 4 =40	9 × 4 =
10 × 5 = 50	9 × 5 = 45

Teacher: When we compare the 9's which we have answered to the 10's, what difference do we see in the answers? What happens in the case of the 9's which did not happen in the 10's?

Class: Each step we move up in the 9's, one is lost.

Teacher: How do you mean?

Class 9 × 1 is one fewer than 10 × 1, 9 × 2, is two fewer than 10 × 2, and 9 × 3 is three fewer than 10 × 3. That is why we get the answers 09, 18, and 27.

Of course, finding this principle may not come as easily as the foregoing dialogue might suggest. The teacher might need to do quite a lot more "fishing," by rephrasing the question and perhaps even offering some hints. The speed with which a class comes to see for itself principles which are new to it depends much upon what atmosphere has been established, and, of course, on the brightness of the students.

The teacher next helps students see that as in the 10's, the first digit goes up one each time, 09, 18, 27. By this time, the stage should be set for supplying the missing answers.

Teacher: Now think carefully about what we have learned. since 9 × 2 = 18 and 9 × 3 = 27, Gary, what is the answer to 9 × 4?

Gary: 36.

Teacher: Why?

Gary: Well, if the first number increases by one for each larger table, and if we lose one in the last number of each table upward, it would have to be 36.

Teacher: You already know the answer to 9 × 5. Judy, does it check with the idea which we have learned?

Judy: Sure, the first number will be one larger, and we will have lost five numbers from the second number. That makes 45.

The reader should not be misled by the foregoing hypothetical dialogue. In order to economize on space, students have been pictured as saying the right thing the first time. In an actual classroom situation there would be more hesitancy, more fumbling, more tries on the part of students and teacher. But the process would remain essentially the same.

The class now is ready to deepen its insights in relation to the multiplication process.

Teacher: Look again at the first digit of each answer. (Teacher points to the 9's through 9 × 5.) Look at each of these digits in relation to the multipliers, 1, 2, 3, 4, and 5. do you see anything interesting?

Gary: Why, the first digit of the answer is always just one number smaller than the multiplier.

Teacher: Why do you think this is so?

Gary: Would this be caused by losing a number each time—I mean, losing a number as compared with the 10's?

The teacher has succeeded in evolving the insight (at least in Gary) that when one multiples by 9 rather than 10, there is a loss of one at each step, including the first. The answers "never catch up," so to speak. They keep falling behind, but according to a definite and predictable pattern.

Still another relationship may be taught the class:

Teacher: Look carefully at the answers which we have so far. (The teacher points to 09, 18, 27, 36, and 45.) Add the two digits of each answer and see what happens.

Class: The sum of the digits is the same in each answer. The sum is always 9.

Teacher Yes. 0+9 = 9; 1+8 = 9; 2+7 = 9. why is this so?

Class 9 x 1 = 9, then the first digit always increases by one, and the second digit decreases by one. They kind of balance each other, so the sum remains the same.

By this time the stage has been set for teaching the remaining combinations involving the 9's. when asked the answer to 9 × 7, students should reason that the first digit of the answer will be 6 (7 – 1) and that the second digit should be 3 (9 – 6). The class now should be able to complete the table through 9 × 10 easily. At 9 × 11, the first digit of the answer becomes two less than the multiplier. (Why?) Furthermore, the sum of the two digits of the answer does not equal 9, as it did in each preceding step. (Again, why?) Students will know the answer is 99. The problem is why? Answer 9 × 10 = 90; at 9 × 11 "we start around again"— 90 + 9 = 99. At 9 X 11 the first digit of the answer has lost two from the multiplier: 11–2=9, so in 9 × 12 the first part of the answer is 12–2 or 10. For the sum of the digits to add to 9, the last digit is 8. Thus, 12 × 9 = 108. This can be extended into a game.

13 × 9 = 117
14 × 9 = 126
15 × 9 = 135

The class members now are ready to test their new insights to see whether they will work. The teacher may suggest to his better students that they put into words the insights they have learned. However, it should be borne in mind that it is not always necessary for one to put an insight into words in order to use it.

In what specific ways does this lesson in arithmetic differ from traditional procedures used in teaching the multiplication tables? The answer to this question will express the significance of field psychology for learning and teaching. This lesson reflects the teacher's assumption that learning is an insightful process. The teacher is attempting to aid students in improving their understandings or insights in regard to multiplying by 9 and doing it in such a way as to heighten their abilities to achieve new insights independently; he is not merely giving students a gimmick.

4

Teaching and Intelligent Behaviour

Owing to the historical sequence of emerging psychologies of learning, the psychological underpinnings of moderns education are extremely diverse and inconsistent. Once a point of view is developed and popularized, centuries are required for its influence to cease to be felt. As new positions are developed, they do not displace the old; they are grafted on to it. The eventual result is a hodgepodge of bewildering complexity. In the resulting educational atmosphere, one of the most perplexing problems involves the relationship of teaching to intelligence. Consequently, a key to significant differences in outlooks of teachers is the way they define, treat, and foster *intelligence.*

Representatives of all schools of thought take at least some interest in intellectual development of individuals. However, they do not all define intelligence in the same way, and they differs sharply in regard to whether intelligence should be the immediate end of education or merely a subsidiary goal or by-product. Each psychological position has its own characteristic way of defining intelligence and evaluating a proposal that promotion of intelligence be the central goal of education.

We take the position that the most useful way for teachers to define intelligence is as capacity to act with dependable foresight and that it is a product of the interaction of a person and his psychological environment. Hence, a person's intelligence is capable of improvement with education.

WHAT ATTITUDES HAVE BEEN TAKEN HISTORICALLY TOWARD THE NATURE AND PROMOTION OF INTELLIGENCE?

Prior to the 1600s it was thought that little, if anything, could be done to improve the intelligence of an average man. Until the coming of the "Age of Enlightenment" of the seventeenth and eighteenth centuries, it was generally assumed that attempts to improve the quality of the intellect of an ordinary person were doomed to defeat. This pessimistic and fatalistic view of the human race dated from ancient times. However, a much more optimistic view developed in the eighteenth century. Liberal thinkers of France, England, the American colonies, and elsewhere, influenced by Locke's *tabular rasa* theory of sense empiricism, concluded that the intelligence of any normal person could be improved indefinitely through education. Faculty psychology, too, contributed to this line of thinking; intelligent behavior was assumed to be a product of the use of certain faculties (such as reason, memory, and imagination), which were strengthened by exercise.

Those who were optimistic about improvement of intelligence tended to favor extension of education to the lower classes and improvement of education for everybody. However, the mental discipline approach to learning was at that time the only one known; hence, those who felt what education could improve the intelligence of students assumed that benefit could come only from disciplinary drill or reading of the classics.

So far as eighteenth-century school people were concerned, improvement of intelligence could hardly have been much of an issue. For one thing, the concept of intelligence was not well developed. Nothing like a modern definition, in operational terms, of what it means to be intelligent was available. For another thing, the aims of education were many, and production of "thought power 170 by no means given central place. Moral training probably was regarded as more central to the educational enterprise. Today, however, in much of the literature of education, development of the capacity to thin, i.e., to make intelligent decisions, is a paramount goal. This is not to say that moral education is disregarded but rather that the method of intelligence is recommended in this area as well as in others.

Why do so many educators of today stress development of intelligence as a primary goal of education? One reason is the relation between the level of general intelligence and successful functioning of democracy. This relationship has been noted for many centuries, often for the purpose of proving that, since the masses were so lacking in intelligence, democracy was an impractical ideal. However, by the late eighteenth or early nineteenth century, democracy had come to be widely accepted in a few countries not only as an ideal social arrangement but also as a practical system of human relations. Those who thought democracy practicable, like Thomas Jefferson, felt that its potential for good could be realized only as the masses were educated. Jefferson recommended free public education—not much, but a little—for everyone. His assumption was that a system of free, compulsory public education would raise the general level of intelligence.

Possibly most people today would say that intelligent behavior among the masses is prerequisite to successful functioning of democracy and that education is essential to mass intelligence. It is likely that the average person does not have a very clear conception of what it means to be intelligent. He is for intelligence up to a point; but when its application has reached a certain intensity and comprehensiveness, he becomes frightened of it. He regards a limited amount of intelligence as a necessity and any amount in excess as subversive.

Many social scientists and other students of society, while committed personally to democratic values, are not now so much concerned with the use of intelligence to bolster democracy as with its use to insure human survival. Perhaps there are few who fear that *Homo sapiens* will disappear from earth; but a great many highly educated people genuinely fear that human existence may degenerate to a kind of brute level. They are alarmed because of the failure of man, up to the present, to eliminate certain threats to his continued civilized existence. The greatest such threats probably are uncontrolled population growth and atomic war.

Although there might be disagreement as to the seriousness of problems now confronting mankind, there probably would be little objection to the statement that numerous social difficulties exist which people have so far failed to alleviate to any significant degree. In addition to population growth and war, we should include in our list extreme poverty and outright hunger in large parts of the world, political and economic centralization, growing mechanization of life in industrial countries, and increasing pressures toward conformity.

To what extent can gains in the general level of intelligence help us achieve solutions or partial solutions to problems like these? no one can answer with certainty. In some areas of life we allow intelligence to operate in comparative freedom. In science and technology the method of intelligence seems firmly established. A scientist or technician is rewarded for discovering flaws in old scientific or technical ideas, particularly ideas relating to design and manufacture of material goods. An inventor who devises a new military weapon or a new design for an automobile motor may become a national hero. It does not matter seriously that his invention makes obsolete all that has come before it. Here, at least, intelligence is highly rewarded.

But as James Harvey Robinson pointed out, "...Out most important opinions—those, for example, having to do with traditional religious and moral conviction, property rights, patriotism, national honor, the state, and indeed all the assumed foundations of society—are, as I have already suggested, rarely the result of reasoned consideration, but of unthinking absorption from the social environment in which we live. consequently, they have about them a quality of 'elemental certitude,' and we especially resent doubt or criticism cast upon them." Thus, we live in a paradoxical world. We use the method of intelligence with boldness and zest in certain areas of living and we reject it with great determination in others.

Each basic psychology of learning—mental discipline, natural unfoldment, apperception, S-R associationism, and cognitive-field psychology—has its unique meaning for the concepts *intelligence* and *intelligent.* During the development of modern education, each psychology has had its turn at the center of the stage. With every change in dominant psychology, schools have shown the consequences of the meaning of intelligence then in vogue. Consequently, confusion in regard to the nature of learning has carried with it a parallel confusion concerning the nature and meaning of intelligence.

Mental Discipline and Intelligence

According to the doctrine of mental discipline, the chief purpose of education is to strengthen the mental faculties, especially will and reason, through appropriate kinds of drill. Although mental disciplinarians often fail to define their terms carefully, it is evident that their view of the meaning of intelligence is different from that of persons who reject this approach to education. To mental disciplinarians, intelligence is a condition characterized by relatively high development of the faculty of reason. An intelligent man is a highly rational man. The faculty or reason, when well exercised and developed, supposedly qualifies its owner to reason intelligently—accurately and logically—in regard to any matter.

Until the end of the nineteenth century, American formal education was dominated by the doctrine of mental discipline. During this period, education was regarded as necessarily unpleasant. The schoolroom atmosphere was at least austere and sometimes harsh. Teachers usually were dictators, sometimes benevolent, sometimes even spiteful. Children were expected to be respectful and obedient and to accept at face value whatever a teacher told them. Curriculums were relatively fixed, with an almost exclusive emphasis in elementary schools on the fundamental skill subjects and in secondary schools on such "disciplinary" subjects as Latin, history, and mathematics.

There always have been persons who opposed austere, disciplinary education. Undoubtedly some of these dissenters rejected mental discipline because they felt sorry for children. The deplored extremely difficult assignments, stern rules governing conduct, and severe punishments. However, kindness toward children was not likely to be carried very far in a culture based upon the psychological and philosophical premises of Puritanism and kindred outlooks. One who accepts the "bad-active" principle of human nature logically regards it as a favor to a child to "break his spirit." If a child's natural impulses are evil, crushing these impulses should help the child—not only to acquire immortality, but also to prosper here on earth.

The two most influential groups in the United States who continue to favor a disciplinary approach to education are some Church officials, particularly those dedicated to parochial education, and those liberal arts professors who are under the influence of faculty psychology and the classical tradition in education. In addition to these there are many thousands of persons, including some public school teachers, who gravitate toward a theory of mental discipline. All of them to some degree assume the validity of faculty psychology. They think that learning is a matter of strengthening, or disciplining, the faculties and that certain faculties combine to produce intelligent behavior.

Persons whose theory of mental discipline is tied to a theology are likely to stress strengthening of faculties such as will, moral discernment, and religiosity. Those whose theory of mental discipline is related to nonreligious humanism, e.g., "pure" classicists, are likely to stress such faculties as reason, memory, and imagination, all of which might work together to produce "intellectual capacity."

Professor Arthur Bestor, who may be called a modern classicist, writes as follows: "...The school exists to provide intellectual training in every field of activity where systematic thinking is an important component of success. It exists to provide it for every citizen who has the capacity and the will to apply intellectual means to the solution of the problems that confront him." Repeatedly in his writings Professor Bestor reiterates his contention that the foremost role of schools is "intellectual training." Other modern classicists who argue in the same manner are Robber Hutchins, Mortimer Smith, and Bernard Iddings Bell.

Roussellian Natural Unfoldment and Intelligence

Any drastic departure from a disciplinary approach to education is possible only with adoption of fundamentally different assumptions about the nature of man and the universe. As we have seen, Rousseau supplied these assumptions. Let us follow the train of thought which emerged as a result of Roussellian influences.

If man is a part of nature, and if all of nature is intrinsically good, then man is naturally good. (This line of reasoning is developed in considerable detail in previous chapter) If a child is born good, and his natural tendencies lead him to remain so, then it follows logically that children should be reared *permissively;* there is no need for their being disciplined at any time. A permissive classroom is one in which there is *unlimited freedom.* A permissive situation is laissez faire—meaning literally "let people do what they choose." *Permissive* may be considered the opposite of such terms as *teacher-centered, centralized, directed, and autocratic.*

Permissiveness should not be confused with democracy. A democratic group is led; it may be subject to a variety of restraints. in a democratic classroom there is not unlimited freedom but, rather, equally limited freedom. We may think of democracy as an emergent synthesis arising from the inadequacies of both anarchic—laissez-faire—and autocratic forms of organization.

How exponents of natural unfoldment define intelligence is not entirely clear. Conceivably, they might employ any of the extant definitions. What is clear is that they regard the development of intelligence as something which "just naturally happens." To be consistent with their over-all out-look, the would reject any kind of formal teaching for the purpose of stimulating intelligence. They would stress student-planned activities, including highly permissive types of projects, as the means for releasing of developing intellectual performance.

Eighteenth-century Roussellian "romantic naturalism" greatly influenced nineteenth-century thinking of leaders such as Pestalozzi and Froebel and reasserted itself in twentieth-century "Progressivism." Not only did Heinrich Pestalozzi (1746–1827) favor broadening the elementary curriculum by adding subjects with a natural appeal to children; he also believed that children should learn actively through inquiry and investigation. Compared with practices which were to develop in the twentieth century, Pestalozzi's approach to teaching does not appear highly permissive. However, it was much more "child centered" than most elementary education of that century.

Friedrich Froebel (1782–1852), a German educator and founder of the kindergarten, appears to have favored permissivism more than did Pestalozzi. Froebel said, "What one tries to represent or do he begins to understand." This seems to mean that "we understand what we do for ourselves." There surely is merit in such an idea; however, Froebel developed the idea to mean that children can set their own standards and should be allowed to do so. All self-initiated activity is creative, he argued, and can be justified on educational grounds. The curriculum he advocated consisted almost entirely of relatively spontaneous, free activity.

Without some qualifications, the foregoing statement would be an exaggeration; Forebel apparently did feel that certain activities were more valuable than others. He listed a large number of such activities, including games, plays, handwork, collecting, music, gardening, storytelling, construction projects, and democratic self-government. However, in a Froebelian kindergarten children were more free than in any previously know school. Here teaching practices *looked* different, dramatically different. Anyone could sense the difference in atmosphere between a school where children were encouraged to do what they liked and happiness and gaiety were promoted and a school where the teacher was a dictator deliberately trying to make life unpleasant for children.

Herbartian Apperception and Intelligence

There are two broad types of associationisms: (1) early mentalistic associationisms which had association of ideas in a mind as their focal point, and (2) more modern physicalistic associationisms which concern themselves with formation of connections in a brain and peripheral nervous system or between organic responses and environmental stimuli.

Herbartian apperception has been the leading example of the first type of associationism. Although Herbart's associationist psychology was built on fundamentally different premises from the natural unfoldment theory of followers of Rousseau, it was equally incompatible with mental discipline. Hence, Herbartian teaching, like Roussellin permissiveness, can be considered a counter influence to mental discipline. The formal, rigid approach of Herbartians, however, coupled with what appeared to be emphasis upon rote memorization, made theory teaching appear on the surface much like the kind of education practiced by the mental disciplinarians. Herbart's prescription for good teaching, as implemented by his followers, became highly mechanical. Both apperception and mental discipline made a teacher equally central and dominant in the educational process. The Herbartian five steps seemed to put teaching on a different plane from that of mere drill an rote memorization. However, the Herbartian teachers were like all other associationist in one respect: the teacher was the dominant figure and students were permitted little opportunity for creative reflection.

Psychologists in the tradition of early associationism had a characteristic manner of defining intelligence. Remember that they regarded learning as a process of storing away ideas. Hence, they equated intelligence with capacity to associate and retain ideas and call them forth when needed in proper association with one another. To them a mind acts somewhat the way a boy managing his marbles does: except for those in use, he keeps them put away, but they are stored in a sufficiently organized manner so that the boy can easily get his hands on his favorite "shooters" as well as his cheap, expendable glass marbles when he needs them *Intelligence* refers to a person's general effectiveness at storing "mental marbles" in organized fashion and selecting efficiently those which he wants to use as the need arises. The active nature of intelligence, however, resides in the "marbles," not in the container.

S-R Associationism and Intelligence

In the first quarter of the twentieth century the two dominant S-R associationistic psychologies were Watsonian behaviorism and Thorndikean connectionism. Today's S-R associationisms are modifications and refinements of these two earlier psychologies.

If we permitted them to substitute "physical bonds" for "ideas in association," the later associationists would accept about the same definition as apperceptionists. To them, a person's capacity to form links in the nervous system between stimuli and motel responses, to retain these links, and to repeat the proper sequence of motion when confronted with a stimulus at any time in the future constitutes intelligence. Since, to them, intelligence has a physiological basis and a given person's neural structure is not likely to change, it is only logical to suppose that the potential of an organism for intelligent behavior will not change. And indeed this is what the generation of associationists who were in the forefront during the 1920s and 1930s did believe.

S-R associationists regard intelligence as an innate, relatively fixed neural structure; once physiological maturity is reached it does not change. It is measured by tests which attempt to sample what a person has learned as well as how effectively he can solve problems (most of which involve one's ability to see relationships). Once a person's "mental age" is derived by means of such a test, an IQ score is obtained by dividing mental age by chronological age and multiplying by one hundred. Intelligence, so measured, supposedly is innate, and IQ supposedly is constant throughout life.

John b. Watson was convinced that in any normal person the capacity for forming neural bonds was so great that he would never make full use of it. He therefore assumed that an average person does not learn up to capacity, and the amount he does learn is purely a function of the environment. Watson believed, the, that almost any normal person could acquire the same complicated conditioning that, say, a skilled surgeon (or even a philosopher) could achieve. Thus, on the matter of intelligence, Watson was an environmentalist.

Watson's followers were less optimistic. Generally speaking, American behaviorists have assumed not only that intelligence is a fixed capacity but that the limitations of neural structure do prevent most persons from performing above a given (and definable) level. these psychologists place great faith in the ability of intelligence tests to reveal the level for any particular person.

Implications for education of this mechanistic concept of intelligence are clear. First, education can do only so much; each person is limited by his inborn neural structure. Second, all education can do is take advantage of what capacity a child has for forming dependable S-R linkages. His capacity for intelligent behavior depends upon how many good links can be formed and retained. Hence, the best—in fact, the only—way education can serve the cause of intelligence is to condition children effectively.

In a classroom situation where the guiding educational psychology is based upon S-R associationism, conditioning takes the from, for the most part, of committing facts to memory and selecting the proper one of several suggested answers. Students learn to repeat verbal statements when given the appropriate stimulus. Obviously, there is little which is reflective or creative about this, but persons who operate in terms of an associationist psychology have never regarded learning as basically reflective or creative. Associationists, however, do assume that conditioning may be the basis for future intelligent behavior.

Any psychology which explained mental functioning as either an association of ideas or an association of stimuli and responses is likely to lead to a characteristic manner of classroom instruction. Such psychologies (all the associationisms) usually assume that learning is a mechanical process which can operate only in the presence of an environment directing it.

Hence, a teaching who accepts an associationist psychology selects ahead of time the precise ideas or response inculcate in his students. Through drill or exercises students reproduced the desired ideas or responses until they are fixed. Then, as a final step, the teacher tests the students to see whether they can accurately reproduce the learned material.

Appropriate responses become the associationistic basis of courses of study, textbooks, and unit plans. A teacher's role is to get the responses fixed in students. If, life Thorndike, one defines a habit as a fixed way of responding to a given stimulus situation, then the object of education under S-R associationistic psychology becomes the fixation of as many habits as possible as permanently as possible. Successful teaching of a maximum number of habitual responses seems to required somewhat rigid time scheduling and minimum indulgence of students' natural interests.

Classrooms of teachers education in associationistic psychology often have the appearance of classrooms of mental disciplinarians. The chief difference perhaps, is that an associationist includes "practical" subjects like shop and home economics, whereas a mental disciplinarian, influenced by the classical tradition, stresses subjects like philosophy and classical literature to discipline immature minds.

Cognitive-Field Theory and Intelligence

The cognitive-field definition of intelligence is one's capacity for accurate foresight as it is revealed in one's ability to solve problems in areas of concern. This conception of intelligence assumes that problem-solving ability, although influenced by hereditary factors, is susceptible to change in a normal per and can improve through education. If one's education includes not only opportunity for problem solving but also opportunity to study the problem solving process as a process and to achieve generalized insights about it most new problems it is assumed, will be approached more intelligently than they would have been before. As a person acquires more, and more adequate, generalized insights he become more intelligent.

Capacity for accurate foresight is closely related to the quality of one's perceptions. We cited earlier a highly provocative article on this subject published by Arthur Combs in 1952. Combs begin by stating that, there is a growing tendency in psychology to view behavior as a function of perception. Anything which limits the scope and clarity of a person's life space—perceptual field——detracts from his capacity for intelligent action.

At any given time the nature of our perceptions is influenced by certain factors. First, our perceptions are affected by our purposes at the time; what seems relevant one time will be quite irrelevant another. Often we unknowingly distort "what is there" in an attempt to serve our purposes better. Second, there are physiologic limitation to perception. some of these are not obvious and are difficult to demonstrate—such as differences in the functioning of neural structures in persons who appear physiologically normal, other pysiological differences are obvious: e.g., the nearsightedness of one of the authors often leads to behavior which to an observer appears "stupid." Exhaustion or illness, too can significantly limit the quality of perception. Third, the range of experience which is represented in a stimulating environment has a great advantage over one who does not.

It Combs' thesis is valid, learning necessarily plays a major role in determining a person's habitual level of intelligence. In fact the range intelligence among persons who are not physiologically defective may be explainable largely by differences in learning. At least, we have no conclusive evidence to the contrary. In any case, we now have good reason to believe that virtually everyone can make significant gains tin intelligence under the right environmental circumstances. Combs emphasizes the role which our perceptions of self play in intelligent behavior; a person who becomes convinced that he has certain limitation s tends to have these limitations, and a self-confident person, in contrast, is likely to perform at an increasingly high level.

Exponents of cognitive-field theory, more than representatives of any other system of modern psychology, have emphasized that capacity for intelligent behavior is modified by learning. Advocates of the cognitive-field position do not like to talk in terms of any limitations of intelligence. For example, Combs and Snygg tell us, "...the possibilities for human perception seem almost infinite. Given a healthy physical organism to provide the vehicle for perception, enough time, a stimulating environment, challenging and fruitful problems, and a non-restrictive self concept, there seems no end to the perceptions possible to the individual." Given the proper conditions there is no reason why the intelligence of a person should not increase during his entire lifetime. of course, old age may produce physiological deterioration which reduces the capacity for differentiating new perceptions. On the other hand, it is possible to cite numerous cases of persons who have retained a remarkable capacity for intellectual growth and creativity until the age of 90 or beyond.

In consideration of the foregoing point of view concerning flexibility of intelligence, a word of caution is necessary. It is by no means easy for a person continuously to improve the number and quality of his perceptions. Although one's perceptual field, or life space, undergoes continuous modification, these changes tend to apply to minor attitudes, values, and beliefs—to items which are not central to one's personality structure. Religious convictions, for example, are not likely to change readily—not, for example, like one's taste in clothing or automobiles. The essential ingredients for continued growth in intelligence are *open-mindedness to new ideas and willingness to criticize one's most cherished convictions.* since for most persons attainment of these ingredients is very difficult, their intelligence quotients, as revealed by any known measuring device, do not change markedly over the course of time; and in the case of some persons the IQ remains stable, or may even regress. There is reason to suppose, however, that one's degree of open-mindedness and one's ability for self-criticism *are largely a function of his education.*

In discussing intelligence we have said nothing about another dimension of experience—emotion. Faculty psychologists have treated emotional capacities as faculties, able to operate quite independently of other faculties. The faculty of reason, too, was susceptible to independent development; and for reason to function efficiently it must be freed from entanglements with emotion.

Likewise, associationists have tended to separate emotion and thought. They think of all behavior as a product of conditioning. A person could be conditioned, they thought, to be coldly objective when decisions had to be made; or he could be conditioned to make decisions "emotionally." Both of these outlooks can be criticized because of their separation of thinking and feeling (emotion).

To cognitive–field psychologists, thinking never occurs apart from feeling. A person who habitually displays a high level of intelligence experiences emotion as he thinks. Emotion is one aspect of the process we call thinking. Of course, some types of feeling, if experienced with intensity, may hinder rational decision. One of the most common is the fear a person feels when he thinks some aspect of his self is under threat. However, the most careful thought may be accompanied by considerable amounts of fear, discouragement, elation, or other feeling states.

How a teacher conceives the nature of intelligence has great bearing upon how he teaches. Furthermore, whether a teacher is an exponent of mental discipline, natural unfoldment, apperception, S–R associationism, cognitive–field theory, or some combination of these greatly affects how he defines the aims of education, organizes a curriculum, and conducts classes. Most teaching procedures reflect influences of a combination of learning theories. But quite often teachers do not recognize the inconsistencies which their teaching represents. Consequently, there tends to be considerable confusion over the proper relationship of teaching and intelligence.

WHY THE CONFUSION CONCERNING TEACHING AND INTELLIGENCE?

Obviously, there are many contradictions in policies and operations of American education. However, so far as the psychology of teaching and learning is concern, the one central contradiction is an *incompatible marriage of society–centered, authoritarian traditionalism and child–centered permissiveness.* Traditionalism is an approach to teaching based upon either mind training or the passive assimilation of factual content through drill. Child–centered permissiveness is the approach to teaching based upon giving children free reign to design their own learning activities, with steady emphasis upon self–expression and reliance upon self–control. Child–centered permissiveness considers intelligence innate ability which naturally unfolds as a person develops through successive salutatory stages. Traditional teaching, in contrast, proceeds on the assumption that societal imposition is essential to intellectual growth; minds must be trained, apperceptive masses must be built, or organisms must be conditioned.

In the conflict between *traditionalism* and *child– centered permissiveness, neither has bee able conclusively to win the field. Consequently, as a convenient* modus vivendi *both outlooks have come to be practiced side by side.* A teacher may rely for a while on highly traditional instruction—as if a psychology of learning on which traditionalism is based were valid. After a time he may begin to feel guilty. After all, one's teaching should be up to date! This rationalization is likely to be assisted by the fact that students are becoming restless. So the teacher shifts gears. He assigns handicraft projects and for a few days allows students relatively free expression—as if a psychology of learning upon which free expression is based were also valid. The rub lies in the disharmony of the two psychologies; since they rest on incompatible assumptions about the nature of human beings, they cannot both be valid.

This is not to suggest that students will not learn something under either approach. They possibly may learn equal amounts under both, whether much or little. The point is that the learning process which actually is operating may be quite different from what a teacher assumes it to be; students may be learning things in ways the teacher does not suspect and does not want. The teacher is caught, usually unknowingly, in a situation which he does not understand. What may happen can be illustrated with a concrete example.

How Is Confusion Apparent in Today's Schools?

Mrs. R had taught for 25 years in the same city school system. She was regarded favorably by her administrator and by most of her students. Her areas of specialization were social and English.

Mrs. R began a unit pertaining to the geography and the culture of France by assigning the textbook chapter on France. She stressed the importance of memorizing factual details, such as the leading rivers, towns, industries, and seaports. She also told her students that they must learn some of the facts of French history, such as the dated when various heads of government were in office. All of these facts were given in the textbook and in reference books available in the room. At the conclusion of the unit, Mrs. R gave a test consisting of true–false items on the facts.

Daily recitation involved question–and–answer sessions in which Mrs. R asked students to recall facts given in the textbook. On one occasion the class was permitted to play a game. The class was split in half, and the halves took positions on opposite sides of the room. From each group a "questioner" was chosen.

His job was to ask questions about France of students in the other group. When a student missed a question, he had to take his seat, as in a spelldown. The questions asked involved highly specific facts of the kind which Mrs. R had stressed as being important.

On two different days students worked at their desks with dittoed sheets supplied by Mrs. R. These were verbatim copies of textbook material, except that two or three words were omitted from each sentence. Blanks were substituted for the words, and students were required to refer to the text and fill in the blanks with the rights words.

In addition to the work in class, Mrs. R assigned each student a project. Projects were to be originated by the students and completed outside of class, with no help from Mrs. R. Mrs. R gave no specification, except to say that projects must involve some kind of handwork and must bear some relationship to France or French history.

After several rather turbulent days spent in trying to find a project, one of the students, Sally, hit upon the idea of etching a map of France on a piece of plywood with a woodburning set. After etching the map, her plan was to paste pictures on the wood indicating industries or products of particular provinces. Since Sally did not draw well, she persuaded her father to sketch in pencil on the plywood the outline of France, with its rivers, provinces, and major towns. She then selected one of the woodburning styli and began tracing in the sketched map. In the process, she burned a severe blister on one finger. After a number of tearful request, her father finished tracing the lines on the map with the styles.

After searching through a good many magazines, Sally discovered that she could not find pictures representing a range of French industries and products. The products portrayed most often were alcoholic beverages—wine, champagne, and brandy. Her father suggested that she confine the pictures to one industry and make use of the pictures of alcoholic beverages.

The teacher accepted the map and gave Sally a mark of B for it. However, when it came time to display the various projects on classroom walls and tables, Mrs. R put Sally's map away in a cupboard. Mrs. R is a teetotaler.

A few months later Sally's father asked Sally what she remembered from her study of France. Her reply was, "I learned that you have to be awfully careful with a woodburning set or you will burn yourself."

The foregoing illustration is reasonably typical of all the units studied in this class during the course of the year. Note that it combined more or less rote fact learning with supposedly free activity. Most of the time the class was fact centered and teacher dominated, but where the projects were involved the teacher veered to a highly permissive approach. Such vacillation between teacher–dominated drill on facts and relatively undirected project work characterizes much of today's teaching.

To summarize, we may say that today's teaching often reflects an incompatible marriage: the *wedding of teacher–dominated drill over highly specific factual material and relatively undirected project work.* It is based on different, and incompatible, psychological assumptions. How, how has the rise of such self–contradictory teaching occurred and what is to be done about it?

How Has John Dewey Influenced Teaching Practices?

John Dewey generally is considered America's foremost twentieth–century philosophy was unique in that he was convinced that we should be able to validate any tenable philosophical position by placing it in operation in our public schools and reaping beneficial consequences. Dewey's thinking developed at the same time that S–R associationism and Gestalt–field theories were being advanced. Exponents of both schools of psychology have attempted to harmonite their respective theories with Dewey's relativistic philosophy. This practice has given rise to much conflict and confusion and many contradictions in the thinking of modern educators.

Dewey thought that the primary goal of teaching should be improvement of intelligence. Consequently, his psychology placed central emphasis upon teaching students an inclination toward, and the skills necessary for, reflective thinking. Dewey's book *How We Think* reflects his central pedagogical interest. He argued that teachers should stimulate students to think by maneuvering them into problematic, or "forked path" situations. Such situations have the qualities of raising doubts about existing convictions and requiring students to seek alternative solutions, each to be studied on its own merits.

In addition to his positive emphasis on development of capacity for accurate foresight—intelligence—Dewey attacked much of the formalism inherent in both mental discipline and the mental and physical associationisms. He insisted upon treated children kindly, recognizing their interests, and encouraging them to participate actively in the educative process. Because this personal emphasis is stated so strongly in some of Dewey's works, such as *Democracy and Education,* many of his "followers" associate Dewey with those who argue of highly permissive treatment of children. However, careful reading of Dewey's concept of a democratic classroom was not one of laissez faire any more than it was one of cloaked autocracy.

However much quarreling there might be about Dewey's exact position on teacher–student relationships, there is general agreement that his impact served to weaken the arguments of mental disciplinarians and all other formalists. Dewey's philosophy and psychology seemed to demand introduction of much greater flexibility and freedom in classrooms.

It is probably easy to overestimate the immediate influence of Dewey on American education; many classrooms show very little, if any, Dewey influence. Probably one reason is the fact the Dewey's thinking was complex and his writing extraordinarily hard to read. Many "followers" undoubtedly never understood what Dewey meant about some matters. They tended to overemphasize out of all proportion the small streak of Roussellianism which appeared in Dewey's early writing and to ignore

Dewey's constant, tough–minded insistence on placing reflective thought at the heart of the educative process. Often they introduced innovations into education which they attributed to Dewey's inspiration but which actually were inspired by educational reformers who preceded Dewey by a long time.

The Progressive Education Association was the chief organization within which contradictions in educational thinking, particularly in regard to the role of schools in relation to intelligence, became apparent.

WHAT WAS THE PROGRESSIVE EDUCATION MOVEMENT?

Progressive Education has deep historical roots in both the United States and Europe. The revolt against what seemed to be mechanical, rote teaching and learning reached such proportions by the time of World War I that the situation was ripe for launching an organized movement for a new kind of education. Hence, the Progressive Education Association was founded in 1919, had its first national conference in 1920, and established its journal, *Progressive Education,* in 1923.

Francis W. Parker often is considered the pioneer of Progressive Education in this country. Parker was director of the Cook County Normal School of Chicago. He urged that his students, as teachers, develop and employ a theory of education along the lines developed by Pestalozzi and Froebel. Parker wanted the native endowments of a child, rather than formal school subjects, made the center of attention in a school. He displayed a reverence for childhood of such magnitude that he could not think in any terms other than those of a child–centered school.

In 1901, a well–to–do admirer of Parker financed a private school in Chicago for implementing Parker's ideas. Over the years, the Francis W. Parker School graduated hundreds of boys and girls. many of them became distinguished citizens. The school also attracted numerous visitors from this country and abroad. Parker died in 1902.

In 1894 Dewey became head of the Department of Psychology, Philosophy, and Education at the University of Chicago. In 1986 he established his experimental school, the University Elementary School, at the University. From this time on, he was claimed as the guiding light of the Progressive Education movement. In his book *School and Society* (1899) he advocated introduction of activity programs into schools through which students might learn, through experience, greater freedom of creative expression and attention to social as well as academic aims. However, Dewey did not in this book advocate Roussellian permissivism.

What Were the Key Tenets of Progressive Education?

What did the early Progressives believe? Mr. Cobb has summarized the Progressive creed under 10 major points. He maintains that these 10 points represent principles upon which virtually all Progressives agree; extreme views which reflect personal idiosyncrasies are omitted.

1. Health most come first. This principle means much more than the mere promotion of bodily fitness through calisthenics and proper medical care. It means that "...the school life from beginning to end should be adapted to the developing nervous system of the child. It means movable seats; more freedom of movement in the classroom; elimination of strain from academic work; abundant handwork and motor–activity of different kinds to balance the head work; avoidance of large classes with their overstimulation for small children; longer recesses and more use of the out–of–doors; and close cooperation between school and home for detection and cure of pathological conditions, whether of body or of mind."
2. Learning comes from doing: let the hands aid the brain. According to this principle, activities should be introduced

into all subjects insofar as possible. The means physical activities—work with the hands. Cobb says that this principle is justified because a majority of children in today's world are "motor–active and love doing rather than reading."

3. Classrooms should be freed from unnatural restraints, and "exterior compulsions" should be transformed into "interior compulsions." A great amount of freedom with respect to both the work and general discipline characterizes a Progressive school. Specifically, Cobb says, "...The children feel the school to be theirs. They help make the rules which govern their own academic and social conduct...Progressive education introduces into the school life the freedom and democracy which have long since been expressed in political life and which are now manifesting themselves in the home...Children are best behaved when they learn to control themselves..."

4. Education should be adapted to the different of individual children. Progressive schools, according to Cobb, do not merely allow for differences in personality; they encourage such differences. Such schools continually fight against standardization and conformity. Each child is assumed to be unique and to require unique treatment.

5. Group–consciousness and social–mindedness should be developed in children: social adjustment and character training are as important as academic progress. Progressive schools, as Cobb sees it, de–emphasize competition. Progressive teachers abhor the use of competitive marks and rewards. They seek to develop in children social and cooperative, rather than competitive, aggressive, and exploiting, qualities. To achieve this end, much use is made of group projects.

6. A child should have abundant opportunity for creative expression. "Education should be a process of expression rather than of impression—a natural unfolding of the powers and potentialities of the Child." Self–expression calls for

much use of the arts, although not in any formalized way: "Expression first, with form subservient to it."

7. A child should be enabled to acquire thorough control of the tools of learning rather than merely to acquire facts. In Progressive schools the emphasis is not on fact learning but rather on the learning of research methods. children are taught to know how and where to gather required information, and how to use it.

8. The method of creative expression should be introduced into academic work, so that education shall be joyous. Mr. Cobb is not as definite as he might be about what he means here. He suggests that the same principles employed in the teaching of art should be applied to academic subjects "so as to introduce inspiration and creativeness as preliminary to the acquirement of technique by drill." If this is done successfully, children will "work hard" and "accomplish marvels."

9. The tyranny of marks and examinations should be abolished. We shall let Mr. Cobb speak for himself on this point: "Progressive schools do not entirely abolish marks and tests, but use them in such a way as to eliminate strains and anxieties. Progressive educators as a rule use no marks in the classrooms...Children are encouraged to express themselves and to compete, not with other children, but with themselves to surpass their previous records and achievements."

10. The teacher should be a leader and a guide, not a taskmaster. A teacher should be of the "artistic rather than of the bureaucratic temperament." He should have a personality which will permit awakening the creative gifts in children. This means he will be a friendly helpmate who tries to encourage and stimulate. He tries to erase the old-fashioned barriers between teacher and students.

An analytical reader can see a strong element of Roussellian "natural unfoldment" along with a lesser element of authoritarian imposition in these 10 principles. Although Cobb and virtually and other Progressive educators do not advocate turning children loose to do entirely as they please, they reiterate time and again the need to encourage self-expression. Under item 6, Cobb makes the point in typical Roussellian language: "Education should be a process of expression rather than impression—a natural unfolding of the powers and potentialities of the child."

Confusion Within the Progressive Education Movement

One of the few defensible statements which can be made about the Progressive Education movement is that it embraced a diversity of views, united only in that they were all opposed to a mental discipline approach to teaching. The movement represented a revolt against the notions that children are innately bad, that child nature must be remolded, that this can be done only through the stern discipline of rod and unpleasant subject matter. The movement likewise represented a revolt against learning characterized exclusively by drill and rote memorization, or mechanical procedures.

During the early years of the movement, the urge to rebel was so strong in the minds of members of the Association that they failed to see clearly the differences among themselves. The Roussellians, whom some persons have labeled the "super–Progressives," were at the beginning and remained, perhaps the dominant element in the movement. However, during the 1930s and 1940s an important non–Roussellian segment within the Association began to see clearly the implications of the Roussellian overtones of the movement. The group began to protest and to withdraw support. One of the more important of these critics was Boyd H. Bode, who spent the latter part of his professional life at Ohio State University. In his book *Progressive Education at the Crossroads* Bode attempted to state the crucial issue as he saw it.

Progressives, Bode said, talked and acted as if educators could determine the aims of education merely by studying children.

Such study, the Progressives felt, would reveal the needs of children. Reference, of course, is to so–called "child–centered needs"—needs based upon instinctive urges. Once the needs of children were known, a curriculum could be devised to cater to them. Bode countered this view by arguing that needs arise out of interactive situations, and hence neither the social nor the physical environment can be disregarded. No formulation of children's needs is possible apart from a study of the culture in which a child lives.

For example, according to Bode, we live in a culture which is straining to become more democratic and so requires from its members certain kinds of attitudes, values, beliefs, and knowledge. The schools in the United States have an obligation to teach thought patterns compatible with democracy. However, since each person's needs arise from interactive situations, a teacher cannot be guided only by the demands of the culture. Rather, he must study each child in an attempt to see what "needs" arise from the mutual impact of perceptual selves and cultural forces. (The situational concept of needs is described in the last part of further Chapter.)

Bode did not stop with Dewey's psychological formulations; he developed psychological concepts in his own way, introducing a terminology similar to that used by some of the field psychologists. His over-all point of view, however, is clearly derived from Dewey.

The followers of Dewey, or at least one group of them, irritated by the persistently Roussellian tendencies of other members of the Progressive Education Association, became increasingly intransigent. Ultimately, many of them dissociated themselves entirely from the Progressive Education movement or, if not that, remained as rebels within the ranks. The disharmony within the movement tended to confuse not only the general public but school teachers and administrators as well.

A point of view other than Roussellian unfoldment or that of Dewey could also be detected within the Progressive Education movement, based upon a quite different school of thought in psychology—Thorndikean connectionism. We note in previous Chapter that Thorndike was extremely influential in teachers' colleges during the 1020s and 1930s. His textbook in educational psychology.was the first in its subject to be published in this country and enjoyed nation-wide usage. Although Thorndike's connectionism seems to represent an entirely different theoretical viewpoint from that of either Roussellieań or Deweyan psychology, nevertheless it was adopted, at least in part, by numerous persons who identified themselves with Progressive Education. Most of the persons who did this were teachers and administrators without a sophisticated grasp of the ramifications of different psychological viewpoints. Hence, they were unaware that Thorndike's psychology logically calls for an approach to teaching quite incompatible with either the Roussellian or the Deweyan approach. However, a great many professors of education also were not immune to this kind of eclecticism.

For example, William H. Kilpatrick, a well–know figure in the Progressive Education movement, went through stages of promoting a connectionist psychology. Kilpatrick's influential *Foundations of Method* (1926) unequivocably states a Thorndikean connectionist psychology, rooted in the reflex-arc concept. Although Kilpatrick later veered to a configurational psychology of the Gestalt-field pattern, his *Philosophy of Education* (1951) contains a reaffirmation of his debt to Thorndike's laws of learning. Kilpatrick's basic premises appear to be inconsistent. An associationist psychology, such as Thorndike's connectionism, harmonizes with a neutral–passive conception of human nature as developed by John Locke. But when Kilpatrick discusses what part a child is to play in the educative process he usually advocates permissivism. Time after time in his writings he has urged that children be allowed free choice in determining what to do and how to do it. Thus, he seems to assume validity of the Roussellian good–active concept of human nature, which is incompatible with the Lockian view. It should be noted, though that Kilpatrick is not consistently an advocate of permissivism; at times he says dictation by a teacher is necessary.

One of the slogans popularized by Progressives in education is "Children learn by doing." The implication of the statement seems to be that learning accompanies action—any action. This is the kind of statement which a connectionist or behaviorist, but not a Gestalt–field theorist, would make. To the latter, overt action is not necessary to get change in insight and, in fact, often is not accompanied by learning at all. The "activity programs" which so often characterized curriculums of Progressive schools, as well as the concept of project teaching (as popularized by Kilpatrick), seem much more in the tradition of an associationist psychology than in the Gestalt–field tradition.

What Are the Psychological Implications of Contemporary Educational Procedures?

Although Progressive Education is now virtually defunct as an organized movement (it ceased publication of its journal in the summer of 1957), it has unquestionably been highly influential in American education. Its impact may be observed almost everywhere. However, the movement has not been fully victorious. Almost any school still retains practices that are in keeping with the tenets of mental discipline and apperception. During the 15 years prior to this writing, traditionalism—as exemplified in mental discipline and apperception—even enjoyed a marked upsurge. Not all the reasons for this are entirely clear, but one reason would seem to be the generally conservative temper of the country during the period. Another reason was the inadequacy, in the minds of the public, or some of the practices of Progressivism.

Since Progressivism itself is eclectic in its psychological background (a combination of natural unfoldment, Dewey's personal-social psychology, and Thorndike's connectionism) and since traditionalism is also a combination of divergent positions (mental discipline, with both its classical and faculty psychology emphases, and the associationist psychologies) *it is evident that the psychological underpinnings of contemporary educational procedures have been inherently self-contradictory.*

Even though the inharmonious elements in present-day educational psychology are not recognized by many persons who are in charge of our schools, steps in the direction of development of an adequate and harmonious psychological basis for education would definitely contribute to the quality of education and a greater enhancement of human intelligence. Perhaps a more adequate psychological basis for teaching is to be achieved through emphasis upon the method of intelligence.

WHAT IS THE METHOD OF INTELLIGENCE?

In harmony with cognitive-field psychology, the primary aim of education is to *foster intelligent solution of all manner of problems which confront people.* Schools should give major attention to communicating to students the *method of intelligence* so that they may use it where they will.

It may seem at first glance that this objective of education is just as sweeping, overly general, platitudinous, and meaningless as the highsounding objectives in the lists which one encounters so often. However, we have already gone a long way in the present book to state in operational terms what it means to behave intelligently. Further chapter concludes with a section in which we described an act of reflection in step-bay-step terms and state some of the assumptions governing the reflective process. Later chapters in the present section of the book carry this discussion farther by showing the operations a teacher performs when he promotes reflection. A person who acts reflectively acts intelligently—in fact, for our purposes here we may consider the two terms virtually interchangeable.

To many persons, a single statement of the primary objective of education will seem to by-pass a large number of specific and valid objectives with which schools must be concerned. Surely, it will be argued, a class in say, woodworking must have its own specific objectives and these will differ drastically from the specific objectives of a class in English literature. We grant that this argument can hardly be denied; but our intent here is to focus on an aim of democratic education which applies to any subject field and the achievement of which hinges on a grasp of fundamental psychological principles.

Is Education for Intelligence Too Risky?

This question is likely to inspire the quick retort, "How can a gain in intelligence be risky? Does not the risk lie in failure to improve intelligence?" The retort usually ignores the full implications of educating for intelligence. In order to make these implications clear, it will be necessary to clarify further and to amplify our definition of intelligence.

Among other things, but perhaps most centrally, intelligent behavior is acting with foresight—that is, with regard to consequences. This implies ability to foresee, to forecast, to see ahead, which is possible only with the aid of experience. Experience gives us generalized insights—general ideas, rules, principles. For example, experience with thunderstorms leads to the generalization that lightning tends to strike high, exposed places. This generalization can be used during future storms to forecast where lightning is most likely to strike. We may then behave intelligently—stay away from high, exposed places if we want to live, or seek such places if we prefer suicide.

So much for how the general principle of foresight works. But there is more to intelligence than this. Certain rules govern the formation of experientially derived generalizations and their application in new situations. They are the rules of the scientific process itself. One rule is that there can be no limitations on the possibilities of a situation: an experience may seem to suggest a rather obvious insight; nevertheless, the insight may seem to suggest a rather obvious insight; nevertheless, the insight may be wrong. Of the possible insights suggested during an experience, which is the best? Obviously, it may be a highly unorthodox or socially unpopular one, as is evidenced by the frequency with which, historically, shocking ideas have proved eventually to be the most accurate—or wise (for example, Galileo's hypothesis about the solar system).

If experience is to enhance intelligence, it should be clear that one must approach life situations with an open mind and that the prevailing intellectual climate must permit completely free exploration. There can be no censorship, no tabooed lines of thought. All available pertinent evidence must be regarded as worthy of scrutiny.

Furthermore, there appears to be a correlation between capacity for intelligent behavior and capacity for critical thought. An intelligent person is always something of an iconoclast—he is suspicious of all that is settled and taken for granted. He enjoys examining ideas which frighten persons of lesser intelligence.

Still further, he likes to turn the light of intelligence on any and all areas of life, particularly the "closed areas". Also, a positive correlation seems to exist between intelligence and creativeness. An intelligent person tends to get fresh ideas, to think in novel terms. His solutions to problems frequently have an original flavor. The method of intelligence has been designated aptly as "that peculiar species of thought which leads us to change our mind."

To drive our point home, we might illustrate the difference between an intelligent an an unintelligent approach to a specific problem. A few years ago a major controversy raged in the Pacific Northwest over whether the Snake River should be dammed and power installations built by the federal government or by a private power company (the notorious "Hell's Canyon controversy"). The arguments offered in connection with this issue provided excellent examples of intelligent and unintelligent approaches to problem solving. On both sides of the dispute there was name calling and a tendency to impugn the motives of the opposition. This activity was not intelligent because it contributed nothing to a sensible solution of the issue.

The proponents of private development labeled the plan for government development "socialistic." This behavior was unintelligent because it substituted a poorly defined, extraneous issue for the real one, namely, how could people of the Northwest get maximum electric power, flood control, and irrigation at minimum cost. Some of the proponents of government development claimed that those who wanted private development were agents of a private power lobby which was trying to extend its grip over the economy for selfish purposes. This was equally unintelligent behavior, for the same reasons.

Those who approached the problem intelligently kept their sights at all times on the objectives of the project: a combination of cheap power, water for irrigation, and flood control. They then tried to work their way to a conclusion which would be in accord with all the pertinent facts.

Necessarily, they drew heavily upon previous experience by studying examples of both public and private river development, comparing the effectiveness of each, and they trying to determine whether factors unique to the northwestern situation would invalidate conclusions drawn from the results of experiments elsewhere.

They refused to be sidetracked by ideological issues irrelevant to the main problem. Their approach was flexible and pragmatic. Needless to say, different persons might approach a given problem intelligently and yet come up with different conclusions, as was the case in the Hell's Canyon controversy.

In a school situation, it should not be too difficult of an impartial observer to determine whether a teacher is trying to promote habits of intelligence. Obviously, a teacher who gives his students pat answers which are not to be questioned is not serving the cause of intelligence. Nor is a teacher who refuses students access to relevant categories of facts for fear study of all the facts might lead students to adopt conclusions unsanctioned by the teacher or community. Apparently, in a number of communities, school boards or community pressure groups want students to behave intelligently only in certain "safe" areas and fear the general extension of the method of intelligence.

What Are Some Requirements for Educating for Intelligence?

If he accepts the analysis of cognitive-field psychology on the matter of intelligence, what can a teacher or counselor do to promote intelligence among students? The main avenue for achieving this aim is, of course, reflective teaching and counseling. Specific techniques of reflective teaching are treated in further Chapter. But reflective teaching by itself may be insufficient. In the case of youngsters with certain types of handicaps, reflective teaching alone may have little effect in enhancing intelligence. Combs and Snygg list several concerns which should be taken into consideration; the following points are suggested by them. (We have added and deleted and take full responsibility for departure from Combs and Snygg's treatment.):

1. Do everything possible to improve students' physical condition. Various studies have shown that improvements in health may lead to marked gains in IQ scores as well as in capacity for steady intellectual growth. Of especial importance is the problem of faulty sensory equipment. The quality of perception is closely related to how well one's senses are functioning. A child with impaired vision or hearing may appear stupid; with the necessary correction, he may make startling gains.

2. Make certain that students have maximum opportunity for achieving new and higher–quality perceptions. Perception occurs only when a meaning is grasped. If a learning situation is meaningless because of its nature, it can hardly be expected to lead to gains in intelligence. We treat the problem of meaning in connection with "understanding level" teaching in further chapter. Readers should not underestimate the importance of meaningfulness of experience.

   The meaning of course materials may escape some students, not because it would be impossible for them to make sense of the materials, but because anxiety about other matters or distractions of some sort may prevent their giving the necessary attention. Classroom atmosphere itself may interfere with perception. In the now famous experiments of Lewin, Lippitt, and White, it was demonstrated that in the United State either an authoritarian or a laissez-faire classroom is less favorable for effective perception than is a democratic one.

3. The capacity of a person to improve his perceptions may be increased if some of his most pressing goals are met. If a child desires something strongly, he may be able to think only about his want. A child or youth's most urgent wants may involve out–of–school matters over which a school has little control; however, a school may aid a great deal in the satisfaction of certain kinds of wants. For example, a child who is starved for love, prestige, or friendship may find gratification through steps which teachers or counselors can take; as a result, his ability to perceive in, say, the area or geography may increase.

   An excellent example of how satisfaction of a pressing want may improve over-all performance is found in the experience of unmarried and married college students. In study after study it has been demonstrated that typically the work of a college student improves as a result of marriage. Of course, some of the gain is attributable to the increase in his responsibility—his greater need to do well. However, college counselors, on the basis of interviews with students, seem inclined to attribute part of the gain to the simple fact that with marriage satisfaction of a student's heterosexual desires ceases to be a time–consuming distraction.

4. We can help a student achieve more useful perceptions if we stop trying to hand perceptions to him on a platter. Most of the time, as Combs and Snygg put it, "He [the student] is lectured, required, shown, exhorted, and coerced to perceive what someone thinks he should." It would seem that, if a student can be made to feel a problem an if he is then given considerable leeway in exploring solutions, his capacity for achieving new perceptions is greater than if

less freedom prevails. The foregoing statement is in no sense advocacy of the ultrapermissive, child–centered approach to education advanced by Roussellians. It means that the more opportunity we can give students for relatively *independent* perceptual situations, the more likely we are to foster intelligence.

5. Schools should do what they can to help children achieve adequate concepts of self. This may well be the most important of the recommendations we can make. To a large degree a person's achievement is limited to what he thinks he can achieve. Virtually everyone eventually develops definite ideas about his limitations. It seems likely that, more often than not, people "sell themselves short." Parents or teachers often act as if they think children are lazy and dull. If this happens frequently enough, children come to accept this evaluation of their abilities. As Combs and Snygg ask, "What differences in the richness and variety of perception might result from a generation of people with 'I can' rather than 'I can't' conceptions of themselves?"

6. Teachers and counselors should make every possible attempt to relieve threat whenever it is suspected that a child is handicapped in his perceptions by it. By "threat" we are not referring necessarily to the threats a teacher might hold over students: "If you don't learn your 6's by Monday, I will keep you after school." Rather, we mean anything in a child's life space which he sees as endangering his self–respect, or the integrity (inner harmony) of the inner–personal area of his life space. The most pressing threats, in this sense, are ideas which appear to jeopardize present self–structure. Awareness of an inconsistency in one's beliefs is often threatening; in this case, feeling of threat can be relieved only by achieving some reconciliation of the incompatible beliefs.

Obviously, any situation calculated to produce serious reflection contains some degree of threat to established convictions. Otherwise, why bother to reflect? What we are referring to in this section, however, is threat of such magnitude that all a child's efforts must be devoted to combating it. Threat of this kind is often quite irrelevant to the learning task before a child. It may reflect a family situation or inadequate relations with peers. A child who carries too heavy a burden of threat usually displays a rigid, defensive mind–set. He finds it virtually impossible to be open–minded about anything. Furhter chapter, on schoolroom "climate making," deals extensively with steps teachers and counselors may take to reduce threat.

HOW CAN SCHOOLS MORE EFFECTIVELY PROMOTE INTELLIGENCE?

Learning situations may be classified according to where they are placed on a continuum which ranged from "thoughtless" to "thoughtful." It is convenient to divided the total range of learning situation, however, into three broad classifications—memory–level, understanding–level, and reflection–level learning.

1. *Memory-level Learning:* Memory-level learning is the kind of learning that supposedly leads to committing factual materials to memory and nothing else. We all know how this can be done; it is possible for a person to memorize virtually any type of material, including that which seems quite nonsensical. The more meaningful the material learned, the longer it tends to be retained. However, a collection of nonsense syllables might conceivably be remembered for a lifetime if a person had sufficient reason for retaining it.

At first glance, rote–memory learning seems to exemplify the S–R theory of learning; simple linkages are formed between stimuli and responses with no particular thought or purpose involved. A cognitive–field psychologist denies that this is the case. He insists instead that insight of a sort is always present, if anything is learned at all. What characterizes rote learning, to a cognitive–field theorist, is that the insights acquired usually have no significant relationship to the material being studied. However, the learned material is patterned by the learner during the process of his learning it. Even "nonsense syllables," when learned, are not completely nonpatterned.

The capacity to memorize and retain material probably bears no relationship to the capacity for intelligent behavior. Geniuses are notoriously forgetful, although not usually in their areas of major interest. Conversely, a mentally defective person may be highly proficient in memorization. One of the authors once had an opportunity to study a 13–year–old girl with the mental capacity of an imbecile. Polly had a quite brilliant memory of the "shotgun" variety. That is, she memorized indiscriminately anything she heard, and could often repeat verbatim an overheard conversation or a radio newscast after hearing it once. She could recite faultlessly the words of every popular song being broadcast at the time. Nevertheless, Polly's "thought power" was so impaired that if asked to close an outside door of the house she could not tell on which side of the door to stand to avoid shutting herself outdoors.

Every experienced teacher can recall numerous students who developed a considerable capacity to memorize standard curricular materials in most or all school subjects. Such students usually make high marks. However, when put in situations requiring reflection, they may be at a loss. If, occasionally, they take a course from a teacher who employs problem centered teaching, they may become extremely frustrated and do poorly. Conversely, an experienced teacher can recall students whose marks were spotty but who achieved magnificently once they got out of school. There is a fairly good chance that in such cases poor achievement in school is a result of rebellion against required rote memorization.

Memory–level teaching may, of course, contribute indirectly to intelligent behavior. If memorized facts become pertinent on an occasion when a problem requires solving, they contribute to usable background and hence to the effectiveness of the problem solving. However, memorized facts usually contribute little. One reason is that, as already suggested, they tend to be forgotten quickly. Another reason is that a large proportion of the facts memorized in school are irrelevant to future thought needs.

It is no longer a matter for speculation that not much in the way of durable or useful results can be expected from memory-level instruction. Its contribution to intelligent behavior is too unpredictable and undependable for us to set much store by it as a favored instructional procedure. Yet there is no reason to suppose that most teachers are dedicated to any other approach. No matter how much talk is raised against straight memory-level instruction, there are numerous pressures placed on teachers to confine teaching to this level. Furthermore, they may have no vision of anything different. The chance of a prospective teacher's experiencing much instruction in college on a level above sheer memorization is not very great; it would be possible for a person to complete a college education and never once experience a class taught on any other level.

In spite of all the legitimate criticisms we may make of rote memorization, it would be unrealistic to suppose that a teacher can always avoid it. In any ordinary school situation, on occasion even the most imaginative teacher will have no better approach than memory–level teaching. This may occur on days when lack of time has prevented planning anything else. Or it may occur when the teacher does not know how else to handle the material to be covered.

It is perhaps defensible to argue that material which can be treated only on a memory level should not be included in the school curriculum, but for as long as one can see ahead, teachers will be asked to teach subject-matter which is difficult to make problem centered or even meaningful. One also can ask, can the fundamental skills, such as spelling, be taught otherwise than through a process of straight memorization, using drill procedures? Generally speaking, they can be taught more efficiently through other procedures. However, much more study will be required to develop procedures for all the fundamental skill subjects which will get us entirely away from memorization by rote.

2. *Understanding–level Learning:* The term *understanding* has been used so ambiguously by psychologists and educators that teachers are likely to use it rather glibly, without being able to define it clearly. A teacher may ask his students, "Are you sure you understand this?" and not himself know the meaning of his question. One may be fairly sure his students do not know either.

Although a careful analysis of the nature of understanding must wait until further chapter, which is devoted to understanding–level learning, our purposes require a short definition here. A common definition of understanding is "seeing the use to which something may be put." For example, if Johnny knows a use to which he can put his knowledge that Columbus sailed to the West Indies in 1492, we may say that he "understands" the date.

A more sophisticated definition retains the idea of purposeful use but includes another element: the relationship between the general and the particular. A fact or group of facts is said to be understood if their evidential relationship to a principle is seen. That is, if a student sees that a particular fact either supports or casts doubt on some principle, he understands the fact. Likewise, the ability to hypothesize further facts from a principle is evidence of understanding.

Now what is understanding–level teaching? It is teaching that seeks to acquaint students with the relationships between the general and the particular, between principles and solitary facts, and which also shows the uses to which principles may be put. When a teacher tries to teach students *rules* governing the use of say, subjunctives, he is trying to keep his instruction on an understanding level. If he succeeds, his students will be able to identify cases in which a particular rule applies and use the rule as a guide. We are seeking the same thing when we try to teach rules of spelling, rules of dividing fractions, or rules for repairing a motor. We are likewise operating on the same level when we teach theories in physics, chemistry, or football. (A rule or principle is at the same time a theoretical statement—by definition.)

A contrast may be drawn between understanding-level and memory–level teaching as follows: if understanding–level teaching is successful, students will know, in addition to facts, the principles by which the facts are related; memory–level teaching tends to ignore principles, or at best handles them on such a superficial level that they have no meaning.

From the standpoint of an educational psychologist, understanding–level teaching is much to be preferred over memory–level teaching. In fact, few educational psychologists would settle for anything less. They would argue that much of the inefficiency in education which research has exposed stems from the way most school subjects are organized and presented. Subjects often remain meaningless to students, not because of the intellectual deficiencies of students, but because a human mentality works in such a way that the subjects, *as organized and taught, have little meaning for them.*

Understanding–level teaching gives students a tool for more intelligent behavior. It equips them with generalized insights which can be applied in problematic situation inside and outside of school. It provides them with a mental kit of rules. If the rules learned are the best which are know at the time—by people in a position to have expert knowledge—then students have at least gained something from their education.

By this time readers may have sensed that there is still something lacking. Understanding–level teaching, if it remains merely that, depicts the student as a passive and the teacher as an active agent. A teacher tells, a student listens. Understanding–level teaching may be highly uncritical an authoritarian. The principles taught by the teacher may be wrong—and sometimes are. Understanding–level teaching may lead to more intelligent behavior on the part of student but it does not carry with it the quality of experience needed to enhance intelligence to the fullest.

3. *Reflection–level Learning:* Reflection–level learning leads to understanding, but with reflection the search for understanding is pursued in different fashion from that described in the preceding section. Instead of being given a collection of facts and generalizations by a teacher, students are confronted with something

which is unclear or puzzling. Reflective learning may being with what a student brings with him to school—his own attitudes, beliefs, values, and knowledge. If he can be convinced that there is something seriously inadequate about his present mental furniture, he may be led to reflect. Or reflective learning may begin with some observed inadequacy in the subject-matter; inconsistency, incompleteness, irrelevance, etc. In any case, a problemic situation appears about which a student centers his thinking and research. In the process, he examines facts and generalizations, and we hope, he tries to seek out new ones.

There are these crucial differences between understanding– and reflection–level teaching: the latter requires more active participation of students, more criticism by them of conventional thinking, and more imagination and creativeness. The classroom atmospheres associated with the two approaches differs markedly. Reflective teaching and learning lead to the development of a classroom atmosphere which is more alive and exciting, more critical and penetrating, more open to fresh and original thinking. However, the type of inquire pursued in a reflective classroom may be even more rigorous—and more "work producing"—than that pursued in an understanding–level classroom. In contrast a memory–level classroom is easy on everyone, teachers and students alike, unless they are overcome with boredom.

One reason why reflective learning is more consistent with the requirements of intelligent behavior is that intelligence usually implies behavior which is active, exploratory, and original. This is not to suggest that intelligent behavior ignores established facts and ideas. It never cuts completely loose from the past. But it does have a tendency to seek something better than what is commonly accepted.

Many will argue that this chapter states a hopeless idea. The will insist that an average man is incapable of showing any more intelligence than he now does. The argument can command impressive supporting evidence; after all, what indications are there today that an average adult approaches critical issue intelligently? To all indications, he does not. But at this point we feel impelled to adopt the essential optimism of James Harvey Robinson when he says that the only hope of civilization is the application of human intelligence to the solution of human problems. What other choice do we have except to try this remedy?

5

Climate Making and Method

A teacher's success in inducing reflective learning hinges upon his ability to bring students to be involved in issues and yet be curious and open-minded in regard to their resolution. The aim of this chapter is to consider how to keep learners involved to the point of perplexity and yet not frustrate them, and to explore ways in which they can be made more receptive to points of view based on evidence more scientific than the common run.

For this purpose we shall draw rather heavily from experience in fields outside formal education. Specifically, we shall survey briefly some findings from psychiatry which bear on the problem of reducing emotional blocks to learning. We shall also examine the areas of study known as "democratic group leadership" in an attempt to see what an understanding of the dynamics of democratic adult groups may reveal concerning classroom practice.

It should be noted at the outset that we make no attempt to apply directly to classroom practice the procedures which have been developed for use in therapeutic groups or normal adult groups. Many of these procedures are inapplicable in school classes. However, experience with them does suggest important clues for making learning more reflective, functional, and permanent.

HOW MAY CONFLICT BE RESOLVED FROM A PSYCHOANALYTIC POINT OF VIEW?

Psychotherapists differ in their interpretation of causes of emotional conflict. Freudians attribute conflict to a combination of instinctive drives and early childhood experiences. Neo-Freudians are more inclined to emphasize a patient's present environment as a source of conflict. Therapists likewise differ in their approach to treatment, one group assuming that therapy should expose and help a patient reinterpret early experiences in life, and another that therapy should focus on changing a patient's contemporary life situation. Another source of disagreement is in the question of how directive a counselor should be during counseling sessions. Still another issue relates to whether, in treating certain forms of mental illness, individual or group therapy is the more valuable. Because they are particularly pertinent to our present problem, we shall explore briefly the last two of the issues mentioned.

Directive vs. *Nondirective Therapy*

In the language of psychotherapy, the issue posed here is between directive and nondirective (or patient-centered) therapy. What is probably the first attempt at careful description and defense of a nondirective approach to therapy was made by Rogers.

We can best describe nondirective therapy through comparisons and contrasts. Rogers suggests that virtually all historical approaches to psychotherapy place a therapist in an authoritarian position with reference to a patient. These approaches assume that a counselor can and should determine a socially accepted goal for a patient and help him rearrange his personality structure or his life situation so that he can achieve it. A patient may be told what to believe and do by subtle and indirect methods, but told he is nevertheless.

Nondirective therapy avoids substituting a therapist's purposes for a patient's. A warm and permissive atmosphere is created in which a patient feels perfectly free to talk about his problems. The counselor accepts, recognizes, and clarifies feelings expressed by the patient, who talks his way through his problems, moving successively from a phase of "blowing off steam" to a phase of better self-understanding and heightened capacity for reflective handling of his own problems. Although nondirective therapy places more emphasis upon emotional adjustment than do some other approaches, it is assumed that an *outcome of therapy will be reflectively achieved insight*. The responsibility for this outcome is placed squarely on patients; whatever decisions they make are theirs alone.

We shall confine ourselves to one further point: in contrast to Freudian approaches to the theory of neurosis, nondirective therapy assumes that, rather than being largely internal and psychic, conflicts have a large cultural component. That is, they are mostly a result of one's present relationship with his environment: they grow from "some new cultural demand which opposes individual need."

This appears to be saying much the same as is said elsewhere in the present book: that most emotional conflicts are a result of a person's internalizing, or incorporating within conflicts are a result of a person's internalizing, or incorporating within the self, discrepancies of his surrounding culture, i.e., conflicting beliefs and behaviors.

A nondirective approach to psychotherapy has important implications for teaching. Although a teacher probably should not be "nondirective" in the sense described by Rogers, the idea of encouraging individuals (including students) to formulate their own purposes and solve their own problems in the presence of an adult who, rather than dictating, merely gives encouragement has broad significance for group management in a democratic society. Limitations of the Rogerian outlook for school use will be treated later in the chapter.

Individual and Group Counseling and Behavioral Change

Psychological counseling which acquaints a patient with "the facts" concerning his situation may fail to produce logically implied changes in behavior. For example, Rogers says, "It has come to be recognized that we do not change the client's behavior very effectively simply by giving him an intellectual picture of its patterning, no matter how accurate." Change in knowledge leads to the adoption of new values. But if a situation rewards old values, they will continue to dominate the new. When this is the case, behavior reflects the old values and remains unchanged.

One reason a counselor may not succeed in bringing about significant changes in behavior is that the behavior of every individual is firmly rooted in the persons with whom he associates. That is, actions of a patient are largely controlled by groups to which he belongs and can be changed only as behavior of the group themselves changes.

A deep-seated desire of human beings is for security. A common means of achieving security is through membership in a group. When a person feels that he has a place in a group, that he "fits in," that he is wanted, he feels secure. As Lewin points out, "The social climate in which a child lives is for the child as important as the air it breathes. The group to which a child belongs is the ground on which he stands. His relation to the group and his status in it are the most important factors for his feeling of security or insecurity." One achieves membership in a group by conforming, at least to a degree, to the mores of the group. To be accepted in a group of thieves, one must act like a thief; to be accepted in a group of saints, one must act like a saint.

This is not to say that an individual is completely subject to group control. He may develop beliefs and values which are novel to a group and may get them accepted by others in the group. With widening acceptance, the new beliefs and values become effective in controlling group behavior. The extent to which an individual can project his own unique personality into group life, and thereby change a group, depends on the situation, e.g., whether the group is itself democratic and the extent to which the larger culture outside the group is hostile or friendly to the changes, and on his own capacity for persuasion. A modern sociologist is likely to regard the process of interaction itself as the basic social datum; every group is constantly shaping individuals in it and simultaneously is being shaped by them.

Though interaction is always present, we cannot imagine that large changes will occur in individuals outside their relationship to their primary group associations. A psychotherapist is constantly aware of the fact that there is little he can do to help a patient reorganize his personality as an individual. such reorganization as may occur must fit exigencies posed by a patient's associations—the various needs and pressure, often highly subtle and complex, which grow out of the fact of group membership itself. This is particularly the case where values are concerned, and even more particularly, values in "closed areas."

During World War II, experiments in group psychotherapy were under-taken out of necessity. There were not enough therapists or facilities for individual counseling. The results of counseling with groups of patients were often gratifying. Now, in certain situations group therapy is seen as having advantages over individual therapy. The reason appears to lie in the previously mentioned supposition that it is easier for an individual to change his values and behavior if other persons with whom he is in intimate contact are also changing.

There is disagreement as to whether in group therapy the therapeutic effect comes primarily from the relationships of each member to the therapist or from relationship of members to each other, but the latter interpretation seems to be growing in popularity. In some instances a patient can express himself more freely in a small face-to-face group than in individual relationship to a counselor, perhaps because he feels less alone, the group gives him courage, and other members have established precedents for speaking frankly. Through the give-and-take of free discussion some persons may come to see their own problems better than through individual counseling situations. Patients accept censure, suggestions, and guidance from each other more readily and with less disturbance and hostility than from a therapist.

> "One of the most important constituents of the ground on which the individual stands is the social group to which he 'belongs'"

A group situation may also stimulate one to deal openly and creatively with his own conflicts. Foulkes summarizes this possible therapeutic effect of a group: "... Lectures, exhortations, sympathy, pity, advice, medicaments, explanations, encouragement, all can help a little, but they cannot move the patient out of his fortress of entanglements. In the long run, they can only help him to entrench himself deeper in it... If he is, however, brought into a situation, which he himself is continuously helping to create, to shape, he is forced to come out into the open with his own reactions and their contradictions."

Whether a patient benefits more from group than from individual therapy depends in large part on the nature of his illness. Group therapy is regarded as of limited usefulness for the mentally unbalanced and probably for extreme neurotics. The nearer a patient is to normality, the more effective group therapy is likely to be. Its greatest value may be, as Hobbs points out, "in the neglected field of therapy for the moral person with debilitation situational conflicts..."

What is the significance to classroom teachers of clinical experience in individual and group psychotherapy? The hypothesis is suggested that a wide range of personally felt problems may be handled successfully among normal persons, including adolescent youth, with resultant permanent changes in outlook and behavior, if they are encouraged to air problems freely in the give-and- take atmosphere of a face-to-face group. Although this general idea is not new, modern psychiatric practice offers clues as to the most effectual managerial techniques for such learning situations.

WHAT IS THE DEMOCRATIC GROUP-LEADERSHIP MOVEMENT?

Related to the development of group psychotherapy is the democratic group-leadership movement. This movement embraces a body of experiments and practices with normal adult and youth groups. Its aim is to translate a democratic philosophy into action on a group level and to compare the learning and behavioral results of democratic groups with those of nondemocratic groups. An understanding of the dynamics of groups is valuable to teachers. In the concluding section of the chapter, we make applications, and also show why, because of differences in aims and competence of most adult groups involved in experimentation, certain aspects of the management of adult groups are not transferable to classroom situations.

The democratic group-leadership movement is rooted in a democratic social-political philosophy dating in the United States from the Jeffersonian period, and from earlier than that in Europe. The modern concept of group work combines our traditional democratic philosophy with an understanding of group psychology which in human affairs is relatively recent.

In a large sense, the democratic group-leadership movement is a counterpart, for normal groups, of group psychotherapy for the abnormal. Although there is disagreement as to just how directive a leader can be and still remain "democratic," democratic group leadership appears to be an application of some of the principles of nondirective group therapy. It is to be expected, therefore, that among the contributors to our understanding of group process are numerous psychiatrists and psychologists. Haiman suggests that modern methods of group leadership "find their origin in the work of Sigmund Freud and follow the patterns of the psychiatric tradition which has flowered since his time." Because there are significant relationships between the concepts of psychiatric medicine and of leadership of normal groups, psychiatrists have transplanted their philosophy and methods to normal group situations.

Although the contribution of psychologists and psychiatrists to an understanding of group dynamics has been great, it is perhaps no more significant than that of experts in management-worker relations. Of studies along this line, possible the most notable were those conducted by staff members of the Harvard Graduate School of Business, F. J. Roethlisberger, W. J. Dickson, and colleagues, at the Hawthorne Works (Chicago) of the Western Electric Company between 1927 and 1932.

It was found from these studies that labor contentment and efficiency rose when workers were (1) organized in terms having a sense of common purpose and (2) made participants in an interview system where they could talk freely about whatever they wished.

Among other experiments conducted with self-governing adult groups is the famous Peckham Experiment, involving the work of the Pioneer Health Centre of Peckham, England. This health center was established to give family groups a program of mental and physical preventive therapy. In the main, the extensive program is run by members themselves without centralized direction. Marked—sometimes revolutionary—changes in the apparent values and behaviors of many members are noted by skilled observers.

It is from experiences and experiments like these that we have gained much of our knowledge of group dynamics. New concepts have developed as to how a democratic group functions and the role of a leader in it. It has become clear also that the idea of a democratic group, as developed in the democratic group-leadership movement, is very similar to the idea of a therapeutic group, as developed in the field of group psychotherapy.

The Nature of a Democratic Group

Democracy is a philosophic concept. We define democracy as a social arrangement in which all members of a group share equally in determining which freedoms and restraints shall apply. It is presumed that, in general, freedoms and restraints shall apply with the same force to all. But democracy must allow for the granting of special powers for special purposes (as in the case of its executive officers). It we think of democracy as a system of *equally limited* freedom, characterized by shared decisions regarding which specific rules are to prevail, then we have a simple criterion for distinguishing democracy from other social arrangements. A social system may provide *unlimited* freedoms, in which case it is called anarchy. Or it may provide *unequally limited* freedoms, in which case it is called autocracy.

A democratic group is self-governing. But it must provide for situations where disagreement occurs. Ideally, democratic decisions are by consensus, i.e., mutually agreeable decisions reached through discussion and compromise. Then, by common consent, action is taken. If consensus is not possible, a democratic group votes. Each person has an equal vote, and a majority vote wins. Votes are taken to facilitate action, not to enforce belief.

Successful and permanent operation of democracy seems to require that a group maintain certain conditions which, although not a part of the central idea of democracy, contribute to its functioning. For example, if participation is to be full and free, a group must establish an accepting atmosphere—an atmosphere in which every member is considered important and has his opinions guaranteed a hearing. Participation implies reasonable freedom of communication, and freedom of speech and thought. If any single individual or minority group gains disproportionate control over agencies of communication and opinion, the society has lost equality of participation in decision making.

It would also seem that, if a democratic society is to survive over time, a majority of its members must learn to make reflective decisions where socially important questions are involved. A democratic society assumes competence on the part of its members; any different assumption would lead to distrust and rejection of the principle of equal participation. We assume that without wise leadership no society can solve its problems and endure. In a democracy wise leadership is a function of wise citizenship. If democracy is to survive, its members must take steps to insure that the principle of reflection is employed as widely as possible in making choices of group concern. Among other things, this means that a democracy should always be in the process of reducing the number and extent of its closed areas.

The Role of Democratic Leadership

Behavior of a group is influenced significantly by its leaders. Particularly if a group is immature, its over-all emotional and intellectual climate and its direction and extent of growth depend largely on the conduct of its leadership. As a group matures, it becomes less dependent on particular leaders. It develops capacity to produce leaders from its own ranks and reject and select leaders according to need.

The role of democratic leadership is to *help a group realize its own potentialities for growth.* Such a statement becomes meaningful only when growth is defined in operational terms. One attempt at definition specifies a number of "dimensions" of group growth, including the following:

1. Progress toward fuller intercommunication among members. This includes growing acceptance and understanding by members of mechanics of language, with particular reference to meaning.

2. Progress toward viewing objectively the functioning of the group. This includes ability of all members to make and accept interpretations about member and group functioning and ability to collect and use pertinent information about itself.

3. Progress toward developing shared responsibilities. This includes growth toward a sharing of leadership functions, participation in setting goals, and cooperation in achievement of goals.

4. Progress toward developing group cohesion. Cohesion should be adequate to permit assimilation of new ideas without group disintegration, assimilation of new members

in a way to strengthen rather than disrupt the group, holding to long-range goals when a situation requires, and making constructive use of internal conflicts.

5. Progress toward developing ability to inform itself, to think straight, and to make creative decisions about problems. This includes learning to make full use of the contribution potential of all members, to detect and correct fallacies in group thinking.

What specific functions does a democratic leader perform if a group is to move in these directions? He may execute or administer, serve as judge or arbiter, be an advocate (or shaper of opinion), or render expert advice. He may also play the role of discussion leader. Although a discussion leader may on occasion assume any of the above roles, his function is distinctively different from and more inclusive than any of them. He helps a group to achieve self-growth. Or, as one writer puts it, he tries to "releases the creative talents of the members of a group, help them solve their own problems, and reach their own decisions."

Some Significant Experiments with Groups

We have already mentioned the experiments in group climate conducted at the Iowa Child Welfare Research Station by Ronald Lippitt and Ralph K. White. In this study matched groups of 11-year-old boys were subjected to variations in leadership and resulting behavior was noted. Leadership conformed to three contrasting patterns, defined as authoritarian, laisses-faire, and democratic.

Perhaps the greatest significance of these experiments for our purposes rests in the light they throw on insightful outcomes of three possible types of leadership situations. For example, work habits learned under democratic leadership, more than those learned under authoritarian leadership, may have significant carry-over into situations where an adult leader is not present. That is, learning in a democratic group "cuts deeper." However, results of these experiments should not be regarded as conclusive or as suggesting characteristics of "basic human nature." They involved groups having rather special purposes and boys who were products of a culture which prides itself on being democratic. It would have been surprising if these boys had not preferred and functioned better under democratic leadership.

Another group of experiments pertaining to our general theme include those in food use made World War II, likewise conducted at the Child Welfare Research Station of the University of Iowa. In this case, the effects on behavior of lecture and group discussion were compared. Three adult groups of housewives were lectured on nutritional value and contribution to war effort of wider use of beef hearts, sweetbreads, and kidneys. Three other groups *discussed* the problem of getting "housewives in general" to make grater use of these foods and as groups resolved to make use of them in their won families. A resource person who could supply recipes and other information was available to each discussion group.

Of the women lightening to the lecture, only 3 percent who had never before served the meats served one of the them. Of the women in the discussion groups, 32 percent who had never before served the meats served one of them. Apparently discussion followed by group decision was much more effective than lectures in producing behavioral change. Experiments designed to increase home consumption of milk showed similar results.

Lewin also cites experiments designed to test the relative effectiveness of individual instruction compared with group discussion and decision. In this case, a number of mothers received individual instruction on medically approved practices of feeding infants. Other mothers were formed in groups, received instructions, and then were given an opportunity for discussion and group decision. In this experiment, discussion and group resolve were found to be much more effective than individual instruction in producing behavioral change. We are reminded of experience in group psychotherapy, cited earlier, which indicated that group situations may sometimes be more effective than individual counseling in producing changes in beliefs and behavior.

Lewin concludes that, if group discussion and decision are to produce significant change, leadership must be democratic. It must avoid high-pressure methods and be sensitive to change. The burden of decision must be placed on group members themselves. Changes is likely to be greater, too, if a goal is set on which consensus is possible; majority rule is less effective because minority members who are outvoted sometimes deliberately resist the decision. An object in achieving change is not to apply pressure from outside but to remove counterforces within individuals. Such removal seems to occur best in relatively permissive group situations.

It was also found that less resistance is encountered if subjects are asked to discuss a problem as it relates to other persons, e.g., "How might it be possible to induce the housewives of the nation to use more milk?" Then they do not feel that their own habits are being selected as objects of criticism. This approach reduces resistance to a serious consideration of opposing practices. As a evidenced by their own changed behaviors, group members seldom fail to apply the problem to their own situations.

We shall describe one other experiment which appears significant for teachers. Shaw reports an experiment conducted at Columbia University in which graduate students tackled problems individually and in groups. In each instance, small groups of students, working cooperatively on problems, attained a much higher proportion of correct answers than the same number of students working individually. Also, groups were able to solve problems cooperatively which were too difficult for students working individually to solve. Investigators attributed the results to a tendency of members of a groups to criticize and cross-check suggestions raised within the group.

In all the experiments cited, the groups employed were essentially democratic in structure and function, as we have defined this term. The implication is that in our culture a face-to-face group which is democratically structured permits its members to achieve grater ideological and behavioral change, and more permanent change, than any other acceptable organization for learning. Also, if we may generalize from rather scanty data, members of such groups tend to be more productive intellectually and to show more wisdom than individuals working alone. Further, they exhibit better "mental health"—as conventionally defined—than members of either authoritarian or laissez-faire groups.

HOW MAY CLASSROOM TEACHERS FUNCTION AS DEMOCRATIC LEADERS AND CLIMATE MAKERS?

In order to understand the task of teachers as its relates to the problem of crating open-mindedness and willingness to change beliefs and behaviors, we need to examine in detail how emotional blocking can prevent such changes. Only as a teachers understands the process of blocking and how it manifests itself can be take steps for its removal.

Deficiency of Perception as a Cause of "Closed Minds"

In just what way does blocking interfere with reflection? It might be supposed that, no matter how strong one's emotional attachment to a belief, if he is confronted with facts which clearly question it, then question it he must. Any other course would appear highly unreasonable. Yet a normally intelligent and perfectly sane person may seem blind to evidence which others find thoroughly convincing.

Such behavior is not to be interpreted as willful irrationality. We agree with Wertheimer when he says that human beings usually have a "willingness to face problems straight, a readiness to follow them up courageously an sincerely, a desire for improvement, in contrast with arbitrary, willful, or salvish attitudes." What occurs, as a result of emotional blocking, apparently is *deficiency of perception, which is not understood by the person involved and which without help he cannot prevent or overcome.*

What is deficiency or perception? Answering this question raises complex technical as well as philosophical issues. At any given moment of consciousness a person has a "perceptual field." It is that part of has physical and psychological environment of which he is aware.

There is disagreement as to whether a person can directly perceive the physical, social, and psychological surroundings which are assumed to exist. Philosophical realists assume that he can. The position taken here is essentially that of field theory, which maintains that a person imposes *pattern, order, and meaning*—psychological reality—on the data of sense experience. This imposed pattern is what we mean by insight. Insights are dependent not only on the nature of the environment, or confronting situation, but also on the influence of one's experience and one's purposes at the time. Thus, in a given situation we cannot expect the insights of any two persons to be identical. Nor can we assume that for an individual any reality exists except the insights which he holds.

The literature of psychotherapy usually defines deficiency of perception as "loss of contact with reality." The goal of therapy is the re-establishment of accurate perception, or the re-establishment of contact with reality. What does this terminology mean? In the present book, when we say that perception is accurate, or that a person is in touch with reality, we mean that his insights are accurate guides to action. That is, they have been or can be verified experimentally or experientially. They are consistent with the verified data of past experience (*facts* as we use the term here) or they produce the consequences which a person anticipates when he acts on them. This is what we expect of any scientific theory.

When we say that a person is suffering from a deficiency of perception, we mean either that his insights are inconsistent with one another or that deductions made from them do not check with the data of observation. Now it is true that a person who is out of touch with reality may deduce consequences from a proposition and make observations to see if the anticipated events occur. But he is likely to make faulty deductions and faulty observations; that is, he is likely to claim the occurrence of events which a disinterested public cannot detect, or deny the occurrence of events which, to others, clearly happen.

Ideally, perception brings events of one's physical, social, and psychological environment into a person's consciousness with a minimum of distortion. But in normal life it is probable that most persons frequently perceive events which others do not and fail to perceive those which other do, or exaggerate or minimize the significance of events which they see. Rationalization, as defined in further chapter, is creating or disregarding facts in order to support a foregone conclusion. Most of the time it is quite unverbalized; in fact, when we become conscious that we are reading into a field what we want to see there instead of what might enable us to make more accurate predictions, we tend to become uncomfortable.

A person is especially likely to experience a deficiency of perception when he is under heavy emotional pressure. If he feels insecure or frightened, particularly with respect to the integrity of his own personality, he tries to read into the perceptual field whatever immediately appear most likely to restore his security. In other words, if he feels that a cherished belief is under attack, he will read the facts of perception in such a way as to protect and preserve the belief.

Deficiency in perception is most likely to occur in the closed areas of belief and value. Here a person simply *does not see facts as data.* To him they remain an insignificant—perhaps entirely undifferentiated—part of his perceptual field, bearing no relevance to the issue under consideration. Consequently, the facts do not change his thinking or behavior. We can hardly expect a person to incorporate data into his thinking when he remains unaware of their presence or significance. As Lewin says, "Since action is ruled by perception, a change in conduct presupposes that new facts and values are perceived." Simply telling a person that data are there is often futile. If his perception does not permit his to see them, we must approach the problem in such a way as to remove the distorting factors.

We have not yet distinguished clearly the role of perceptual deficiency in blocking changes in behavior. Deficiency of perception may prevent changes in insight. But very often changes in insight appear to occur, without the accompanying changes in values (and their corresponding behaviors) which we would expect. When this is the case, it would follow from a theory of learning consistent with a cognitive-field view that other, competing insights remain which furnish warrant for the old values. In short, we assume that all values and related behaviors issue logically from insights, and the former will not change unless the latter change also. But a person may hold to competing and contradictory insights (with corresponding contradictory values and attraction toward contradictory behaviors). In this case, the insights, attitudes, and behaviors which seem most attractive at the remain dominant.

With the foregoing interpretation we may explain a phenomenon noted earlier in the chapter, namely, that a person appear to accept a new set of facts, opposed to what he has heretofore accepted, without *observable* changes in behavior. If we understand that an individual in such situations is dominated by one of tow competing patterns of insights and corresponding behavioral sets, then clearly he is a victim of inconsistency, either recognized or unrecognized. Deficiency of perception in this case is a failure to recognize the inconsistency.

Once a person is aware of inconsistency, we assume that he will take steps to change one of the two competing outlooks (and its corresponding behavioral pull). But if he has a strong emotional need to follow his old (and, to disinterested observers, perhaps less wise) pattern of behavior, he is likely to try to minimize the conflict, to try to live with it, or to escape through some neurotic response. However this may be, it is apparent that failure to adjust behavior to what seems to be a change in insight indicates a problem of inconsistency and pedagogically it should be treated so. In a democratic school, such incompatibilities are studied reflectively.

What are the conditions under which perception achieves maximum accuracy? How can we set the stage so that a person will most easily adopt new outlooks or see his inconsistencies?

Insofar as experimental evidence allows an answer, it appears that the first requirement is a *nonthreatening* emotional atmosphere. We referred to this need for acceptable nonmenacing atmospheres earlier in the chapter as we discussed experience with psychotherapy and work with normal groups. What are the specific conditions of a nonthreatening climates? A *threat*, as the term is used here, is anything said or done by others which *appears to a learner* to jeopardize his present beliefs. It is the equivalent of an anticipated attack on the self. A normal individual wants to maintain a feeling of consistency and adequacy in his beliefs and values, which feeling is what we mean when we refer to integration or integrity of personality. A person's knowledges and values may be shot through with inconsistency and confusion, but if the person is not aware of this, he may continue to feel integrated. If he feels that someone is trying to destroy his integrity of self, he is likely to resist.

Rogers describe this problem very well: "Experience which, if assimilated, would involve a change in the organization of self tends to be resisted through denial or distortion of symbolization. The structure and organization of self appears to become more rigid under threat; to relax its boundaries when completely free from threat. Experience which is perceived as inconsistent with the self can only be assimilated if the current organization of the self is relaxed and expanded to include it."

For a climate to seem nonthreatening, it is necessary for a subject to feel that no one is trying to judge him. He needs to feel completely accepted. He is particularly likely to resist criticism if it comes from someone he regards as having arbitrary power and authority over him. He needs to feel complete freedom to express his opinions without danger of censure, no matter how ill formed or unorthodox they may be.

The type of climate in which a person feels so secure that he dares entertain evidence contrary to present knowledge and values seems best achieved in a small, face-to-face group in which warmth and considerable permissiveness have been deliberately cultivated. Some techniques which a teacher may use in creating such a situation, and in leading a class to change its views and behavior, are discussed in the following section.

Classroom Techniques for Assisting Conceptual and Behavioral Change

Reducing Threat and Promoting Open-mindedness: We have suggested that a student feels threat to his ago if he regards his beliefs as under fire. The intensity of threat depends on its source, its power, and the valuation placed on beliefs which are in jeopardy. Unless threat can be largely eliminated, a student is not likely to entertain evidence contrary to present beliefs or, when facts warrant, to change his mind. Several techniques are available for keeping a sense of threat to a minimum.

One rule is that a teacher should treat student opinions with respect. This does not necessarily mean that a teacher expresses approval; but he avoids ridicule or sarcasm, or any expression which might be so interpreted by students. He does not cast aspersions on the intelligence or motives of students who render serious opinions. Opinions offered in good faith are taken for what they are—the best insights which students have been able to achieve up to then.

On occasion, as during relatively undirected discussion preceding serious study of an issue, it may be advisable for a teacher to give students plenty of opportunity to express the very beliefs which he hopes later to bring under question. It may even help for him to express considerable sympathy with these ideas, for the time being to "go along." Lewin, for example recommends that a group leader may get farther by letting members of a group freely express the very values which he hopes to change because "a feeling of complete freedom and a heightened group identification are frequently more important at a particular stage of re-education than learning not to break specific rules."

When a teacher wishes to challenge an opinion expressed by a student, he should do it in such a way conflict is internalized. That is, the student is made to feel the conflict within his own personality. He may not feel a problem, or at least not the problem which the learning situation demands, if he sees the conflict merely as a contest between him and someone else.

When a teacher wishes to contest the opinion of a student, he may best handle it something like this; "You have an opinion, and I think I understand and appreciate your reasons. But there are contrary opinions which are widely held in this country. I wonder if there is any merit in a point of view such as...?" The student is thus asked to entertain, not an opinion of the teacher or a classmate, but simply an opinion which "some persons" hold. Experiments cited by Lewin and noted earlier in the chapter suggest that, when a group is presented with a problem to discuss, beliefs and behaviors contrary to those accepted by group members are more likely to be seriously entertained and later adopted if the problem is discussed with reference to persons other than themselves, at least in early phases of discussion.

Another means of inducing students to internalize conflict is to arrange the learning situation so that facts "speak for themselves." Other things being equal, facts—especially if impersonal, sharply relevant, and simple enough to be easily grasped—are more likely than expressions of opinion to break through an emotional barrier, particularly if the facts come to students in life situations. It may then only be necessary to remind a student of their relevance and their bearing on a problem. For example, a trip to a slum may speak eloquently against the notion that everyone is adequately housed, or the witnessing of a congressional investigation over TV may show quite convincingly that traditional American principles of fair play are not always employed. Lewin has suggested that "An individual will believe facts he himself has discovered in the same way he believes in himself or in his group."

In most instance it probably pays to minimize, or at least not encourage, emphasis on personal opinion in discussion. Issues may be handled as issues and propositions discussed on their merits. The learning enterprise should focus on raising questions about what will come of acting in accordance with a given proposition or hypothesis. An opinion may be converted to a proposition by saying, "Here is an opinion which is before the class. Let us take it as a proposition to be tested. If it is true, what consequences may we deduce from it?" If propositions are relevant to beliefs of students, then students often make their own connections. Even though beliefs are not studied directly, significant revisions may come. It is necessary, of course, that student *see* connections; if emotional blocking prevents this, steps must be taken to expand perception. Perhaps only mentioning the connections will be enough; perhaps patient effort will be needed further to reduce emotional barriers.

Encouraging Group Decision: A student is more likely to drop prejudices, revise his moral values, or make almost any other type of significant change if he is a member of a group *which is making the same change together*. Assuming that a teacher does all he can to produce a nonthreatening climate, what can be done to from a class into a true in-group, a "team," so to speak, and help them, as a team, to change basic outlooks?

Although significant learning may occur in discussion groups formed of strangers, learning in areas of strong prejudice (such as in the closed areas) seems more likely to occur in groups characterized by friendships and some degree of mutual intimacy. There may be sound pedagogical advantages in helping students become well acquainted with each other, whether simply through classroom informality or by deliberately fostering out-of-school contacts.

Cliques, self-contained groupings based on religious or social-class affiliations, racial groupings, or associations based on academic achievement may develop within any school and be reflected in a single classroom. Such groupings may entirely omit certain students, who in turn became social isolates. With development of subgroups of this sort, especially if chauvinistic attitudes are involved, a class may become badly split and team spirit difficult to achieve. If observation or use of sociometric devices suggests to a teacher that an unhealthy social situation exists in his classroom, he should take steps to alleviate it.

In establishing group feeling, there are possible advantages to be gained from group study and group projects. When this sort of thing is attempted, it is usually necessary to divide a class into small groups and to see that the same students do not always work together. A committee system can ordinarily be made to work fairly well for gathering information. Whether it can be made to function in reflective evaluation of data and the productive solution of problems depends on the maturity of students and their familiarity with the rules of reflection. Generally, a teacher must be central to reflective deliberation if it is to be productive.

Encouragement of full and free communication among members will heighten the cohesiveness of a group. If students understand each other, they will almost inevitably work together better as a group. A teacher should urge and help students to state opinions and propositions meaningfully. He should discourage use of emotive language, particularly when students are inclined to direct personal jibes at each other. He should make certain that every member has a chance to be heard and is correctly interpreted.

Although important, these suggestions concerning the development of "groupness" are peripheral to the problem. In a given learning situation, group spirit probably hinges primarily on whether all members of a class feel personally involved in the problem under study. If motivation to study a problem is high, a common interest exists which transcends lack of acquaintance, clique interests, or personal antagonisms. In the final analysis, whether group spirit is achieved at the point where it needed—where a problem is to be studied and beliefs are to be changed—depends largely on a teacher's skill in focusing effort on a common goal.

No matter how great their internal rapport, groups do not change beliefs automatically. As we have observed, the most effectual situation for producing group change appears to be a democratically led discussion. For purposes of this analysis, probably the most important requirement of discussion (or other modes of study) designed to change basic attitudes is that it have the quality of freely permitting self-learning. (This should not be taken to mean absence of directedness). We have already noted, in our discussion of threatening situations, that students resist outside pressure to change opinions. As Lewin has indicated the object in achieving change is not to apply pressure from outside but to remove counterforces within the individual.

Although a teacher can and usually must help in eliminating these counterforces, students must perform the actual removal. If they can explore a problem independently, feeling no authoritarian pressure from above to explore it in a particular way or emerge with particular conclusions, they are much more likely than otherwise to undergo real and permanent changes in conceptual patterns. They need to be encouraged to use investigatory techniques of their own, to explore by themselves provocative readings, trips, interviews, radio and TV programs, and the like. A teacher's role here is to suggest possible directions of exploration and to help students evaluate facts which are exposed.

For maximum change, permissive discussion of problems should culminate in group decisions. That is, in addition to discussing and studying a problem, students as a group should consider what conclusions are warranted, what the conclusions mean to them, and what if anything they intend to do about them. Students need to communicated their views to each other, so that intentions of each are known to all. It it is evident to individuals that most members of a group have revised their outlooks and expect to change their behavior in stated ways, then members who are reluctant to change because of long-standing attachment to certain beliefs may find change easier. This should not be interpreted to mean that a group or its leader should pressure individual members to accept conformity. We are referring to changes which individuals see the logic of making find difficult because of opposing forces. The opposing forces are often social pressures exerted by peer culture, community mores, or parental dictates. These may be combated more successfully if a student feels that others intend to combat them with him.

Ideally, group decision should represent common consensus. Proposed changes in belief should be kept within the bounds of what is possible for all. If a group is in agreement on the rules of reflective methodology, if it confines its learning operations to the testing of propositions which may be defined operationally, and if the threat-removing techniques employed by a teacher are sufficient so that without serious inhibitions all students are able to examine pertinent facts, then at least some degree of consensus is likely. This point of view assumes that for many problems there will be at a given time a "best" answer, in the sense that one hypothesis, more than any other, will adequately harmonize data relevant to it. This is a denial of the common belief that "every problem has two sides" and the further implication that "one opinion is as good as another." Of course, if the perplexity is of such nature that consensus based on reflection is impossible, no attempt should be made by a teacher to force it.

A Teacher's Role in a Democratic Classroom

Within a democratic framework there is room for disagreement as to the amount of centralized direction which is required. According to definitions previously suggested, a democratic group is distinctively different from a laissez-faire or authoritarian group. It would seem as unreasonable to try to establish there as completely hard-and-fast categories as nay other differentiated concepts. A democratic group might, under certain circumstances, operate with a minimum of neutralized leadership and appear to approach the laissez-faire extreme. On the other hand, it might delegate to particular persons positions of such authority as to appear to approach the authoritarian norm. (The former extreme might be illustrated in a small adult study group, the latter in a democratic nation which, during a war, grants extraordinary powers to its executive branch.)

We would place a nondirective discussion group, as defined by Rogers and others, near the laissez-faire end of our scale. We would hesitate, however, to place such a group outside the democratic framework. Although under certain circumstances it may resemble anarchy (which is not necessarily the same as chaos), a nondirective group may also produce firm leadership from within its own ranks and formulate and pursue purposes with dispatch and efficiency. When nondirection is employed with an immature group, however, such an outcome is doubtful.

We would place an ordinary classroom, as dominated by a textbook-recitation procedure and arbitrary decision making by a teacher, near the authoritarian end of the scale. Their is not to suggest that, if a teacher has certain types of authority over students, a teaching-learning situation necessarily violates democratic practice. We shall try to show how such authority may be compatible with democracy. Many classrooms, however, gravitate in structure and pattern of leadership toward the concept of an authoritarian group, as defined in experiments by Lippitt and White.

It is not enough simply to say that in a classroom a democratic pattern is preferable. Democracy in a classroom and democracy in adult discussion or psychotherapeutic groups ordinarily take different forms. In examining the form of democracy in a classroom the following points are pertinent:

1. Although it gives us valuable clues with respect to the dynamics of emotion, experience with therapeutic groups is not fully applicable in classrooms. A typical group of students is composed chiefly of normal persons. The conceptual structure of an ordinary student is often inadequate in the sense that it is a poor guide to behavior, owing to erroneous, incomplete and contradictory concepts. But concepts of a typical student are certainly not so inaccurate as to be largely unusable, as is the case with psychotic persons or incapacitate neurotics. Conflicts may be troublesome for

ordinary high school and college students and emotional disturbance may become conspicuous at times, but we do not expect deep neuroses. Basically, then, persons with whom a teacher works are different from those with whom a professional therapist deals.

This difference, between normality and abnormality, immediately suggests some differences in the job of a leader. Emotional blocking which might prevent reflection is probably much easier to remove in a normal group than in an abnormal group. A psychotherapist working with abnormals must usually use extreme and time-consuming methods in order to relieve repression to a point where insights can become reliable predictive tools. Furthermore, a private counseling session or a small discussion group of disturbed adults led by a psychiatrist represents a situation where more drastic means for relieving inhibition may be used. The mores of our culture do not tolerate in school classrooms the freedom of expression which can be permitted in a true therapeutic group. Whenever catharsis requires that a person talk freely about deep personal issues which would seem shocking or embarrassing to others, the case is one not for a teacher but for a trained therapist. One major difference, then, between a class and a therapeutic group is that the former will be free to delve deeply into personal problems, less free to tolerate extreme and shocking expressions of opinion.

Thus, it is both possible and desirable in a classroom to place more emphasis on intellectual experience and less upon catharsis than is done in a therapeutic group. It seems preferable to think of the expression of emotion—of catharsis—as a *tool* for achieving conceptualization rather than as an end in itself. What we want in a classroom is an increase in amount and an improvement in quality of thinking. Emotional release is to be encouraged only as it helps to achieve reflection.

In the literature of client-centered psychotherapy we find the opinion that, if a patient is placed in a nonthreatening, accepting climate and allowed to talk freely about his problems, he will by himself gain more adequate insights, In a classroom, however, a good psychological climate and free discussion are not usually enough to produce accurate insight *because of the difference in learning goals and type of problems discussed*. In a classroom many of the problems treated involve complex social issues and complicated and extensive evidence. Many of the data required to work with them successfully are unknown to students. Although relatively undirected discussion may be desirable to get issues into the open, to expose data from the prior experience of pupils, and to reduce repression, it is not enough. If students do not know what a tariff is, for example, such discussion will not make them more intelligent about tariff issues. A teacher must be charge to lead discussion, inject criticism, suggest research, provide basic data, and in general head the learning enterprise.

2. How far can we go in applying to the classroom principles of democratic leadership as developed through experiences of the democratic group-leadership movement? First, a classroom can and should be fully as democratic as any adult group. There are impelling reasons: school may be the only part of a child's environment where he has a chance to experience, by living it, the meaning of democracy. All too often he experiences authoritarian practices in home, Church, and part-time employment. Not that a person must necessarily be able to live democratically in order to learn to appreciate democracy; it is conceivable that while in a concentration camp a person could learn to appreciate democracy deeply. But probably a child is more likely to understand and value democracy through direct experience with it than in any other way.

Once having stated the necessity for democracy in classrooms, we must make certain qualifications. In a democratic society every member has an equal share in determining the goals and behavioral rules of the society, an equal share in deciding which freedoms and restraints are to apply. But this democratic principles applies only to the larger group, i.e., the entire society, which may limit the jurisdiction of its own subgroupings in any way it pleases. For example, jurisdiction over certain matters is left to adults, under the assumption that children are not competent to decide some things. Within the limits of their jurisdiction, students should have the same right of equal participation in decision making Gas adults.

Let us explore further the question of jurisdiction. Adults have seen fit in various ways to limit the overt behavior of children. For example, children are not permitted to destroy property, to flout community mores, or to loaf through school (when it can be helped). The adult community holds teachers responsible for seeing that the actions of children conform to these rules. In this sense a teacher is a representative, or agent, of the larger community. Although a democratic teacher will encourage his students to discuss problems of behavior, independently formulate rules which are reasonably compatible with those of the larger community, and obey them voluntarily, he must retain the right to overrule students if necessary. On some questions a teacher's vote must remain a majority vote—but only where matters of action or overt behavior are concerned. It is presumed that in a democratic school freedom of thought among students is not restricted; students have exactly the same freedom as adult groups. However, even this statement requires qualification.

We have assumed that, if a democratic society is to govern itself wisely, the principle of reflection will be a necessary adjunct of democratic life. We have assumed future that, *if a democratic society is to live into the further*, the principle of reflection must be extended into all problem areas which seriously threaten democracy. Now not all adult members of a democratic sodity will agree that these needs exist. Many persons may reject reflection and the critical study of certain areas of controversy. But probably a majority of adult Americans do uphold the principle of reflection and the necessity of free and critical thought in all areas of general social concern. If this is the case, then teachers may be regarded as agents of the larger community in acquainting students with the rules of accurate thinking and in encouraging them to think seriously about the most troublesome issues. Even when a local community objects to such practices, a teacher's responsibility to the larger group would seem to obligate him, insofar as he is able, to select methodology and content which are reflective and socially important.

Students in a self-governing classroom might select learning experiences capable of making effective citizens of them; but again they might not. Whether or not students want to think, a teacher must be an instigator of thought. If they want to, the job is easier; if they don't, a teacher has to arouse the desire to think. Whether or not students want to study critical social issues, a teacher must see that, to the best of their ability, they do.

The obligations of leaders in adult democratic groups are no different from the obligations of teachers. But because of their greater competence all members of an adult group presumably are capable to some degree of assuming leadership roles. Although in given cases they may not be, members of adult groups are often somewhat acquainted with reflective problem solving and in a position to decide wisely which problems they should pursue. Student groups, on the other hand, are less mature, less cognizant of the meaning of reflection, less aware of troublesome issues in the culture. By and large, therefore, teachers must play a more dominant role than leaders of adult groups.

6

The Measurement of Learning

Introduction

Throughout this book of readings we have considered the purpose of the schools and teachers to be the promotion of desirable behavior changes. The teacher's first task is to determine what response he wants his students to make. We have indicated that, unless the teacher is clear about the behavioral objectives he wishes the students to achieve, he has no sound basis for selecting particular learning materials, procedures, or activities. We have stated that the objectives which the teacher can select are limited by social and community pressures on the school, but the educational objectives of the community are rarely defined as specific behavior changes. For example, the parent tells the teacher that he wants his child "to know how to read." But "knowing how to read" comprises many behavioral responses. For example, the child must be able to (1) recognize that different marks on the printed page are letters; (2) connect these letters with sounds he has heard; (3) combine them into syllables and words; (4) recognize words by their general shape; (5) connect a word he has read with the same word he has heard; (6) relate words to meanings; (7) discriminate between related words and meanings; (8) pronounce the words he reads—to read aloud; (9) follow directions on the printed page, (10) combine syllables into sounds for new words he has never seen or heard, etc. "Knowing how to read" is not a specific enough objective to guide the efforts of either the child or his teacher. However, specific objectives narrow the selections of appropriate materials and procedures.

The articles in this book have been concerned with the conditions of practical learning situations. For example, there have been discussions of motivation, reinforcement, concept formation, principle learning, transfer. We have also discussed various characteristics of learners, such as ability and modes of communication. In general we have discussed what we know from experimental psychology and the psychology of individual differences, and what we need to know from educational psychology in order to make practical learning situations more efficient. By efficient learning we have meant learning that results in the behavior changes which have been previously designated by the teacher as desirable and which will be preserved over long periods of time for later use by the student. It has been assumed that a greater knowledge of the characteristics of the learning situation will furnish better guidelines for the management of educational activities and increase the likelihood that efficient learning will occur.

This last chapter is devoted to the measurement of learning, that is, testing. We shall take the position of Adkins that testing is an integral part of the educative process. By testing, the teacher tries to find out if the student's efforts to make the designated change in behavior, as well as his own efforts to engineer that change, have been successful. Where they have not been successful it is incumbent upon both teacher and student to take remedial action, perhaps trying quite different procedures for achieving the same change. One cannot consider the teaching or learning process complete until all three of the following requirements have been provided for: (1) selection of the behavioral objectives, (2) selection of appropriate materials and procedures, and (3) testing.

Tidy as this model is, students know from their own experiences that it is only roughly approximated in the schools. We cannot discuss here the carelessness or superficiality with which objectives are selected and defined, or how frequently the objectives are ignored after they have been selected. Nor can we discuss here how haphazardly learning procedures and materials are selected. Testing has received no better, and sometimes even worse, treatment. Teachers frequently see test construction and scoring as an excruciating burden; to them it is a ritualistic practice which must be observed, like erasing the boards, but which is essentially divorced from the serious business of teaching and learning. Students see tests as great trials. Neither teacher nor student seems to understand that unless some careful and constant effort is made to find out whether or not one is learning what one is supposed to be learning, everyone operates in the dark. If a manufacturer, after erecting buildings, purchasing machinery, hiring workers and supervisors of workers, and manufacturing a product, were then to show no interest in the product, we would have a situation similar to that which exists in testing. But in education it is perhaps not a lack of interest that makes us careless or hesitant in finding out how successful or unsuccessful we have been: there may be vague but persistent misgivings about the uses of the test scores.

Not only is testing important for continued learning, it is equally important in the determination of the student's future educational and social advancement. The tests which the student takes, especially in high school and college, are the chief bases for determining his grades. The grades are the basis for many future decisions which affect him later. His parents base their decisions on how much money to provide for his future education on grades. The college bases its decision on whether or not to admit him partly on his grades. His advancement within the school and college is determined by the grades he receives. Employers, who regard education with more favor now than when they were students, base decisions for hiring on grades. All of these individuals are assuming that the information provided by the grades is some indication of how well the student will succeed in some future endeavor. If this information is misleading, there can be unpleasant consequences for both the student and the community. Improved testing can furnish more reliable information upon which to base grades.

Relationship of Readings in Further Chapter

The excerpt from Bloom's *Taxonomy* points up the need for education objectives and considers the range of intellectual objectives possible. Adkins discusses the need for tests and measurement as a means of upgrading the present educational system. Ebel shows how we can improve our tests by careful construction and analysis of them. A second, more controversial article by Ebel raises the question of test validity. The final article is a reply to Ebel from Littell, who believes that testing must have more to do with an empirical "reality" and less to do with other tests.

EDUCATIONAL OBJECTIVES AND CURRICULUM DEVELOPMENT

In the introduction to this chapter the importance of establishing behavioral objectives was discussed. The educative process cannot be efficient unless it is directed toward the achievement of specific tasks. "Exactly what is it that I want the students to learn?" must be the unavoidable first question of the teacher. On closer inspection, however, the teacher often discovers that educational tasks are complex and that it is necessary to reduce them to subtasks arranged in a sequence conducive to efficient learning. Perhaps the most beneficial effect of programmed learning, as discussed in previous Chapter, is that it forces the teacher-programer to make a detailed analysis of the components of complex learning tasks and to experiment in finding out what the best order of presentation might be.

The following reading discusses educational objectives—their sources and classification. The *Taxonomy* is a classificatory system designed for use in constructing tests that would measure significant cognitive change. Although the *Taxonomy* recognizes the importance of simple remembering or the recall of information as an initial educational objective, its chief concern is the classification of intellectual abilities and skills beyond remembering. In general, its particular concern is with the student's ability to use the information he has gained in complex problem solving.

The reading can be compared with those of Adkins and Ebel: (1) How could the testing program described by Adkins fruitfully employ the *Taxonomy?* (2) How does Ebel's scheme for classifying text items compare with that of the *Taxonomy?* (3) What intellectual abilities and skills (beyond remembering) would you specify in a subject or skill area you plan to teach?

We have had some question about the relevance of this section in a handbook devoted to the details of a classification system. We have finally included it because we believe the classification and evaluation of educational objectives must be considered as a part of the total process of curriculum development. Some of these considerations help to clarify the distinctions made in the taxonomy. It is hoped that many teachers will find this chapter useful as a summary of some of the arguments for inclusion of a greater range of educational objectives than is typical at the secondary school or college level.

Problems of developing curriculum and instruction are usually considered in relation to four major types of questions.

1. What educational purposes or objectives should the school or course seek to attain?
2. What learning experiences can be provided that are likely to bring about the attainment of these purposes?
3. How can these learning experiences be effectively organized to help provide continuity and sequence for the learner and to help him in integrating what might otherwise appear as isolated learning experiences?

4. How can the effectiveness of learning experiences be evaluated by the use of tests and other systematic evidence-gathering procedures?

We are here concerned primarily with the first of these questions: the formulation and classification of educational objectives.

By educational objectives, we mean explicit formulations of the ways in which students are expected to be changed by the educative process. That is, the ways in which they will change in their thinking, their feelings, and their actions. There are many possible changes that can take place in students as a result of learning experiences, but since the time and resources of the school are limited, only a few of the possibilities can be realized. It is important that the major objectives of the school or unit of instruction be clearly identified if time and effort are not to be wasted on less important things and if the work of the school is to be guided by some plan.

The formulation of educational objectives is a matter of conscious choice on the part of the teaching staff, based on previous experience and aided by consideration of several kinds of data. The final selection and ordering of the objectives become a matter of making use of the learning theory and philosophy of education which the faculty accepts.

One type of source commonly used in thinking about objectives is the information available about the students. What is their present level of development? What are their needs? What are their interests? Another source for objectives is available from investigations of the conditions and problems of contemporary life which make demands on young people and adults and which provide opportunities for them. What are the activities that individuals are expected to perform? What are problems they are likely to encounter? What are the opportunities they are likely to have for service and self-realization?

Another source of suggestions for objectives comes from the nature of the subject matter and the deliberations of subject- matter specialists on the contributions their subject is able to make to the education of the individual. What is the conception of the subject field? What are the types of learning which can arise from a study of that subject matter? what are the contributions that the subject can make in relation to other subjects?

It is likely that a consideration of these three sources will result in a suggested list of objectives which require more time and effort than the school has at its disposal. The problem of selecting among possible objectives as well as the determination of relative emphasis to be given to various objectives requires the use of some guiding conceptions. The philosophy of education of the school serves as one guide, since the objectives to be finally included should be related to the school's view of the "good life for the individual in the good society." What are the important values? What is the proper relation between man and society? What are the proper relations between man and man?

Finally, educational objectives must be related to a psychology of learning. The faculty must distinguish goals that are feasible from goals that are unlikely to be attained in the time available, under the conditions which are possible, and with the group of students to be involved. The use of a psychology of learning enables the faculty to determine the appropriate placement of objectives in the learning sequence, helps them discover the learning conditions under which it is possible to attain an objective, and provides a way of determining the appropriate interrelationships among the objectives.

It should be clear from the foregoing that objectives are not only the goals toward which the curriculum is shaped and toward which instruction is guided, but they are also the goals that provide the detailed specification for the construction and use of evaluative techniques.

A test of the achievement of students is a test of the extent to which the students have attained these educational objectives. An achievement test is an adequate and valid test if it provides evidence of the extent to which students are attaining each of the major objectives of the unit of instruction.

The cognitive objectives derived from a process like that described in the foregoing paragraphs may, for discussion purposes, be divided into two parts. One would be the simple behavior of remembering or recalling knowledge and the other, the more complex behaviors of the abilities and skills. The following section discusses these two divisions in turn, considering their nature, their appearance in the taxonomy, and their place in the curriculum.

Knowledge as A Taxonomy Category

Probably the most common educational objective in American education is the acquisition of knowledge or information. That is, it is desired that as the result of completing an educational unit, the student will be changed with respect to the amount and kind of knowledge he possesses. Frequently knowledge is the primary, sometimes almost the sole kind of, educational objective in a curriculum. In almost every course it is an important or basic one. By knowledge, we mean that the student can give evidence that he remembers, either by recalling or by recognizing, some idea or phenomenon with which he has had experience in the educational process. For our taxonomy purposes, we are defining knowledge as little more than the remembering of the idea or phenomenon in a form very close to that in which it was originally encountered.

This type of objective emphasizes most the psychological processes of remembering. Knowledge may also involve the more complex processes of relating and judging, since it is almost impossible to present an individual with a knowledge problem which includes exactly the same stimuli, signals, or cues as were present in the original learning situation. Thus, any test situation involving knowledge requires some organization and reorganization of the problem to furnish the appropriate signals and cues linking it to the knowledge the individual possesses. It may be helpful in this case to think of knowledge as something filed or stored in the mind. The task for the individual in each knowledge test situation is to find the appropriate signals and cues in the problem which will most effectively bring out whatever knowledge is filed or stored. For instance, almost everyone has had the experience of being unable to answer a question involving recall when the question is stated in one form, and then having little difficulty in remembering the necessary information when the question is restated in another form. This is well illustrated by John Dewey's story in which he asked a class, "What would you find if you dug a hole in the earth?" Getting no response, he repeated the question; again he obtained nothing but silence. The teacher chided Dr. Dewey, "You're asking the wrong question." Turning to the class, she asked, "What is the state of the center of the earth?" The class replied in unison. "Igneous fusion."

John Dewey's story also illustrates the rote recall nature of some knowledge learning. The emphasis on knowledge as involving little more than remembering or recall distinguishes it from those conceptions of knowledge which involve "understanding," "insight," or which are phrased as "really know," or "true knowledge." In these latter conceptions it is implicitly assumed that knowledge is of little value if it cannot be utilized in new situations or in a form very different from that in which it was originally encountered. The denotations of these latter concepts would usually be close to what have been defined as "abilities and skills" in the taxonomy.

Whether of not one accepts this latter position, it is sufficient to note that knowledge by itself is one of the most common educational objectives. The most cursory reading of the standardized tests available or of teacher-made tests would indicate that tremendous emphasis is given in our schools to this kind of remembering or recall. A comprehensive taxonomy of educational objectives must, in our opinion, include all the educational objectives represented in American education without making judgments about their value, meaningfulness, or appropriateness. Knowledge, therefore, is one of our taxonomy categories.

The knowledge category in particular and, as noted earlier, the classifications of the taxonomy in general range from the simple to the more complex behaviors and from the concrete or tangible to the abstract or intangible. By simple we mean elemental, isolable bits of phenomena or information, *e.g.*., "the capital of

Illinois is Springfield," or "Arkansas contains much bauxite." Thus, our base sub-classification is titled "knowledge of specifics." At the upper end of the knowledge category the sub-classifications refer to more complex phenomena. Thus, remembering a theory is a more complex task than remembering a specific such as the capital of a state. Knowledge of the theory of evolution, for instance, would be very complex. Accordingly, the sub-classification at the complex end of the knowledge category is titled the "knowledge of theories and structures."

The knowledge categories may also be viewed as running from concrete to abstract. Thus, in general, knowledge of specifics will refer to concrete, tangible phenomena: "Insects have six legs"; "Most glass is brittle." But the more complex categories, as, for example, the name "knowledge of theories and structures" implies, tend to deal with abstract phenomena.

It might sometimes be useful for taxonomy purposes to distinguish knowledge with regard to the different specialities, fields of knowledge, or subdivisions of work in our schools. Thus, it would be possible to distinguish knowledge about the social sciences from knowledge about the physical sciences, and knowledge of physics from knowledge of chemistry, etc. Likewise, knowledge about man could be distinguished from knowledge about physical objects, etc. The taxonomy as developed here should be applicable to any of the subdivisions of knowledge or educational units in which school curricula are divided, but no attempt will be made to make all the possible applications or subdivisions in this Handbook. The reader may wish to develop such further classifications as are necessary for his work, using the taxonomy as a basis.

MEASUREMENT IN RELATION TO THE EDUCATIONAL PROCESS

Most teachers know that they must construct and give tests (if for no other reason than that it has always been done), but few know why. Students also expect to be tested, but even fewer students than teachers know why. Of course, both teachers and students know that course grades are largely based on tests, but no one has ever really explained grades.

In the following article, the author attempts to explain what a test is and why we need it. The theory of testing proposed here is based on Skinner's theory of learning. This weaving together of testing and learning is particularly appropriate for an anthology on human learning in the school. In reviewing this article, the student may find the following suggestions helpful: (1) One could almost say that Adkins believes that teaching is testing. How does her description of the "cycle" of the educative process support this view? (2) She has stated that Skinner may become the "sponsor of the century's most massive measurement movement." What is she referring to and how does this relate to her cycle theory of the educative process? (3) What does she believe is the chief purpose of achievement tests? How is this related to transfer of training? (4) What relationship is there between testing instruction, and individual differences? (5) How would Adkins build tests directly into the curriculum? Consequently, how would she report grades? What advantages would this have over the present system?

The measurement of change in the learner—all too often informal, subjective, and unreliable—is an inescapable aspect of various phases of the cycle of activity comprising the educational process. For purposes of clarification, it may be separated into the following steps:

1. Defining behavioral goals or objectives.
2. Planning stimuli (that is, curricular materials) and teaching methods.
3. Predicting the degree to which the objectives can be attained.
4. Applying the teaching methods to the selected curricular content or adjusting the goals or the content and methods.
5. Testing achievement.

6. Defining new behavioral objectives in the light of how well the old ones were met, and so on.

This succession has been called a cycle because it has no boundaries. Each new series must be adjusted upon the basis of the results of the preceding ones. Throughout the sequence, evaluation of either current status of the learner or of change in him must be more or less continuous, whether or not the appraisal is recognized as such or is conducted by means of formal tests.

Returning to the first step, the behavioral goals defined cannot be realistic unless they are based upon a knowledge of the abilities of the prospective learners to reach alternative ends that might be set. At once the necessity of measuring both various kinds of aptitude and previous achievement becomes apparent.

The second phase of the cycle, planning the curricular content and teaching methods, must be related to previously acquired knowledge or skills of the learners and to the readiness with which they can acquire the contemplated new abilities. Again, the decisions need to take into account the learners' present status. Likewise, teaching techniques should be modified in view of the capacities of the learners.

The prediction of whether or not the goals are realistic, listed as the third step, requires consideration of the aims themselves, the selected curricular content, and the proposed teaching techniques in relation to the previous attainments and aptitudes of the learners. Will a particular learner, presented with certain stimuli with specified amounts of reading, explanation, drill, recitation, dosage, and so on, demonstrate the desired behavioral change? Or will his time and that of the teacher largely be dissipated? If a prediction is to be made—as indeed it should be—appraisal of the learners' abilities again must be made.

The fourth phase, the application of particular teaching methods to selected curricular content, can be successful only if the teacher is vigilant in measuring progress toward the desired objectives. If retardation is evident, then teaching technique may be altered, content supplemented, or the goal adjusted. The teacher also should be responsive to more rapid accomplishment of the objective than was anticipated, else otherwise excellent learners will shy away from scholarship through sheer boredom. Here assessment of change in the learner as it is occurring must be prominent.

The fifth step calls for a test of the attainment of the objective of a unit of instruction. Such a test could be regarded as one of current status. Whether or not the achievement reflected in the test can be attributed to the unit of the educational process in question or to the particular teaching involved can not be resolved by a single administration of a test, however. Rather, test results must be interpretable in terms of how much change they reflect. Two comparable tests, given before and after some particular experience, such as exposure to a segment of content by means of certain methods, often will permit an inference as to the extent to which variation in behavior has taken place. Sometimes a conclusion is warranted that such change as is evident is associated with the intervening events, especially if a control group or some other appropriate experimental design has been employed.

The educational process should be dynamic. It should not concentrate fixedly upon an unchanging ultimate goal the attainment of which eventually may be tested. Rather, a series of proximate or intermediate aims should be established, with each subject to constant readjustment in the light of frequent appraisals of the attainment of previous ones. Viewed in this light, the setting of educational objectives can not be divorced from the appraisal of progress toward them...

The ultimate purpose of an achievement test, like that of an aptitude test, is to predict future behavior. Seen in proper perspective, an achievement test must serve this function if it is to go beyond the narrow limits of today's activities. Indeed, were educators completely unable to predict future performance from present achievement, the process of education would become chaotic. Any basis for selecting curricular content, mastery of which presumably would have positive transfer to later situations, would disappear. The inescapable fact, then, is that we are interested in present achievement primarily because it permits a prediction of future performance, however informal and often neglected that prognosis is.

Frank acknowledgement of this fundamental purpose of educational achievement tests should lead to revisions in the measuring devices themselves, in the curriculum, and in teaching methods. Recall with me a study reported by Sidney Pressey in *Psychology and the New Education* in 1933. Students' scores on end-of-course examinations in various high-school and college subjects were compared with their performance on the same examinations after one and two years. To quote, "These students showed a knowledge of about three-quarters of the material covered in the test at the end of the course, less than half after one year and about one-quarter after two years." One hesitates to project these loss of retention curves to even one more year! Pressey himself speculates as to whether solace may be found in the thought that students retain general understanding, principles, points of view, methods of attack, rather than minimally essential facts. Although too many educational achievement tests are limited largely to facts acquired by rote memorization, Pressey concludes by arguing persuasively that we are but little better off in the higher echelons of the thought processes. Finally, he suggests that the slight permanence of much school learning is chargeable to the curriculum, which evidently is not based upon content needed or used outside the classroom.

Yet, while the foregoing argument may hold for, say, algebra, which may appear to fade through disuse, it can scarcely apply to the basic skills of reading and writing, for example, which are practiced quite regularly and in which college students also reveal little permanence of learning.

A repetition of such an experiment in almost any field would yield equally sobering results. The basic difficulty may lie in the fact that materials learned to a level below mastery disappear from our repertoires for the very reason that they are not fully mastered, so that correct responses are not made often enough to get sufficient reinforcement in the normal course of events to perpetuate them. Surprisingly enough, although the advantageous effects of strategic degrees of overlearning upon relearning and eventual permanent mastery have been common knowledge to educators since the 1885 publication of Ebbinghaus' work, teaching practice reflects meager appreciation of them.

The suggested solution will lie in teaching each learner to the mastery level those materials that he is capable of really mastering, by suitable teaching methods and with more or less continuous progress appraisals based upon tests of defined educational objectives. The remedy is not simply to multiply the use of tests. More drastic surgery is indicated. Tests need to be integrated into the entire educational process, as heretofore suggested. To reiterate briefly, we must assess the present abilities of the learners, prepare curricular materials appropriate to the ability levels, adapt teaching methods to the learners and the content to be learned, establish appropriate degrees of overlearning by empirical means, and constantly appraise the learning as it is taking place...

The educational process is expensive, to the society that supplies the dollars and to the learner who contributes the time. As teachers' salaries rise and as the number of pupils increases, the total cost becomes larger. Despite the fact that I think teachers are grossly underpaid, I would at the same time point out that our educational system demands radical improvement. Consider, if you will, the hundreds of hours that are devoted to instruction in English by the time a person becomes a college senior. Then ponder his inability to write. Turn to arithmetic, the time devoted to fruitless drill, and later to algebra and geometry. Then reflect upon the ineptitude of a typical college student in solving the most elementary equation or even in adding a column of figures. Recall the idiosyncrasies in spelling that confront you in personal correspondence. Contemplate the current reading hubbub, by no means without foundation. Shudder at the prevalent superstitions and gullibility of the American public.

This does not mean that we should return to the "good old days", nor that as a people we are worse off than our immediate forbears as far as reading, writing, and arithmetic are concerned. More of us are about equally bad off, and the total effect is thus more devastating. A large part of what transpires under the name of education should be regarded candidly as serving primarily the function of custodial care of the callow. (It also, of course, provides an outlet for members of the teaching profession. And it slows down traffic on school days.) This safekeeping of the young is by no means a thankless endeavor, because it frees parents for several hours a day for other pursuits and hence presumably contributes to their tranquility. Thus the national trend toward starting children to school at earlier ages and keeping them there through early adulthood is not unrelated to the relief of parents from some of the responsibility for their care. As far as progress toward educational objectives is concerned, however, no one believes that schools operate at anywhere near 100 per cent efficiency.

This is not a criticism of individual teachers nor of the profession of teaching. It is an indictment of an educational system within which teachers operate and which is so firmly entrenched by long tradition that no single teacher or group of teachers or school can hope to resist it. Indeed, widespread and drastic educational change is warranted.

Consider a more or less typical fifth-grade group. With a mean age of around 10, it may contain some as young as 8 and others who have repeated a grade or more and who are thus as old as 13, or even older. Their general intelligence, in terms of the rather coarse 1.Q. measure, will vary from perhaps 55 to as high as 170 or more. Their mental ages (equally crude, of course) might range from around 7 to 15 or so. If the school is large enough, some ability grouping doubtless would be used to reduce these ranges. Even so, they are typically pretty large. Children's differences in the several more or less native aptitudes that go to make up the common general intelligence measure are enhanced by the fact that they have acquired widely varying degrees of competence in the many skills and knowledges to which they have been exposed. So what happens? With notable exceptions, every child is given identical assignments, exposed to essentially the same teaching methods with the same amount of learning time, and tested occasionally by identical tests. Teachers are well aware that the amounts learned under such conditions will vary markedly, and achievement tests commonly reveal wide ranges of ability. So inured are we to these differences that their very presence provides a clue to the validity of the tests. When the majority of scores cluster about a particular point, we say that the test is not discriminating among individuals, leading to the conclusion that it is not a valid measuring device. If all learners do well on a test, we plan to replace it by one more difficult in order to reflect the different degrees of mastery of subject matter that our educational system insures will exist.

Under such a plan, the educationally poor become more impoverished, but the rich are not strengthened. By the nature of the system, the weaker student is forced to endure failure over and over again. Aside from the questionable desirability of such negative motivation, the blighting effects of constant frustration upon personality development should be a matter of grave concern. The abler student, on the other hand, often experiences success too readily, with no genuine effort. This painless achievement again may have harmful outcomes when the student later encounters situations that require exertion.

Along what lines a solution, short of providing a private tutor for every child? The first major need is for extensive curriculum revision, in the direction of a large number of learning units scaled according to difficulty within subject-matter areas. Each such area should be limited to a body of knowledges or set of related skills that require the same pattern of abilities, which include both the effects of native aptitudes and previously acquired knowledges or skills. An initial step in scaling learning units would be the testing of these abilities of prospective learners. Then tentative curricular units could be tried out with groups of varying ability patterns by different methods of presentation. Doubtless experienced teachers could effectively reduce the number of methods to be tried by excluding in advance the ones likely to be least effective. Comprehensive subject-matter tests based upon materials taught by whatever method is current in a particular school would provide a start. Then, by some combination of expert teacher judgment and empirical test data, the units of instruction could be placed in appropriate order. The next step would be to develop mastery tests for each unit. These would be entirely different from the tests commonly now administered at the end of a unit of instruction, in which the teacher is disappointed if he can not observe wide individual differences. Rather, the learner would be expected to persist at curricular units of a given difficulty level until he had achieved a standard degree of mastery, at which time he would be ready for the next higher level.

Note some of the features of such an educational plan. The learner is not frequently assigned content entirely beyond his current ability level. Not is he ever wasting time upon materials absurdly easy for him. He rarely experiences failures. The questionable luxury of not exerting effort is disallowed. The learner competes always at his own ability level, not being exposed to content for which he lacks prerequisites. He becomes well acquainted with his limitations as well as with his strengths. His degree of mastery of what he is learning is continuously appraised, so that at all times both he and his teacher can know exactly how he is progressing.

Does this emphasis upon positive motivation and mastery of one learning unit before proceeding to the next mean that by some magic, at the end of several years of exposure to the educational process, we will have been able to eliminate the individual differences so conspicuous at its beginning? Not at all. If anything, the discrepancies will be more pronounced. Moreover, reporting upon such differences as will exist to prospective employers or to higher educational institutions could well be more detailed and far more precise than under the present system. In 1984, we may be able to say to an employer or to a university that John Doe has mastered mathematics unit 1728, English grammar 642, spelling 1021, physics 305, and so on. The personnel officers will by that time have conducted studies to enable them to predict from such data his relative chances of success as an outer-space radiological isotopist or as a student in a modern household engineering curriculum.

Are steps now being taken to reduce the formidable inefficiency and wastage of this mass baby-sitting movement that goes under the guise of the educational process? Undoubtedly isolated schools and rare teachers exist in contradiction to the perhaps shocking phraseology in which I have characterized modern education. But are there discernible trends, omens of significant departures from an educational system geared to presenting identical doses of pabulum to be partially digested within a uniform allotment of time? I am not to be satisfied—nor should you be—by having each teacher know the I.Q. of her every pupil, by further applications of "ability grouping," by myriad "opportunity rooms," or by what need no longer be called "progressive education." What we must seek is a situation in which a sizable share of curricular materials, graded according to the ability pattern and levels required, is presented to the learner in such a way that he can work at his own rate with a record of his progress constantly available to him and to his teacher. The measurement approach must be applied in the scaling of the curricular units as well as in the appraisals of progress. A dearth of such graded learning units exists. In fact, one is hard pressed to cite any aside from Earnest Horn's admirable early work in grading 3500 common words as to spelling difficulty and the contributions of Guy Buswell and others in elementary arithmetic.

A study aimed at the production of graded reading exercises, beginning with ones appropriate for elementary school grade 4 and continuing to the graduate school level, has recently been undertaken by Thelma G. Thurstone in the Psychometric Laboratory at the University of North Carolina. Currently the project involves 4500 items, and once they have been scaled, additional items can readily be added. This study should represent a major advance in the teaching and evaluation of reading skills.

The same B. F. Skinner with whom I have agreed and disagreed in turn in also developing scaled curricular materials as one phase of his work on teaching machines, about which many of you will have heard. Briefly, his plan calls first for the careful preparation of such materials appropriately ordered as to difficulty. Successive elements of each learning unit are presented to the learner in a window of a machine. He is alternately given information, required to practice or apply the information, and tested on each phase until he has mastered the unit. The machine can be set in several ingenious ways, so that, for example, the learner must finally proceed through a mastery test, say, three times in succession without error. Moreover, the robot can reject questions on which the learner has already demonstrated mastery so that he need not devote time to them. Skinner himself, as I interpret him, has misgivings about the reactions of both teachers and testers to his inventive approach to the educational process. He seems apprehensive lest they fear that they will soon be out of business, the teachers because the machine will be presenting materials in their stead and the testers because somehow appraisals of master will no longer be needed. To the contrary, teachers as both curriculum specialists and test construction experts will be needed in large numbers, even aside from their roles as discussion leaders, motivators, socializers, stimulators of creative thought, and so on. Skinner, in spite of his possibly ephemeral scorn of aspect testing, will come to recognize that such measurement is a very integral feature of his teaching machine. If his plans fully materialize, posterity may consign his pigeons to extinction and pay homage to him chiefly as the sponsor of the century's most massive measurement movement.

Pressey experimented with a similar idea in the late twenties or early thirties. He had a machine, like a miniature cash register, by which a student could indicate answers to objective test questions and immediately learn whether his answer was right or wrong. Basically the same idea was adopted by Angell and Troyer in their Self-Scorer. It also provides a means whereby a student taking a test continues to select answers until he obtains the right one, which is revealed by a red mark under the hole on the answer sheet that he has punched out. While we await the commercial feasibility of Skinner's latest venture, a relatively simple and inexpensive device such as this one may help to span the breach between instruction and testing. It is practicable for a small number of questions in daily discussion periods or for longer achievement tests.

On a less dramatic front, such college examiners as Paul L. Dressel at Michigan State University, working over the past several years with the instructional staff on evaluation of the objectives of college courses, has pursued an integrated approach to evaluation and teaching to the extent that they become indistinguishable from many points of view. To quote Dressel: "Evaluation does not differ from instruction in purposes, in methods, or in materials and can be differentiated from instruction only when the primary purpose is that of passing judgment on the achievement of a student at the close of a period of instruction."

The general outlines of an educational system that I have presented and the significant role that I have visualized for measurement in relation to the educational process may seem a far cry from such an institution of higher learning as, for example, Sarah Lawrence College. There, according to the jacket of *Essays in Teaching* edited by its president, Harold Taylor, exists "a freedom of intellectual inquiry unencumbered by the apparatus of assignments and tests." This is so overwhelming that I perforce discredit it. Simply because assignments are not organized or just because they are adjusted to the individual students does not mean that no assignments are made. As for tests, from what I have heard and read about the evaluation of students' abilities, needs, and interests at Sarah Lawrence, far more examining is done there than at the average college. The disuse of end-of-course marks or of any kind of grades that resemble the familiar A, B, C's or the 70-to-100 scale does not indicate lack of measurement. The fact that much of the evaluation depends upon subjective impressions gleaned from examinations does not signify that no measurement is taking place. Conceivably, such testing, based upon close personal contact between student and teacher, may be both less reliable and more valid than many of the objective tests currently extant. As I am sure will be clear by now, however, for a country-wide educational program I would rather place my chips on a more orderly curriculum and a more highly organized plan for measurement, closely geared together at every stage of the educational process.

PROCEDURES FOR THE ANALYSIS OF CLASSROOM TESTS

The question posed by Ebel in this article is "How good are your objective tests?" That objective tests have often possessed only degrees of "badness" can hardly be denied. Frequently they require little more than the recognition of a correct factual answer of one or two words in response to a rather simple-minded question of information. Sometimes the test items are so carelessly constructed that they unwittingly reveal more information than they ask for, and in every case, the items give the correct answer. Students may properly boast about the high degree of test sophistication that they have developed through years of subjection to bad tests. It is even conceivable that in some universities one could obtain a degree by simply "unfoiling" foils on poorly constructed multiple-choice tests. True-false tests have been so poorly constructed that the students who know the most often obtain the lowest scores.

The solution seems to be better tests—of both the essay and the objective type. The following article is limited to a consideration of the latter. In reviewing this article the student may find these questions helpful: (1) What does Ebel mean by relevance? What type of validity would Adkins call this? (2) Ebel has given examples of test items which range from simple recall of factual information to "application" items. Of what characteristic of practical learning situations, frequently referred to in these articles, would such items help to measure the successful outcome? Try to write an "application" item in a subject you plan to teach. (3) What does Ebel mean by discriminating power? If the teacher builds a test using this concept, how would this test differ from many others you have taken?

Defining the Problem

It is generally agreed that classroom tests at the college level, and almost other levels as well, are in need of improvement. Poor tests are the most frequent target of criticism when students rate their instructors and courses. Instructors themselves sometimes admit dissatisfaction with their tests and ask for suggestions as to how they may be improved. But the clearest indications of weakness in typical classroom tests are found in critical and statistical analyses such as those described in this paper.

When a central examinations service was set up at the University of low a decade ago the principal purpose specified for it was to aid instructors to improve their classroom tests. They were relieved of the clerical burdens of duplicating and scoring objective tests so that they might have more time to write better items. Consultation service was offered on testing problems. Files of sample tests were accumulated. Statistical computations, and especially item analyses, were provided. Any or all of these services were offered on request and without charge to instructors or departments. No attempt was made to require instructors to use these services, or to change their examination practices. Under these permissive conditions, which still seem desirable, it has become apparent that test analysis is the most powerful tool for making progressive improvement in classroom tests.

Originally the statistical service offered consisted of calculation of percentile ranks and analysis of items for difficulty and discrimination. While this information was useful, it did not give any simple or reasonably complete answer to the instructor's basic question, "How good is this test?" In an effort to answer the question more adequately, as well as in the hope of making instructors more familiar with the standards of good classroom testing and more clearly aware of the limitations of their tests, we have recently expanded our test analysis service.

The purpose of this paper is to describe this extended analysis and to explain the standards associated with it. No basically new techniques of test analysis have been invented. The main effort has been to apply existing techniques systematically and to develop reasonable standards of excellence for classroom tests.

For several fairly obvious reasons this report will deal only with the analysis and improvement of objective tests. This does not mean that all instructors at Jowa *do* use objective tests, for many do not. It does not mean that we believe instructors always *should* use objective tests, for there are certainly some situations in which essay tests are more effective than objective tests, though many of the reasons given for preferring essay tests seem to be based on prejudice and misconception. It does not mean that only objective tests need improvement, for, on the contrary, the essay tests which many instructors prefer to use are probably as much in need of improvement as are objective tests. To lead a college faculty to use objective tests at the right times and essay tests for the right reasons is a major problem in the improvement of examinations. But it is one which lies outside the scope of this paper.

Analysis for Relevance

The essential qualities of a good educational achievement test or test item are *relevance* and *discriminating power.* Practically all the suggestions offered for good item writing or good test construction relate directly or indirectly to these two basic qualities. When instructors are urged to base test items on course objectives rather than on course content, to emphasize important and useful information rather than trivial or academic details, and to reward understanding and application rather than rote learning or repetition, the purpose is to improve test relevance.

When instructors are urged to select items which most well qualified examines will answer correctly and most poorly qualified examinees miss, to express those items clearly, to make sure the correct response is demonstrably better than any alternative, and to make sure that each incorrect alternative has some basis for attracting poorly qualified examinees, the purpose is to improve the discriminating power of individual items, and thus to improve the discriminating power of the test as a whole.

Some of the important factors in relevance and discriminating power are outlined on the Test Analysis Report form which is shown as Table 6.1. These factors are listed in the first column under the heading *Characteristic.* Desired standards are listed in the second column, headed *Ideal.* Results obtained from the analysis are presented in the third column, headed *Observed.* Verbal evaluations of these results are presented in the fourth column, headed *Rating.* Sample data reported on this form were obtained from the analysis of a carefully developed entrance test, refined in several previous tryouts and revisions.

The analysis shows, for example, that none of the items in this test involve content details. Since such items are undesirable by our standards this aspect is rated "Good." Again, 94 per cent of the Mathematics test items involve application. While it is admittedly easier to write application items in mathematics than in some other areas, this aspect is rated "Excellent" since the desired standard is something more than 20 per cent for this category.

Only one aspect of relevance is covered in this analysis. No attempt is made to indicate the topical coverage and emphasis. All items in a given category are treated as if they were equally relevant or irrelevant when they actually are not. While such other analyses of relevance are most important, they can be made adequately only by an expert in the field covered by the test. The type of analysis reported here can be made by a test specialist, can be applied to most classroom tests, and is by no means insignificant. Over-emphasis on content details, specialized vocabulary and specific factual information, with corresponding neglect of generalizations, understanding, and application, have been observed so frequently that it seems eminently worthwhile to stress this aspect of relevance.

The categories used in the analysis of relevance from this point of view are defined in general terms as follows:

Table 6.1

University Examinations Service	State University of lowa		
Test Analysis Report			
Test Title________	Numer of Items________		
Examinees________	Date of Test________		
Characteristic	Ideal	Observed	Rating
I Relevance			
A. Irrelevant			
1. Content details			
2. Non-functional			
B. Relevant			
1. Information			
a. Vocabulary			
b. Facts			
c. Generalizations			
2. Understanding			
3. Application			
II Descrimination			
A. Item			
1. High (more than. 4D)			
2. Moderate (more than. 2D, up to. 4D)			
3. Low (more than zero, up to .2D)			
4. Zero or negative			
B. Score			
1. Mean			
2. Standard deviation			
3. Reliability			
4. Probable error			

D=Maximum difference (number in either expreme group).
M=Midpoint of range between highest possible and expected chance score.
S=One-fourth of range between highest possible and expected chance score.

1. A *content detail* item deals chiefly with instructional materials rather than with the objectives of instruction, or has no significance out side a particular classroom, or can be answered "correctly" only in terms of a particular source of information.

2. A *non-functional* item is one which is ambiguous or which can be answered correctly on the basis of subtle context clues.

3. A *vocabulary* item is one in which the principal basis for correct response is knowledge of the meaning of a single term.

4. A *fact* item is based upon some specific observation or some statement which is restricted in application.

5. A *generalization* item is based upon the summation of an extensive group of objects, events, observations or experiments, or deals with a conclusion, a principle, a trend, or a general condition.

6. An *understanding* item calls for explanation of a condition or an action, for interpretation of a statement, for knowledge of purposes or determining factors.

7. An *application* item calls for originality on the part of the examinee in dealing with a specific situation, solving a problem, recommending a procedure, or making a judgment, an evaluation, or a prediction.

The following items illustrate each category of relevance. These items were taken from a classroom test in psychology. They were selected to show clearly the differences between the categories. Not all items can be so easily classified as these. Some will appear to be "borderline cases." Others will have characteristics which do not fit any, or fit more than one category. Deliberate judgment is required in these cases, and some "errors" are likely to be made. But it is not likely that enough errors will be made to distort seriously the overall emphasis of the test.

Continental Detail

In an experiment in which anti-aircraft gunners were taught to estimate the distance of approaching planes, it was found that

(1) the responses were made on the basis of interrelationships among several stimuli

(2) gunners could learn to estimate range accurately after a 24-hour period

(3) perceptual reactions depended solely upon the size of the object in the gunsight

(4) the gunners had a tendency to hold their fire until an approaching plane was too close

Non-Functional

In order for regression to occur, the behavior patterns that are re-adopted must have been

(1) emotional in character

(2) operative some time in the past

(3) learned in an emotional situation

(4) a more successful solution of the problem

Vocabulary

Extreme attempts to overcome feelings of inferiority are the main characteristics of

(1) aggression

(2) regression

(3) over-compensation

(4) compensation

Fact

Asphasia is usually associated with damage of

(1) the right hemisphere

(2) the left hemisphere

(3) prefrontal lobes

(4) frontal lobes

Generalization

Studies of personality as a function of birth order have shown that

(1) personality is not related to birth order

(2) the oldest child is usually most independent

(3) the youngest child is usually spoiled

(4) those children who are neither oldest nor youngest are best adjusted

Understanding

Scientists usually work in the artificial environment of the laboratory because

(1) measurements can be made more precisely in the laboratory

(2) statements of truth cannot be made unless they have been verified in the laboratory

(3) events in nature never repeat themselves, and an event must be repeated to be studied

(4) sources of variation in the phenomena studied can be controlled in the laboratory

Application

If a student had at his disposal two hours in which to memorize long lists of dates and foreign words, it would probably be most advantageous for him to

(1) spend the whole two hours in a single unit of concentrated study

(2) divide his study into units of about 5 minutes each

(3) divide his study into two units of one hour each

(4) study in units of from 20 to 30 minutes each

The percentages given as ideal for each relevance category are somewhat arbitrary, and are intended mainly to suggest the desired direction of emphasis. More weight is given to generalization, understanding, and application than to facts, terms or content details. This emphasis does not imply that content details, technical vocabulary, and specific facts are unessential to learning. It does imply that these things are means rather than ends, and that good educational achievement tests should be concerned as directly as possible with the ends, or ultimate objectives, of instruction.

The fact that these categories of relevance are not mutually exclusive is also worth noting. As arranged in the outline they constitute a crude hierarchy in which each succeeding category (except the non-functional) encompasses much of the preceding category but goes somewhat beyond it. Thus, application is based on, but includes more than understanding. Generalizations are based on facts but involve something more in the way of synthesis. And all of these require some knowledge of terms and some acquaintance with content. Hence, when a test emphasizes generalizations, understandings, and applications it is also measuring the other categories indirectly. But a test which stresses content details, terms, and facts is far less likely to reveal knowledge of generalizations, possession of understanding, or ability to make applications.

Analysis for Discriminating Power

For many years our item analysis was based upon complete response counts for upper and lower achievement groups made up of the 27 per cent extremes of the distribution of criterion scores. From these counts percentages of correct response were obtained as indices of item difficulty and correlation coefficients were obtained from Flanagan's table as indices of discrimination. We recommended selection of items in the mid-range of difficulty (40 per cent to 70 per cent) and as high as possible in discrimination (above. .30 if possible). Instructors were told that these policies would result in selection of items which do the best possible job of discrimination.

In time it became apparent that a combined index of difficulty and discrimination could be obtained simply by subtracting the number of correct responses in the lower criterion group from the number of correct responses in the upper. An article by Johnson indicated that while this was not a new idea it had considerable merit. Instead of expressing this upper-lower difference for each item as a proportion of the maximum possible difference as Johnson suggests, we chose to work directly with the "raw" differences. This procedure is somewhat simpler and, in our application, involves no disadvantages.

The standards suggested for this index are again somewhat arbitrary. The maximum possible upper-lower difference is equal to the number in the upper group. Items which yield a difference which is .4 or more of this maximum are called high in discrimination. Those whose difference is less than .2 of the maximum are called low. Experience seems to indicate that these standards are high enough to suggest the need for improvement in most tests, but not so high as to make the standard appear unattainable.

Not all test constructors feel comfortable operating without the guidance of a separate index of item difficulty, especially when they use an index of discrimination such as this which favors items of 50 per cent difficulty. While they agree that items of zero or 100 per cent difficulty are useless, and those near zero or 100 per cent nearly useless, they feel that some distribution of item difficulties between these extremes is desirable. The theory is that difficult items are needed to test the good students, and easy items to test the poor ones.

This theory assumes high item intercorrelation, which is seldom if ever observed among educational achievement test items. Where item intercorrelations are low, selection of items whose difficulty is near 50 per cent tends to flatten the score distribution, to increase the dispersion of scores and thus to improve the discriminating power of the test as a whole. Selection of items to give a range of difficulties, on the other hand, tends to peak the score distribution, decrease the dispersion and thus impair the discriminating power, provided item intercorrelations are low. If item intercorrelations were high distributed difficulty values would give better discrimination than concentration at the 50 per cent level. However, we have yet to see a classroom test in which item intercorrelations were high enough and the concentration of item difficulties about the 50 per cent level close enough even to approach a rectangular distribution, to say nothing of going further to yield the undesirable bimodal distribution which is theoretically possible. Until that happens, item difficulties per se may be safely, even advantageously, disregarded.

Analysis of Score Discrimination

The importance of dispersion in the test score distribution has already been mentioned. The amount of dispersion possible depends partly upon the location of the mean along the score scale. Its location also indicates whether the test as a whole is too easy, too difficult, or about right. If the useful score range on a test is considered to extend from the highest possible score to the expected chance score, the best location for the mean is at the midpoint of that useful score range. For the mathematics test whose analysis is presented in detail in Table 6.1 the highest possible score is 60, since there are 60 items, scored I if correctly answered. The expected chance score is zero, since scores on this test were corrected for guessing. Hence the ideal location for the mean is a score of 30. The observed mean is 27, not far from ideal, but indicating that the test as a whole is somewhat too difficult.

The choice of a minimum standard for score dispersion was again somewhat arbitrary. When 100 or fewer scores are normally distributed, the range is approximately five times the standard deviation. For rectangular distributions the range is about 3.5 times the standard deviation. Since it appears that rectangularly distributed scores, though seldom attainable, would provide better over-all discrimination than would normally distributed scores, the compromise between 5 and 3.5 was weighted in favor of the rectangular distribution, and set at 4. That is, the ideal standard deviation should be at least one-fourth of the useful score range. For the mathematics test of Table 6.1 this ideal minimum value is one-fourth of 60, or 15. The observed value just reaches this standard.

The best single measure of the discriminating power of a test is its reliability coefficient. Experience indicates that carefully built tests of educational achievement can have reliability coefficients of .90 or higher. Experience also indicates that few informal classroom tests are this reliable. Hence .90 seemed a reasonable minimum standard. The odd-even reliability coefficient for the mathematics test of Table 6.1 is .94, surpassing the standard by a fair margin.

The principal reason for reporting probable score errors is to suggest to instructors that the scores on their tests are not perfectly "accurate" even when no scoring errors have been made, and to dramatize the need for more highly discriminating test scores. While a small probable error is better, other things being equal, than a large one, other things frequently are not equal. Because of this the better test may sometimes have a larger probable score error than the poorer. For this reason no standard for probable errors is suggested.

Concluding Remarks

The test analysis described in this paper is certainly not exhaustive. For most tests other aspects of relevance should be considered by the classroom teacher. For some tests a posteriori analyses of relevance (statistical validity studies) are possible and should be made. There probably are some types of educational achievement tests for which other types of analysis would be more satisfactory. But even with these limitations, a test analysis such as we have suggested is a useful tool which promises to be effective in improving the quality of classroom tests. It is a systematic, objective approach to the difficult problem of test evaluation.

MUST ALL TESTS BE VALID?

Asking whether or not a test needs to be valid, in the fields of psychology and education, is like asking whether or not the President of the United States needs to be an American. What is validity? The author of the following article considers several definitions of this term. If the question is, "How well does Johnny comprehend what he reads?" we give him several passages of different levels and types of difficulty to read, ask him some questions which will reveal his understanding of the passages, and then score his responses. If the question is, "How well does the student understand the concept of motivation?" we may give him some examples of motivated behavior and allow him to make inferences about causation. In terms of the educative process as it is understood here, a test is valid if it measures the behavior change the teacher tries to promote.

Of course, as the following article indicates, the question is much more complicated than this. To some extent modern psychological thought has never freed itself from its philosophical and theological origins. This is not to indicate that psychology must completely renounce the past and face only the future. However, the philosophical tradition has often made us suspicious of appearances, and it draws our attention to an "inner reality" as the real determinant of behavior. Much of motivational theory which postulates inner "needs" belongs to this category of thought. Behavior, and as it works out, tests which sample behavior, are but a paltry reflection of the true inner state of man or of his "real" behavior. Therefore an intelligence test is frowned upon because it can never touch the inner reality which is intelligence. And it appears that it will be even harder to touch the inner reality which is creativity. But intelligence and creativity are merely hypothetical constructs, and according to Ebel, they can be little else than the tests we build and use to measure them. If the results of several independent measures of intelligence agree, these instruments give us all the validity we need. Even when we define our course objectives in behavioral terms, as has been suggested by Adkins, the statement frequently looks like a test item. In fact, in the modern school we are relying more and more on test behavior, rather than on direct observation, as a basis for evaluation.

There are many other issues which Ebel raises: (1) How does Ebel's view of validity reflect his philosophical position? (2) How might Ebel's analogy between physical and mental measurement be misleading? (3) Why would he disagree with Adkin's view of predictive validity? (4) How would his concept of meaningfulness be helpful in school practice?

Validity has long been one of the major deities in the pantheon of the psychometrician. It is universally praised, but the good works done in its name are remarkably few. Test validation, in fact, is widely regarded as the least satisfactory aspect of test development. For this the blame is usually placed on the lack of good criterion measures. To assuage their guilt feelings about inadequate test validation, test constructors from time to time urge their colleagues to go to work on the criterion problem.

It is the purpose of this paper to develop an alternative explanation of the problem, and to propose an alternative solution. The basic difficulty in validating many tests arises, we believe, not from inadequate criteria but from logical and operational limitations of the concept of validity itself. We are persuaded that faster progress will be made toward better educational and psychological tests if validity is given a much more specific and restricted definition than is usually the case, and if it is no longer regarded as the supremely important quality of even mental test.

Difficulties with Validity

Definitions of Validity

There are at least four indications that all is not well with the concept of validity as applied to mental tests. The first is that test specialists tend to differ in their definitions of the concept. Gullikesen has said: "the validity of a test is the correlation of the test with some criterion." Cureton writes: "The validity of a test is an estimate of the correlation between the raw test scores and the 'true' (that is perfectly reliable) criterion scores." Lindquist suggests:

> "The validity of a test may be defined as the accuracy with which it measures that which it is intended to measure, or as the degree to which it approaches infallibility in measuring what it purports to measure."

Edgerton says: "By 'validity' we refer to the extent to which the measuring device is useful for a given purpose." Cronbach explains: "The more fully and confidently a test can be interpreted, the greater its validity."

No exact scientist would accept such diverse statements as operationally useful definitions of the same quantitative concept. While there is obviously some conceptual similarity there also are important divergences. The first specifies correlation with a criterion. The second requires estimation of a corrected correlation coefficient. The third avoids statistical terms, stressing accuracy in relation to the user's intent. The fourth makes validity mean utility. The fifth relates it to interpretability of test scores.

It would be difficult to state in words a core of meaning common to all the various definitions of test validity, of which the foregoing is only a sample. Such a conceptual definition, even if it could be formulated satisfactorily, would probably be too abstract to contribute significantly to more effective test validation. What the test developer needs is an operational definition.

Further, the generality of some of these definitions suggests that in the minds of their authors test validity is almost synonymous with test value. But if validity does mean value, then reliability, convenience in use, adequacy of norms, and even the availability of alternate forms become aspects of validity, and we are left without a term for what Gulliksen and Cureton mean by validity. Using the same term for a variety of concepts leads to serious semantic confusions and to procedural pitfalls as well.

Types of Validity

A closely related indication of difficulty with the concept of validity is seen in the diverse forms it must assume to fit different situations. The APA and the AERA Technical Recommendations mention four types of validity: content, predictive, concurrent, and construct. Two of these, content and construct, have little in common with the other two, or with each other Anastasi discusses face validity, and factorial validity in addition to content validity, and various types of empirical validity. Gulliksen has discussed intrinsic validity, and Mosier analyzed face validity into validity by assumption, validity by definition, the appearance of validity, and validity by hypothesis.

Again it may be said truly that these types of validity have some common conceptual elements, but the differences are striking. To encompass all the diverse varieties of validity requires an extremely loose and general definition of the basic idea of validity. It is easy to agree with Guilford that "The question of validity has many facets and it requires clear thinking not to be confused by them." Perhaps one could go farther and suggest that even clear thinking in the frame of reference of the present conceptual structure of validity may not lead to common understanding of a single concept, nor to effective operational use of it. Perhaps what we really need is not clearer thinking about validity, but rather a more concrete and realistic conception of the complex of qualities which make a test good.

Evidence of Validity

A third indication that all is not well with validity is found in this strange paradox. While almost every test specialist agrees that validity is the most important quality of a mental test, almost all of them lament the general inadequacy of test validation. Nearly 30 years ago, in the early years of objective testing, Ruch made this comment—

> There are in use today at least one thousand different educational and mental tests. Convincing critical and statistical data on the validity, reliability, and norms of these measures are available in probably less than 10 per cent of the cases.

One might reasonably expect that the situation would have improved in the intervening years, but this seems not to have happened. In a spaced sample of reviews of 20 tests in the *Fifth Mental Measurements Yearbook* only one was found in which the reviewer judged the evidence of validity to be adequate. Ten tests were criticized for lack of evidence of validity. Nine reviewers made no comment about the validation of the tests they reviewed. This in itself is surprising, if validity is indeed the most important quality of any mental test.

Some years ago, W. J. Cameron in one of his *Ford Sunday Evening Hour* commentaries observed that when someone tries to do a job the wrong way, nature often teaches him his error by refusing to let the job be done. Our failure to demonstrate consistently that our tests possess the quality we value above all other may mean that we have used the wrong approach in trying to gain evidence of it.

Is Validity Essential

A fourth suggestion that something may be wrong with the mental tester's concept of validity is that corresponding problems of validation seem to be almost nonexistent in the realm of physical measurements. Norman Campbell, P. W. Bridgman, and others have written extensively on the measurement of physical properties, but one searches in vain through their writings for a discussion of the *validity* of physical measurements. They show much concern for operational definitions of quantitative concepts, for limitations on the measurability of certain properties, and for accuracy of measurement. But the question of the validity of a measuring procedure seems to arise only incidentally and indirectly. For some properties, such as the hardness of solids or the viscosity of fluids, different methods of measurement yield inconsistent results. But modern physical scientists seem never to ask which of the methods of measurement is the more valid. One is moved to wonder why this difference between mental and physical measurement. It is possible that we have fallen into a trap of our own devising when we find it so difficult to validate our mental tests? Have we, in Berkeley's words, "first raised a dust and then complained that we cannot see?"

Refinements in the measurement of distances—by the interferometer—or in the measurement of time—by the atom clock—are not justified on the basis of superior validity, that is, as closer approximations to the measurement of true distance or true time. They are regarded rather as improvements because they permit reproducible measurement to smaller fractions of existing units of measurement, which is to say that they are justified on the basis of superior reliability.

When a shortcut substitute for some more elaborate standard method of measurement is proposed, the question of the validity of the substitute method does arise with logical legitimacy. In such a situation the concept of validity is simple, and the meaning of the term is clear. We will argue for retaining this concept of validity and of restricting the term to this concept. But to ask about the validity of the basic method of measurement, which provides the operational definition of the thing being measured, would seem to most physical scientists as it does to use to be asking a meaningless questions.

Why the Difficulties

Scientific Adequacy

The observations suggest that the concept of validity itself may be weak scientifically. Most of the definitions of validity can be shown to be derived from the basic notion that validity is the degree to which a test measures what it is supposed to measure.

But how does one know what a test is supposed to measure? On a superficial level, perhaps, it may be suggested by the test title—academic aptitude, mathematics achievement, or social studies background, for example—but these suggestions are by no means definitive.

Does the criterion tell us what the test is supposed to measure? It might if criteria were given to us. Usually they are not. They have to be *devised*, often after the test itself was constructed. Toops has said—

> Possibly as much time should be spent in devising the criterion as in constructing and perfecting the test. This important part of a research seldom receives half the time or attention it requires or deserves. If the criteriaon is slighted the time spent on the tests is, by so much, largely wasted.

The ease with which test developers can be induced to accept as criterion measures quantitative data having the slightest appearance of relevance to the trait being measured is one of the scandals of psychometry. To borrow a figure of speech from Thorndike, they will use the loudness of the thunder as a criterion for their measurements of the voltage of the lightning. Even in those rare cases where criterion measures have been painstakingly devised, the validity of the test is not determined unless the validity of the criterion has been established. This requires a criterion for the other criterion, and so on and infinitum. We can pursue such an infinite regress until we are weary without finding a self-sufficient foundation for a claim that the test is valid. It is an unhappy fact that the general conceptual definition of validity provides no firm basis for operational definitions of validity.

Philosophic Adequacy

The concept of validity is also weak philosophically. It reflects a belief in the existence of quantifiable human characteristics, such as intelligence or skill in arithmetic, independent of any operations used to measure it. Philosophers call this point of view realism but most of them now agree that it is not very realistic. One of Einstein's major contributions was to point out that the concept of time is scientifically meaningless until the clocks used to measure it have been described. As Henry F. Kaiser said in his review of a measurement book recently—

> Chapter 2 repeatedly exhibits the philosophically naïve faith that there "exists" an "actual" or "true" scale for a particular phenomenon; the author seems to assume a degree of absolute truth inherent in nature which went out of style in the nineteenth century.

This naïve faith in the pre-existence of a quantity to be measured is basic to the general conception of validity.

You may recall the story of the three baseball umpires who were discussing their modes of operation and defending their integrity as umpires. "I call 'em as I see 'em," said the first. The second replied, "I call 'em as they are." The third said, "What I call 'em markes 'em what they are." In philosophical terms, the first was an empiricist; the second, a realist; and the third, a positivist. I should like to see test developers be less individualistic in their positivism than baseball umpires are at times, but I think they should be positivists rather than realists. Neither a strike in baseball nor scholastic aptitude in testing is a useful concept until it has been defined in operational terms.

Many of those concerned with mental measurements however, persist in being philosophical realists. They tend to endow abstractions with a real existence. They think of a real trait which "underlies" a test score, and which is meaningfully there even though their best efforts to measure it will never be more than approximations. They think of intelligence as really existing independent of any operational definition such as those provided by the Binet, the Kuhlman Anderson, or the Wechsler. They seek to use tests to discover what critical thinking or creativity really are instead of using the tests to define what they mean when they use such terms. They have not yet learned that realistic philosophy is productive mainly of verbal discourse, and that it must be shunned if mental measurement is to advance.

So long as what a test is supposed to measure is conceived to be an ideal quantity, unmeasurable directly and hence undefinable operationally, it is small wonder that we have trouble validating our tests. Only if we are willing to accept some actual test, or other actual method of obtaining criterion measures, as a basic (if somewhat arbitrary) operational definition of the thing we wish to measure, and only if we have some other test or measurement procedure that we wish to check against this standard, do we find the concept of test validity useful. Further, if the test we propose to use provides in itself the best available operational definition, the concept of validity does not apply. A basic definition needs to be clearly meaningful, but it does not need to be, and indeed it cannot be validated.

One of the by-products of the realistic philosophy is mistrust of appearances and a reverence for the concealed reality. What a test or test item really measures, we warn ourselves, may be quite different from what it appears to measure. But how a person can possibly determine what it really measures without observing something that it appears to measure is never clearly explained. Those who analyze batteries of tests to determine the "underlying" factors trust appearances of what a test is measuring very little, but even they fall back on appearances when they must name the factors discovered or provide verbal descriptions of them.

The source of our concern over the deceitfulness of appearances is probably that what a test appears to measure sometimes seems to be different to different observers or when viewed in a different light. If we resolve not to trust any appearances at all the problem vanishes, but so does our confidence in the test (and probably our sanity as well). A better course of action is to seek to understand why the appearances were not consistent and to find an interpretation which makes them consistent.

Mistrust of appearances, in turn, leads one to seek completely empirical and deductive procedures of test validation. But completely empirical validation is seldom possible. Strictly speaking it is impossible in principle. We cannot escape judgment regarding the choice of a criterion, nor can we escape appearances (i.e., observations) in getting criterion data. To avoid an infinite regress of criterion validations one must stop somewhere and accept or proclaim an arbitrary definition of the thing to be measured. Unfortunately this is seldom done. What happens more often is that we accept highly questionable criteria, obtain discouragingly low correlations, and finally give the whole thing up as a bad job.

Overgeneralization of Validity

A third possible explanation for difficulty with validity is that the concept is too broad. If it is made synonymous with value, or utility, or meaning, if it made to apply to all mental tests including those used to describe persons or control educational processes as well as those used to predict future achievement, it must obviously have many different meanings. Now the trouble with using the same term to mean a variety of different things is that the meanings tend to get tangled up with each other. When the word is used in one particular sense, connotations appropriate to its use in other senses tend to hover about it and suggest irrelevant procedures.

In the case of the term validity, we tend always to expect evidence in the form of a validity coefficient even though such coefficients are completely appropriate only to tests used as convenient operational substitutes for more tedious, if somewhat more precise, standard measurement procedures. But when tests are used to describe educational achievement, or to assist in the control of the educational process, validity coefficient usually are quite irrelevant. The fact that they are not naturally relevant in these situations may account for some of the difficulty we encounter in trying to obtain data from which to calculate them. The obvious natural criteria we need simply do not exist in the real world, and must be conjured up from the realm of abstract ideals. Perhaps this is why evidence for the validity of educational tests is so often inadequate and unsatisfactory. Perhaps the notion of correlating test scores with criterion scores to obtain a basic index of test quality has been overgeneralized. Perhaps we have often sought to use it in situations where it does not logically apply.

It may even be that some of us, unconsciously perhaps, are glad to honor with our words a procedure of test validation which has limited applicability in practice. By so doing we exhibit our good intentions. If the procedure will not work in the absence of a good criterion, and if a good criterion is unavailable, we are excused from further effort to demonstrate test quality. We also have, in the well recognized shortcomings of available criteria, a convenient scape-goat for the lack of good evidence of test quality. It may often be convenient to sweep the problem of test validation under the rug of inadequate or unavailable criteria, especially when we promise ourselves and others to work to get better criteria when we can find the time.

What Is a Criterion

At this point it may be appropriate to ask what, after all, is the difference between test scores and criterion measures? Is the difference one of substance or only one of function? In the case of predictive validity the distinction is fairly clear. Test scores come first. Criterion measures are obtained later. In the case of concurrent validity the distinction gets blurred. One distinction suggested by frequent practice, is that criterion measures should be ratings based on direct observations of behavior under presumably natural conditions. This would serve to distinguish them from test scores, which are almost always based on assessments of output under carefully controlled and hence somewhat artificial conditions. But ratings based on direct observations of behavior have serious and well known psychometric shortcomings. This limits their value as criteria.

Indeed the limitation may be more serious than is commonly realized. Though it has often been done, it makes little sense to judge the accuracy with which a test does the job it is supposed to do by checking the scores it yields against those obtained from a less accurate measuring procedure. If a new method of measurement involves a better (and hence different) definition of the trait to be measured, it obviously makes no sense to judge its quality on the basis of degree of agreement with inferior measures. If the new method does not involve a better definition, but only more precise observations, it does make sense to require that the new agree with the old so far as their respective reliabilities will permit, but in this case it is hard to see the old, inferior measure as a standard or criterion for judging the quality of the new. If the criterion is used as a standard for judging the accuracy of the scores from the test, it should always exemplify a measurement procedure clearly superior to (i.e., more relevant and precise than) that embodied in the test.

In theory this could provide a useful distinction between test scores and criterion measures. In practice it seldom does. What usually happens is that the test developer pours all the skills, all the energy, and all the time he has into the process of making an outstanding test. He has none left over to spend on obtaining measurements "clearly superior" to those his test will yield, and under the circumstances would have no stomach for the task anyway. Small wonder that many good tests go unvalidated or poorly validated by conventional psychometric standards.

Predictive Validity

Predictive validity has long been recognized as one of the standard types, if not the standard type of validity. Cronbach, Mosier, and others have developed the idea that the purpose of all measurement is prediction. There is a special sense in which this is true, though the surveyor or the analytic chemist might be surprised to find himself in the same occupational class as the weather forecaster. Perhaps the statement "All measurement is for prediction" belongs in the same category as the statement "All education is guidance" or even "All flesh is grass." There is a degree of truth in such statements, but if they are taken too literally they can be seriously misleading. If the predictive function of measurement is regarded as the sole function, it leads to the highly questionable conclusion that the best way to judge the quality of a measurement of something is to determine how accurately it predicts something else.

Why should the quality of a Test X as a measure of Trait X be judged by how well it predicts Trait Y when Y is a function not only of X but also of Z, W, and possibly a host of other factors? Is it reasonable to judge the quality of a barometer solely, or even mainly, by the accuracy of the weather forecasts which are made with its help? Or to consider the matter in another way, is it reasonable to suppose that Test X should be itself be a good measure of Trait Y, when Test X consists of verbal analogies, arithmetic problems, etc., while Trait Y is ultimately measured by grades assigned by a variety of teachers in courses from Art to Zoology?

Scores on Test X may indeed be related to measures of Trait Y, and the size of the correlation may indicate, in part, how useful Test X is for a particular task of selection. But loose logic is involved if that correlation is used as a measure of the validity of Test X as a *measure* of Trait X. An academic aptitude test does not purport to *measure* academic success. It should not claim to do more than part of the job of *predicting* academic success.

Specificity of Validity

Validity, test theorists agree, is specific—specific to a given group of individuals tested, to the treatment given them, and to a given purpose for testing (or to a given criterion). Anyone who uses a published test is almost certain to give it to a different group than the one on which it was validated. For any user's group the test may be more or less valid than it was for the test author's tryout group. Quite possibly the user may even have a somewhat different purpose for testing than the test author had in mind. His criterion may be different. Again this means that the test may be more or less valid than the author reported. Under these conditions, how can a test author possibly publish fully adequate data on validity? The best he can do is to report validity under certain clearly specified and carefully restricted conditions of use. For the majority of possible uses of a test, validation becomes inevitably a responsibility of the test user. There is thus an element of unfairness in the common complaint that test publishers fail to provide adequate data on validity.

Alternatives

Meaningfulness and Validity

Whether or not you are prepared to agree that validity has serious shortcomings as the primary basis for judging test quality, you may now be interested in what alternatives might be proposed to replace it. What basis for judging test quality would be better than validity? Cronbach's definition cited earlier, may provide a clue. He said: "The more fully and confidently a test can be interpreted, the greater its validity." The interpretability of a test score depends on its meaningfulness. We would suggest that meaningfulness replace validity in the usual lists of major desirable characteristics of a measuring instrument. Before this suggestion is laughed out of hearing, consider what it implies.

One, but only one, of the kinds of information that help to make test score meaningful is the relation of those scores to other measures of the same persons. When tests are used to predict, or when they are used as convenient substitutes for more exact but more laborious measurement procedures, validity coefficients expressing the relation between test scores and criterion measures may be the most essential basis for meaning. Hence we are not proposing that either the term or the concept of validity be abolished but only that they be restricted to situations in which independent criterion measures are feasible and necessary.

Relationships of test scores to other measures can also add meaning to the test scores even when the other measures do not constitute legitimate criteria. When a test is used in a battery, knowledge of intercorrelations among the scores adds to the meaningfulness of the scores from each test. Such intercorrelations show how much the various tests measure in common, and how much independent information they provide. Campbell and Fiske have suggested a special technique for using this kind of information. From a "multitrait–multimethod matrix" of intercorrelations they secure data on which to base "convergent and discriminant" test validation. Construct validation also depends on relations between measures of various kinds, but thus far it has been of more direct interest and value to the psychological theorist than to the psychometrist.

Unless a measure is related to other measures it is scientifically and operationally sterile. The validity fallacy arises from the assumption that the relation of the measure to one single other measure (the criterion) is all important. The concept of construct validity has helped to break down this unfortunate stereotape.

Operational Definitions: What of the other kinds of information that help make test scores meaningful? Most important of all, scientifically, is a description of the operations used to obtain the scores. Operational definitions have always been basic to the meaning of measurements of length, mass, time, and other physical quantities. Such operational definitions should be basic to mental measurements as well. They would be, I am persuaded, had we not been misled by an overgeneralized concept of predictive validity.

Operational definitions of some kinds of test scores, such as speed scores in typewriting, ability scores in spelling, or vocabulary knowledge scores, are not particularly difficult to formulate. For other test scores, the problems seem more formidable. We must acknowledge that the excellence of many current tests has resulted more from the skilled intuitions of the test constructor than from preconceived excellence of design, recorded in truly controlling test specifications. But there is no apparent reason why an adequate operational definition of the score from any test should be impossible. Such a definition obviously must cover the critical procedures in test construction, in test administration, and in scoring. The development, use, and publication of such operational definitions would, I am persuaded, not only make the test scores more meaningful, but would lead us rapidly to the production of better tests.

Reliability and Norms: There are two other types of information which contribute substantially to the meaningfulness of test scores. These have to do with the reliability of the scores and with the norms of performance for representative groups of examinees. A completely unreliable score is completely meaningless. A perfectly reliable test score is almost certainly meaningful, though it may not be particularly significant or useful.

The importance of norms in making test scores meaningful requires no defense here. In the case of most educational tests they are highly useful. In a few special cases they may be unimportant or even irrelevant.

Importance and Convenience

The stress we have placed on meaningfulness of test scores, subordinating validity, reliability, and norms to it, does not mean that it can be regarded as the sole basis for judging the quality of a mental test. There are two other very important elements. One is the importance (usefulness as a basis for effective or satisfying behavior) of the knowledge or abilities required by the test. The other is the convenience of the test in use. The many factors which contribute to the convenience of a test have been well outlined by numerous authors.

A measurement can be completely meaningful and still be completely useless. For example, the number of hairs on a person's head is an operationally definable measurement. It can be related to other measurements of a person such as his age or his IQ. We could estimate its reliability and get norms for it. But it would remain, so far as I know, an almost useless measurement, one of little or no importance. Quite properly I think, critics of current educational tests are as much concerned with the importance of what the test is measuring as they are with the meaningfulness of the scores or with the convenience of the test in use.

Conclusions

It may be helpful now to summarize in outline form the characteristics which we regard as determining the quality of a mental test or measurement procedure. They are:

1. The importance of the inferences that can be made from the test scores
2. The meaningfulness of the test scores, based on
   (a) An operational definition of the measurement procedure
   (b) A knowledge of the relationships of the scores to other measures, from
      (i) Validity coefficients, predictive and concurrent
      (ii) Other correlation coefficients or measures of relationship
   (c) A good estimate of the reliability of the scores
   (d) Appropriate norms of examinee performance

(3) The convenience of the test in use.

Must all tests be valid? If the term "valid" is not to be made synonymous with the term "good," if validity is a clearly defined concept which can be quantified by finding the correlation between test scores and criterion measures, then the answer is clearly "no," on the basis of the considerations discussed in this paper.

These views may be wrong. If so, and if the current conception of validity is philosophically sound and operationally useful, let us in the name of intellectual honesty, support this claim with some good solid evidence. The time is long past for lame apologies and prolix rationalization of failure to demonstrate that good tests have the quality we have said is more important than any other. Perhaps we should recognize the age-old alternatives so far as validity is concerned. Either put up the evidence or withdraw the claim. It is my view that in general, we have not and will not be able to put up satisfactory evidence. On the other hand we should not stop being concerned about test quality.

What is proposed here is that we stop beating our heads against a stone wall and step back to look for a way over it or around it. There is one, I think, and this article has attempted to elucidate it.

Having followed the argument thus far some will say: "You still want valid tests. All you have done is to propose a different term, meaningfulness, to replace validity." This is surely not what I have been trying to do. I hope that your time has not been wasted in reading one side of a purely lexical debate. I hope that these efforts may contribute to the adoption of a more appropriate and productive procedure than validation has been for determining the quality of a test.

GROUPNESS OF THE GROUP

Are individuals more successful in solving problems when they work alone or when they work in a group? We are reminded by Lorge that before we can answer the question we must have some definition of what a group is. In the Introduction the group was referred to as a method of instruction which can help students achieve particular educational goals. For example, a reading group in the first grade may be a means of giving common instruction to pupils who possess the same level of skill or have the same difficulties in reading. Such groups, in Lorge's terminology, lack "groupness." Psychologically, the group is discussed in terms of the various leader and member roles which are enacted in it and the impact of this behavior on each of the members. The group interaction described by Zander and Cohen in the article which follows later exemplifies some aspects of this groupness. The group which has this quality of groupness may still be an instructional group, but its objectives would relate to social organization, the development of cohesiveness, skill in social interaction, etc.

Lorge's distinction between *ad hoc* (experimental) groups and dynamic (on–the–job) groups recalls the difficulties, referred to by Melton and others, which occur in translating laboratory findings for application in practical situations. The situational factors may actually impose greater restrictions on generalizations in the case of groups than individuals. For example, what limitations does this translation place on generalization which can be made about individual versus group superiority in learning? What concrete proposals for research on groups in the real school situation can the student suggest (in the light of Lorge's discussion)? How would you test for transfer of group learning of social skills?

There is a tendency, among educational psychologists, today to accept some objectives, procedures and content as legitimate curricular goals without assaying the attainability of them. For instance, there seems to be considerable emphasis in the educational and psychological literature on the attainment of groupness and group dynamics. There can be little quarrel with the stipulation of such goals provided that some attempts be made to find out whether the goals as ends, or as means to other ends, are realized or realizable.

From a brief review of group dynamics, it is evident that much attention has been given to the purpose of group dynamics at the elementary school level. The expressed purposes range from the mere learning of specific skills and knowledges to the attainment of the broader aspects of democratic living. For instance, Thelen believes that instructional efficiency can be increased through the teaching of group dynamics in the classroom. He suggests that all students in a subgroup can be brought up to the level originally possessed by the most skilled person in it, if group methods of teaching are intelligently used. It is true that Thelen feels that a primary purpose of group methods in teaching and learning is in the promotion of creative thinking and social organization. When the class discusses and settles the question of how work shall be organized and individual efforts co-originated, he feels that the individuals and the class gain in mastery of decision-making and in problem-solving. Learning in groups is said to satisfy individual needs so that energies may be devoted to solving achievement problems. Indeed, Thelen tends to emphasize not only the individual's gains in the mastering of content, in the accepting of self responsibility, in the motivating of learning, but also stresses the acquiring of group process goals in group feeling and in the understanding of democratic adjustments.

With the current interest in the group and in group dynamics, however, little has been said about what makes a group *a group* as distinguished either from an aggregation or, indeed, from an individual. The popular preference for the word "group" suggests a nuance of an organic unit or a cohesive whole. In the literature, however, the structure of the group is ill–defined and ambiguous. In the references that have been reviewed, the structure of the group, as used in elementary school teaching, may be broadly dichotomized, (1) as that in which the group is considered more in terms of method of instruction than in terms of its organization; and (2) as that in which the group is referred to in terms of role and interaction patterns.

The first obviously does not define a group at all, but gives the flavor of the classroom climate in relation to relative limits placed on child activities both by teacher demands and decisions as well as by the environmental constraints and limitations considered necessary for teaching and learning. Essentially, group structure merely—or really suggests the delicate balancing between the Charybdis of permissiveness and the Scylla of control. The second category asserts that there are differences between an aggregate and a group such as the fact that a group's members have common needs, interests and purposes. This, too, fails fully to specify a group, for in the schoolroom in so far as members have different needs, interests and purposes, they would form different groups. Perhaps, the closest indication of the differential is in the process of interaction among the members of a group. Such an approach to the group leads to difficulties in the appraisal of and even the description of the communications and transactions among the members. Yet, the groupness of any group must represent some sharing of experiences, knowledges, feelings and purposes. Perhaps groupness, or as one writer terms it, "we–ness" is in the sharing of resources, be they intellectual, emotional or material, to accomplish a group purpose of several group purposes.

Even now, however, there is little or no evidence that suggests the degree to which groups achieve any one group purpose, or the extent to which the members as individuals gain from group experience in such objectives as social skills and knowledge, or, more significantly, in the ability to transfer such social gains to other groups. It is too early to expect that the effect of the group experience upon the school children can be appraised. At least, for research, there are hypotheses that should be tested such as: (a) any group benefits are shared equally by all individual members; (b) individual learning is maximized through the group; (c) group experiences strengthen the individual's need to learn; (d) group experience allows the individual to develop at his own rate to maturity; and so on.

It is my belief, however, that it will be very difficult to design research in the effect of the groupness of the group upon the behavior of its individual members largely because the group is so ill–defined.

In the course of summarizing the literature on experimentation with groups in problem solving, we became aware that the psychologist used the term"group" in at least five different meanings. This is not strange. For the lexicographer considers a group to be "number of persons (or things) gathered together and, thereby, forming a recognizable unit; a cluster, an aggregation, or a band" or to be a "number of persons classified together because of common characteristics or community of interest." The difficulty lies in the fact that the dynamic character of the group is lost in the dictionary's definition. Psychologists tend to think of the group as made up of members, each of whom is in close personal relation with every other member. The group implies interaction and communication among two or more individuals whether with, or without, a designated leader but with a tradition of having learned in time and with mutual experiencing to work together. Obviously, such a co–operative amalgamation of individuals who have progressed upward through the stages of organizing, of assaying each other's resources and personalities and of establishing channels of communication into the more significant and higher stages of mutual reinforcement of one another's contributions to solving a problem is not easy to find. Except as described in terms of process observations, the traditioned group has not yet been studied. It is reasonable to assert that such groups have both been utilized in research in groups, either at the elementary or high school levels. And, with the exception of Darley's work with sororities, such groups have not been the basis of research with college students.

The psychologist, however, tends to generalize anticipated values of traditional groups to very many enterprises. Indeed, the psychologist and the educator have failed to recognize that in their research activities, they must necessarily work with groups that are not traditional groups. All of you are familiar with the so–called *ad hoc* group. The *ad hoc* group is usually established by some outside agency (viz., the college teacher as experimenter) to work with, or solve some externally specified task, under the instruction that they do so co–operatively. Such an *ad hoc* group is at least one step away from the more dynamic group. The *ad hoc* group is an artificial assemblage made for the duration of an experiment. Such a group rarely is expected to, and rarely does, continue to develop groupness.

Under an Air Force contract, our research staff has attempted to test the hypothesis that problem solving by *ad hoc* groups of staffs is superior to problem of the random individual. The widely different kinds of problems have been used with two different populations. One type of problem, designated as the field type, is like the familiar O.S.S. task of requiring a cadre of men to cross a mined road without attracting the attention of the enemy and without traces of their route. A series of such problems was given to *ad hoc* teams of college undergraduates to do. In general, the solutions by teams were markedly superior to those of random individuals. Such a result would have been anticipated from the published results of Shaw's well–known experiment in problem solving.

The other type of problem required the solution of a complex human relations difficulty such as taking steps to improve the morale at an Arctic Weather Station under the constraint that the mission of weather reporting must be accomplished. This type of problem was used with officers in the Air Force in the ranks of captain through colonel. The *individual* solutions tended to be as good or better than the average of *ad hoc* staff solutions.

Is it possible that college students work more co–operatively than officers: or is it likely that staffs or teams are superior in those problems for which there is a knowable solution; or is it possible that the responsibility of command makes each member equivalent to a staff? The answers are, of course, unknown. Certainly children in schools today are expected to participate in, and with, groups. Perhaps the future holds bright promise for group decisions and group problem solving if such experience develops a common element of groupness which is transferred positively to all forms of later group experience.

Edward L. Thorndike would certainly have wished to evaluate attainment of the objectives. At Teachers College, three attacks are being made on the nature of the differences in the solutions to problems by groups and by individuals. The first is to compare *ad hoc* groups with random individuals; the second to compare *traditional* groups with *ad hoc* groups; and the third is to create mathematical models to account for the group superiority. As a matter of fact, Dr. Solomon and I have developed two such models to consider group behavior in the solution of the Eureka or knowable solution problem. The models are expressed in terms of two hypotheses: Model A, that group superiority is a function only of the ability of one or more of its members to solve the problem without taking account of the interpersonal rejection and acceptance of suggestions among its members; Model B hypothesizes that group superiority is a function only of the pooled abilities of its members. Modes B implies that each problem is solved in two or more stages.

The use of Models A and B on the Marjorie Shaw data as well as the data for the O.S.S field type problem suggests the *acceptability* (but not the proof) of the formulation that the group is superior to the individual *only* because any group has a higher probability of having among its members at least one solver, or several solvers who can independently solve the various stages of the problem. If this be verified by further researches with a broad range of groups and problems, it reopens the question of the "groupness of the group" and the enduring result as a group activity over fairly long spans of time.

Our own experimental evidence contrasting problem solutions by *ad hoc* teams made up of individuals, who had solved the *same* problem previously, supports the generalization that group superiority may be a reflection of the ability of the best one or two members of the *ad hoc* group. In another experiment, an attempt was made to contrast the problem solutions made by "traditioned" and by "*ad hoc*" teams. The traditioned teams comprised members who worked together at the Air University on all group activities as a staff for three months. The results lead to the inference that the "three–month traditioned group" is equivalent, but not better than, the *ad hoc* group. It must be emphasized that experimental, "traditioned" groups originally had been designated by the authoritarian procedure of selecting individuals from the class at random to make up the group. Hence the "traditioned" group may not have had in it members who would have developed the group cohesiveness that is so essential to a dynamic group with groupness.

No interest group, as sophisticated as educational psychologists, would be tempted to overgeneralize these results. First, the subjects in our experiments were adults who may have overlearned those ways of working out problems that stressed the individual; second, the solutions did not have to be carried into action. While the individual adult, student or officer, may have made a decision or solved a problem as well as or better than the group, this does not suggest that the individual solution must, necessarily, be carried out as well as a group solution or decision; and third, no attempt was made to ascertain what each individual as individual got from the group process of deliberation and closure.

The three limitations to generalizations about individual over group superiority should suggest that educational psychologists must develop hypotheses and the means for evaluating them; the attainment of curricular objectives not only for relatively immediate consequents but also for long time transfer the the tasks and problems that living affords. Indeed, the groupness of the educational psychologist lies not so much in the affiliations with other interest groups; but in the common purposes and needs to get at the facts, generalizations and applications that will lead to better teaching and better learning among themselves and for those that must learn. Groupness for educational psychology is a function of our communications and transactions.

GROUP PROBLEM SOLVING

The conflicting adages, "Too many cooks spoil the broth" and "Two heads are better than one," may well serve to illustrate the confusion about a current problem in education: which is better, individual learning or group learning? In answering this question we have also to consider the free–floating anxiety that we may lack individual resources and are objectly dependent on the team, or group, and exquisitely attuned to its moods and demands. Such phrases as "organization man" are rather high abstractions with emotional auras that obscure their meaning and maximize their threat. It is never quite clear in what way an "organization man" is different from one who is "non–organizational," especially in a society where only a few artists and country physicians manage a livelihood without much institutional involvement. Even some of our most prominent scientists have become organization men: they work in teams in what must be one of the biggest organizations in the world—the Federal government. It would be a bit of Sophoclean irony if we could produce evidence to show that no child is more organizational than the offspring of child–centered parents eager only to foster his independence. The question may not be conformity versus nonconformity but what type of conformity and who decides the type.

Any investigation of social learning must not ignore the aspects of the cultural milieu reported above. Such research is further complicated by the fact that individual differences rapidly multiply when one is attempting to find both stimulus and the response variables in the group. Marquart's study has shed some light on this issue. The student may consider the following questions: (1) How does Marquart's treatment of the data differ from Shaw's (as described in the report)? (2) How did this alter the conclusions Marquart reached? (3) What might have occurred if she had used more complex problems? Why? (4) What cultural factors may have reduced the quality of the group of performance as compared to the individuals'? (5) As revealed in this study, what seems to be the chief characteristic of this situation which accounts for superiority of either group or individual?

A. The Problem

A number of studies have been conducted to determine the effects of various types of social stimulation upon the performance of individuals. We are fairly certain that simple tasks are performed more rapidly when spectators are present than when the subject is alone and that the presence of a co–working but non–competitive group increases the quantity of work done but decreases the quality of the work. However, few attempts have been made to compare the efficiency of a group and of individual problem solving.

The experiment upon which the present research is based was published by M.E. Shaw in 1932. Miss Shaw compared, as shall we, the performance of individuals and of groups on problems which require more complex thought processes than do those used by Watson. She employed six problems, one–half of which were to be solved by individuals working alone and one–half by individuals working in groups of four members each. She analyzed her data in terms of the total number of correct solutions attained relative to the number of possible solutions and found a very strong advantage for the group over the individual. Her individuals attained correct solutions on 7.9 per cent of their attempts and her groups on 40 per cent of their attempts.

It is the belief of the writer that the method of experimentation employed in Shaw's study is good, that the problems are well selected, but that the method of treatment of the data could be improved upon. Miss Shaw does not consider that group performance is superior to individual performance only if the performance of the group is better than the performance of the top member of the group. Thus, if one of the members of a group can solve a problem when working alone, there is no proof of the advantage of group performance if the group as a whole can solve the same problem.

The purpose of the present study is to determine whether the advantage of group performance in problem solving will meet this more rigid criterion. Does a group solve problems of the type used by Miss Shaw more readily than does the top member of the group? We shall also reanalyze Miss Shaw's data to check for the attainment of this criterion.

B. Subjects and Apparatus

Subjects

The 66 subjects employed in this study were students in a course in experimental psychology at the University of Arizona. They were all of junior, senior, or graduate standing, and most were majors in psychology. All of the subjects had formerly completed at least one year of general psychology and two other courses in the field; most had completed far more than this.

Apparatus

Eight problems were utilized: four for the first experimental session and four for the second. Each problem was typed and enclosed in a separate envelope. The first four problems were either the same or closely parallel to four of those used by Shaw in her study. They were:

1. Use the disks H1, H2, H3, W1, W2, and W3. (For the present disregard the symbols on the reverse side of the disks.)

On the A–side of the river are three wives (W1, W2, W3) and their husbands (H1, H2, H3). All of the men but none of the women can row. Get them across to the B–side of the river by means of a boat carrying only three at one time. No man will allow his wife to be in the presence of another man unless he is also there.

2. Use the disks marked M1, M2, M3, C1, C2, RC. (The reverse side of the disks just used.)

Three missionaries (M1, M2, M3) and three cannibals (C1, C2, RC) are on the A–side of a river. Get them across to the B–side by means of a boat which holds only two at one time. All of the missionaries and one cannibal (RC) can row. Never under any circumstances or at any time may the missionaries be outnumbered by the cannibals. (Except, of course, when there are no missionaries present.)

3. The enclosed slips of paper containing words will when put in the proper order form the last three lines of the unfinished sonnet below. Arrange them as nearly as possible in the proper order.

> Knowing this man, who calls himself comrade mean, underhanded, lacking all attributes real men desire, that replenish all worlds men strive for; knowing that charlatan, foot too,masquerading always in our colors, must also be addressed as comrade—knowing these and others to be false, deficient in knowledge and love for fellow men that motivates our kind.

Nevertheless I answer the salutation proudly, equally sure that no one can defile it, feeling deeper than the word the love it bears, the world it builds. And no man, lying, talking behind back, betraying trustful friend, is worth enough to soil this word or mar this world.

4. A consolidated school is to be built in the rural district shown in the diagram. The capital letters (A,B,C, etc.) indi-

cate points (not towns) where pupils are to be picked up by two school buses. The mileage between each point is indicated on the diagram. The capacity of each bus is 35 pupils and the driver. Find the most desirable location for this school and give the route each bus must take. The buses may start at *any* point and need not necessarily start from the school each morning. Following are the number of pupils to be picked up at each point (see Table 6.1):

Point	Pupils	Point	Pupils	Point	Pupils
A	6	D	4	G	3
B	13	E	2	H	10
C	17	F	5	I	3

The second set of problems were as follows:

1. A man stopping at a hotel ran out of money and would have no more for 23 days. The landlord would not trust him, but, as he had a heavy gold chain of 23 links, the landlord agreed to accept one link in payment on each successive day and to restore the chain on receipt of the money. The owner was anxious to preserve the chain as intact as possible. How many links was it necessary for him to cut? Show how he was able to pay the landlord one link

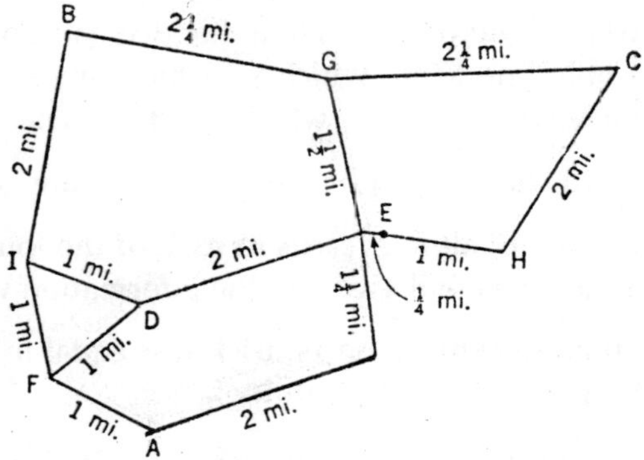

Figure 6.1

on each successive day for 23 days, and yet cut only this small number of links of the chain. (Time limit 30 minutes.)

2. Six bathing beauties stood in line facing the judges.

The prize was given to the only girl whose name began with the same letter as that of her state; only, of course, the judges did not know this until the contest was over.

From the description below, you will be able to write each girl's name opposite her state, and then pick out the prize winner.

Miss Ohio was not on speaking terms with *Dorothy Olga* was engaged to *Miss Delaware's* Brother. *Mary* and *Miss Maryland* were at opposite ends. *Dorothy* was at the judges' right, next to *Miss Maine*. Neither *Maude* nor *Vera* represented Ohio.

Miss Vermont was between *Katie* and *Miss Delaware. Miss Kansas* was between *Olga* and *Miss Maine. Vera* 'was not next to the girl at the judges' left. (Time limit 25 min)

3. A milkman has a 14–quart can full of milk. He wishes to divide his milk into two equal portions. In addition to the 14–quart measure, he has a 5–quart measure and a 9–quart measure. How does he make the division without any waste using the three measures only and not guessing at the amounts? (Time limit 30 min.)

4. In the first four tricks of a four–handed game of cards, there was only one King, which was the highest card played. There was only one Six, which was the lowest card played.

No two cards of equal value were played in any single trick.

Find the value of all four cards in each of the four tricks. The following statements will give you the information you need.

(a) The highest card in the 1st trick was equal in value to the 2nd highest card in the 4th trick.

(b) The lowest card in the 2nd trick was equal in value to the highest card in the 4th trick.

(c) The second highest card in the 2nd trick was equal in value to the lowest card in the 3rd trick. (Time limit 25 min.)

C. Procedure

The 66 subjects employed in the present study were divided into 22 groups of three subjects each. This division, except for an equation of sex, was done on a chance basis. All groups except three were comprised of two men and one woman. These three groups were made up of two women and one man.

Two experimental sessions were utilized for each subject. The first session, of approximately two and one–half hours, was devoted to the solving of the four problems which were identical or closely analogous to four of those used by Shaw. The subjects solved two of the four problems by the group method and two by the individual method. As can be seen in Table 1, one–half of the subjects worked first as individuals and then as groups; one–half worked first as groups and then as individuals. Also, one–half of the subjects worked on Problems I and II first, and one–half of the subjects worked on Problems III and IV first. No time limits were set for the solution of these problems. When working as individuals, the subject were together in one large laboratory room; when working as groups, each group used a small room.

The individuals, when working alone, were told—

> You will be given two problems; solve them in order. Do not be content with your first solution but work until you are fairly certain that you have the correct answer. Record tentative and final solutions on paper so that they can be turned in and scored. Keep a record to the nearest minute of the time required for the solution of each problem. Include the time required for the writing of the solution. If you find it impossible to solve any problem, you may turn in a sheet containing a description of your partial solution.

The groups were told—

> Solve the two problems in order. Do not be content with your first solution but work until you are fairly certain that you have the correct answer. One of you is to act as a recorder, that person is to record tentative and final solutions on paper so that they can be turned in and scored. Also, keep a record of the time required for for the solution of each problem. Include the time required for the writing of the solution. The recorder is to take an active part in the solution of the problems. Please try to work together as a group as well as you can. Do not work in a parallel manner and then select the best of the three solutions. If you find it impossible to solve any problem, you may turn in a sheet containing a description of your partial solution.

The experimenter observed brief sections of the working periods of the individuals and of the groups to assure herself that the directions were being followed.

The second experimental session, which was held one week later, was devoted to the solving of the second group of four problems. Again, one-half were solved by the individual method and one–half were solved by the group method. The groups were the same as those used during the first session and followed the same procedural order (see Table 6.1). The only difference is that Group XXII was broken by an absence, and that data for it was discarded in this part of the study.

Table 6.1

Procedure Followed by Each of the Groups Employed in This Study

Group	*First one-half of session*		*Second one-half of session*	
	Problems	*Method*	*Problems*	*Method*
I	1 and 2	individual	3 and 4	group
II	1 and 2	group	3 and 4	individual
III	3 and 4	individual	1 and 2	group
IV	3 and 4	group	1 and 2	individual
V	1 and 2	individual	3 and 4	group

Group	First one-half of session		Second one-half of session	
	Problems	*Method*	*Problems*	*Method*
VI	3 and 4	individual	1 and 2	group
VII	1 and 2	individual	3 and 4	group
VIII	1 and 2	group	3 and 4	individual
IX	3 and 4	individual	1 and 2	group
X	3 and 4	group	1 and 2	individual
XI	1 and 2	individual	3 and 4	group
XII	1 and 2	group	3 and 4	individual
XIII	3 and 4	individual	1 and 2	group
XIV	3 and 4	group	1 and 2	individual
XV	1 and 2	individual	3 and 4	group
XVI	1 and 2	group	3 and 4	individual
XVII	3 and 4	individual	1 and 2	group
XVIII	3 and 4	group	1 and 2	individual
XIX	1 and 2	group	3 and 4	individual
XX	1 and 2	individual	3 and 4	group
XXI	3 and 4	group	1 and 2	individual
XXII	3 and 4	group	1 and 2	individual

All directions for this part of the experiment were given while the subjects were together in groups of approximately 20 members. The subjects were told that they were to follow the same procedure as the previous week, that they were each to solve two problems as individuals and two as groups, and that they were to be even more careful to do their group work as a unit.

They were told that the only difference in procedure from that of the previous week would be that there would be a time limit of 30 minutes for Problems I and III and of 25 minutes for Problems II and IV, that they were to use no more than this time per problem, and that they were to examine their solutions carefully before they decided that the solutions were correct and ready to be turned in.

D. Results of the First Experimental Session

When the results of this study are analyzed in the same manner as that used by Shaw, her findings are corroborated. That is, if one considers the ratio of the number of solutions obtained to the number of possible solutions, the groups solved many more problems than did the individuals. Since there were 66 subjects and each worked on two problems individually, 132 solutions were possible. Twenty–nine solutions were obtained if Shaw's criterion for the answer of the fourth problem is used. The author questions whether an answer which makes the two buses travel a total of one–half mile farther is not as good or better than her solution. If the solutions allowing the buses to travel this additional one–half mile are allowed, the ratio of solutions to attempts is 35 to 132.

Forty–four problems were attempted by groups. Using Shaw's criterion, there were 17 successes; using our more lenient requirement (either 12 or 12 $\frac{1}{2}$ miles for Problem IV), there were 19 successes. The ratio of successes to attempts is either 17 to 44 or 19 to 44.

There seems to the writer to be a question of the validity of this statistical treatment. It counts one individual as equal to one group and makes no allowance for the fact that a group solution might be the result of activity of any one of the three individuals rather than of the group as a whole. One can reanalyze the data for individual solutions by viewing the individuals as grouped. If any one, or more than one, individual in the group solves the problem, the group working individually can be given credit for the solution. For example, when working as individuals, one member of Group I solved Problem I. According to this method of calculation, Group I working as individuals solved Problem I. On the same basis, two members of Group IX solved Problem I and the group is given credit for an individual solution of Problem I. No member of Group IV solved the problem; thus the group working as individuals is credited with a failure on the problem. When this is done, 61 per cent of all problems attempted by the groups working as individuals were correctly solved. Only 43 per cent of all the problems attempted by the groups, as groups, were solved.

This difference between solutations by 61 per cent of the groups working individually and by 43 per cent of the groups working as groups is not significant. The chi–square value obtained from using the test of independence is 3.684 with one degree of freedom. This value attains the 5.7 per cent level of significance.

When one considers the problems separately, there are some slight differences in trends (see Table 6.2). Problems I, III, and IV were solved slightly more readily by individuals than by groups. Problem II was solved slightly more readily by groups than by individuals.

Table 6.2

Results of the First Experimental Session Viewed with Individuals When Working Alone Still Considered As Grouped

Problem	*Per cent Solving correctly*		*Average time required for solutions**	
	Individuals	*Groups*	*Individuals*	*Groups*
I	75%	50%	9.2 min.	6.6 min.
II	25%	50%	13.3 min.	31.0 min.
III	80%	33%	8.3 min.	15.8 min.
IV (12 miles)	10%	17%	14.0 min.	19.5 min.
(12 ½ miles)	50%	17%	11.0 min.	15.5 min.
Total	61%	43%	10.8 min.	15.5 min.

*The average time required for solution is an average of the times required for each group to solve the problem correctly. Incorrect solutions are disregarded.

Only one of these differences even approaches significance. The difference for Problem III between the proportions of groups solving as individuals and of groups solving as groups attains the 3.5 per cent level of significance when the chi–square test of independence is employed.

The average time required for correct solutions by the groups working as groups is slightly higher than the average time required for the groups working as individuals.

E. Results of the Second Experimental Session

The results of the second experimental session are very similar to those of the first session. Using Shaw's method of treatment of the data and allowing as correct a cutting of four or fewer links in Problem I (2 only need be cut), 36 out of 126 possible correct solutions were attained by the individuals, 22 out of 42 possible correct solutions were attained by the groups.

When one analyzes the data in terms of groups working individually as compared with groups working as groups, there is a slight advantage for the individual rather than the group method of solving problems. Sixty per cent of the solutions attempted by groups working as individuals were attained, while 52 per cent of the solutions attempted by groups working as groups were correct. This difference is not significant.

Again there is a variation between the problems (see Table 6.3). Problems I, III, and IV were solved slightly more often by groups working as individuals than by groups working as groups. Problem II was solved slightly more frequently by groups than by individuals. None of these differences even approach significance.

Table 6.3

Result of the Second Experimental Session Viewed with Individuals When Working Alone Still Considered As Grouped

Problem	*Per cent solving correctly*		*Average time required for solutions**	
	Individuals	*Groups*	*Individuals*	*Groups*
I (2 links cut)	0%	10%	—	10 min.
(3 links cut)	9%	10%	30.0 min.	20 min.
(4 links cut)	36%	10%	25.2 min.	6 min.

Problem	*Per cent solving correctly*		*Average time required for solutions**	
	Individuals	*Groups*	*Individuals*	*Groups*
II	27%	40%	22.3 min.	24 min.
III	80%	73%	17.7 min.	22.4 min.
IV	90%	64%	13.4 min.	17.4 min.
Total	60%	62%	20.25 min.	18.95 min.

*The average time required for solution is an average of the times required for each group to solve the problem correctly. Incorrect solutions are disregarded.

The average time required for a correct solution was, in this case, slightly greater for the groups working as individuals than for the groups working as groups. However, as can be seen in Table 3, this trend is due entirely to differences in the time required to solve Problem I.

F. Summary and Conclusions

We have believed for some time that group performance is better than individual performance, that one cannot simply add together the results of the production of the individual members of a group and arrive at a group production. We claim to have demonstrated this phenomenon in our psychological laboratories. And we group our scientists together in order to assure the accomplishment of the scientific aims of our period.

The writer feels that the results of the experiments which have been performed to demonstrate group superiority are inconclusive. This does not mean that our national research accomplishments do not seem to reveal an advantage of group performance over individual performance. Watson found that a group can construct more words out of the letters found in a longer word than can the best member of the group. He also found that the group performance is the positively related to the individual performance of the best member of the group (r = .53), negatively related to the performance of the poorest member of the group (r = –.19), and only negligibly related to the performance of the average number of the group (r = .16). Does this not sound as though the results are due to a simple summation? Considering this and the nature of the task, it would seem that for the group to be regarded as superior to the members of the group working individually, the performance of the group would have to surpass the total production of the individuals. This was accomplished by only five out of 20 groups.

Shaw found that in the solving of problems requiring reasoning the average group surpassed the average individual. She did not check to determine whether the performance of the group is superior to the performance of the top member of the group. If one makes such an analysis from her data, one finds that 12 of the 30 solutions attempted by the groups were correct and that 9 of the 30 solutions attempted by the groups working individually were correct. This gives an advantage, although very slight and not significant, to the group over the top member of the group.

Our results are similar to those obtained by Shaw. If we analyze our data in the same manner as does Shaw, we find an advantage for the group over the individual. But when we analyze our data to determine whether the group results surpass the individual results of every member of the group, we find no significant difference. The trend, in fact, favors the top individual of the group over the group as a whole.

Perhaps the advantage of the group over the individual members of the group appears only when the problems are even more complex. That is, when the amount of background work that must be done is so great that no one individual can possibly accomplish it. If there is a difference in the problem solving behavior of groups and of individuals using the type of problem employed by Shaw and in the present study, it must be in approach rather than in the merits of the solution. The only alternative conclusion would be that our pleas for co–operation were not followed and that superiority can appear only if our training methods are changed in such a way as to increase the co–operative nature of our culture and to decrease its competitive nature.

References

American Educational Research Association. Committee on Test Standards. *Technical recommendations for achievement tests.* Washington, D.C.: AERA, 1955.

American Psychological Association. *Technical recommendations for psychological tests and diagnostic techniques.* Washington, D.C.: APA, 1954.

Anastasi, Anne, *Psychological testing.* New York: Macmillan, 1954.

Bridgman, P. W., *The logic of modern physics.* New York: Macmillan, 1927.

Buros, O., (Ed.), *The fifth mental measurements yearbook.* Highland Park, N. J.: Gryphon, 1959.

Campbell. D. T., & Fiske, D. W., Convergent and discriminate validation by the multitrait-multimethod matrix. *Psychol. Bull.*, 1959, 56, 81–105.

Campbell, N. R., *Foundations of Science.* (Originally published as *Physics: The elements.)* New York: Dover, 1957.

Cronbach, L. J., *Essentials of psychological testing.* (2nd ed.) New York: Harper, 1960, (a)

Cronbach, L. J., Validity. In C. W. Harris (Ed.), *Encyclopedia of educational research.* New York: Macmillan. 1960. (b)

Cureton, E. E., Validity. In E. F. Lindquist (Ed.). *Educational measurement* Washington, D.C.: American Council on Education, 1951. Pp. 621–694.

Edgerton, H. A., The place of measuring instruments in guidance. In Wilma T. Donahue, C. H. Coombs, and R. M. W. Travers (Eds.).

Shaw. M.E., A comparison of individuals and small groups in the rational solution of complex problems. Amer. J. Psychol., 1932, 44, 491–504.

Watson. G. B., Do groups think more efficiently than individuals? J. Abn. & Soc. Psychol., 1928—29, 23, 328–336.

7

The Trial-and-Check Process in Learning

Structuring an approach is only the initial step in many learning tasks. In mastering language, computational, musical, or other complex skills, both *repeated trials* and *checking their consequences* are equally important and long-continued steps. When we analyzed learning into seven essential conditions, we separated these two closely articulated conditions and designated them "repeated trials" and "perception of effects." Actually, in the goal-directed trial-and-check process of learning, they are complementary and often occur almost simultaneously. In this chapter, therefore, we shall discuss them together, but we shall define the distinctive role which each has. Although "practice" sometimes implies repeated trials only, we often give the term a broader connotation to include both the making and checking of provisional trials. As an introduction to a systematic analysis of these conditions of learning, let us observe their operation in a rehearsal of such a typical complex skill as madrigal singing.

During regularly scheduled practice periods and in repeated trials, the signers strive for improvement in ensemble attack and release, blend and balance, suitability of dynamics, and musical discrimination. To check the correctness of their goal-directed trials, the members and director of the group ask themselves after each performance (sometimes recorded): "Are the attacks clean? Are the releases exact? Were the soft and loud passages contrasting and appropriate so as to produce the desired musical effect?" In the evaluation of provisional trials, correct procedures are confirmed as a basis for more confident performance next time. And the faulty passages to be remedied in a subsequent rehearsal are marked on the score.

From this description, we can see the intimate relationship between provisional trials and checking results. But let us also try to see the unique role of each factor.

The Role of Repeated Trials in Learning

Experience has taught us well that long-continued practice extended over several years is necessary to attain high levels of proficiency in any subject or skill–language, mathematics, science, music, art, or sports. To attain virtuoso skill on the violin, for example, may take ten or twelve years of three to five hours of daily practice. The archery scores shown in Figure 7.1 typify the gradual improvement which results from such practice.

The young adult whose record is reproduced in this figure used a 6–foot bow which required a pull of 44 pounds. His arrows were 28 inches long, and his 48–inch target had a 10–inch bull's–eye. The target was set at a distance of 40 yards and had a 14–foot square of muslin screen around it to permit registering outside shots. Because of his talent and his opportunity to study and observe other learners for two weeks prior to beginning his own overt practice, this individual's initial score is much better than that of the usual beginner. Despite these advantages, however, he is still–after more than 1,300 shots (12 per day)—far from championship performance. In the trial-and-check process, which constituted his practice (in the broad sense) and produced the fluctuating but gradually improving scores, he tried out different methods in successive trials. He eliminated interfering

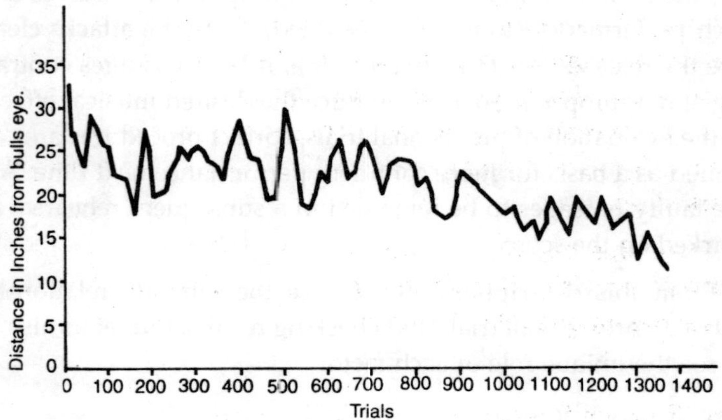

Figure 7.1. Progress from Practice in Archery for Subject C, who Achieved the Best Final Score of Several Subjects, in over 1,300 Shots. (Championship Scores at The Time Were 8 to 11 Inches from the Bull's-eye.) (After K.S. Lashley, Papers from the Dept. of Marine Biol., Carnegie Inst. of Washington, 1915, vol. 7, p. 117.)

habits, achieved insights into better methods, and improved adjustments in aiming and loosing arrows.

The mastery of many school tasks requires similar amounts of practice. For example, a record of a five-year-old child's progress in reading shows that he gradually advanced from recognition of no word on the first day to recognition of 43 different words on the thirty-fifth day. Words were presented to him on separate cards and it was found that several presentations of each world were required before he could recognize the world immediately and confidently. School, for example, required 18 exposures. among a group of third grade children, it was found that the discovery and memorization of the correct products for 39 multiplication combinations (3 × 7 to 9 × 9) required an average of 19.2 repetition per combination.

Sometime, however, concept is mastered in a single trial, as was demonstrated by the third grade child whose introduction to borrowing in subtraction followed his mastery of carrying in addition. He immediately grasped the significant generalization and announced: "Why, it's just the opposite of carrying," In other instances, despite large amounts of practice, improvement does not occur. From the sixth to the fifteenth week of practice in archery, for example, Davies's uninstructed college students failed to make appreciable gains.

In other learning activities, practice seems to impair proficiency. Seashore and Bavelas report an instance of deterioration rather than improvement from practice. In a succession of 15 trials, the experimenters coaxed 18 children to "draw another man; this time a better one." Bored with the repetitions and receiving no approval for their efforts, the children–with two exceptions–tended to draw more more hurriedly and to produce poorer drawings. One subject's deteriorating performance is graphed in Figure 7.2.

These illustrations indicate that practice plays a complex role in the learning process. They show that practice may improve, leave unaffected, or even impair proficiency. Although experi-

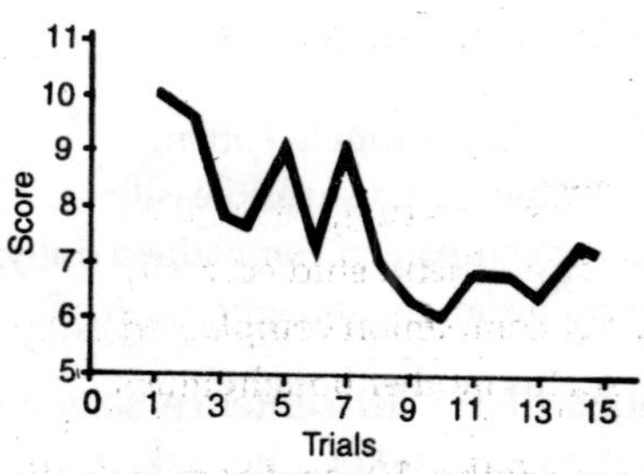

Figure 7.2. *Bored Repetitions of Drawing a Man Produce Deterioration of A Child's Performance, as is indicated by a Tendency to Include Fewer Differentiated Features. (Adapted from H.G. Seashore and A. Bavelas, J. Genet. Psychol., 1942, vol. 61, pp. 279-314.)*

ence demonstrates that practice is an essential condition of learning, its effectiveness apparently depends upon the nature of the practice, as well as upon the simultaneous operation of the other conditions of learning.

What Practice Is

An industrial arts supervisor was perplexed to observe an adolescent boy melting solder into the joint of two pieces of metal. Apparently the boy had no effective goal-directing idea since he was not checking the consequences of his efforts. To the supervisor's query on what he was doing, the boy answered: "I am practicing welding." The supervisor responded: "But you are not making any improvement. You're just pouring the solder on in a way it can't possibly hold the pieces together," The boy replied: "That's why I'm practicing my welds haven't held, But if I practice, I'll get better, won't I?" As we shall see, such confidence in sheer repetition is most naive.

Practice as Repetition. Several experiments demonstrate that a mechanical repetition of concepts or skills does not produce improvement in them. In one of these experiments, Thorndike read and re-read to his adult subjects sentences like the following:—

> Jackson Craig and his son struggled often.
> Charlotte Dean and her friend studied easily.
> Mary Borah and her companion complained dully.
> Norman Foster and his mother bought much.

After 10 repetitions of the 10–sentence selection from which these sample sentences are taken, he asked his subjects such questions as—

> What word came next after "and his son struggled often"?
>
> What word came next after "Norman Foster and his mother"?

Although the facts needed for answering these two types of questions had been repeated an equal number of times, the percentages of correct answers for them were distinctly different. For the first question, in which "struggled often" had been followed 10 times by the beginning of the next sentence, only 2 per cent of the answers were correct. The 10 repetitions yielded practically no learning. For the second question, calling for the predicate of the sentence beginning "Norman Foster and his mother," 81 per cent of the answers were correct. In this instance the 10 repetitions produced a relatively high degree of mastery of the sequence. On the basis of these results and similar data from other experiments, Thorndike concludes that "repetition of a connection in the sense of mere sequence of the two things in time has then very, very little power, perhaps none, as a cause of learning." He explained the advantage of the second type of sequence by his principle of "belonging." It is fitting to complete "Norman Foster and his mother" with "bought much." But as a sequel to "and his son struggled often," "Charlotte Dean" does not belong.

It is also possible, however, to explain the memorization of the sequence "Norman Foster and his mother" and "bought much" in terms of our seven conditions of effective learning. Besides repetition, several other conditions were present which facilitated learning. Supplying a predicate for a subject is a product of *transfer* from much prior experience with sentences. It is *perceived* (checked) as making sense. And completing a logical sequence–resolving an unfinished problem–is *motivationally satisfying* or reinforcing.

Experiments with school subject matter also bring out the relative ineffectiveness of repetition alone in learning. Symonds has shown that "pure repetition of correct form" alone is insufficient for mastery of correct language usage. From such practice, sixth grade pupils made no appreciable gains in correction of usage errors. Only when the teaching incorporated the learning of general grammatical principles, when there was teacher guidance in applying rules for choosing correct constructions, and when both correct and incorrect forms were presented and perceived as right or wrong–only then did appreciable gains occur.

Other experiments show that degree of mastery is not directly proportionate to frequency of repetition of concepts. In teaching 26 concepts in fractions and denominate numbers to fifth grade children, Harap and Mapes found no relationship between extent of mastery of these concepts and the frequency of their repetition in arithmetic projects. In functional study units which involved making candy and conducting a candy sale, the children learned and used the concepts as they had need for them. For example, concept No. 2 (multiplying an integer by a common fraction) was used 51 times, while concept No. 10 (dividing a common fraction by a common fraction) occurred only once. Yet the percentage of mastery for both concepts was 94. The rank order correlation between frequency of repetition (ranging from 0 to 112 times) of all the concepts and the percentage of mastery of them was found by the writer to be zero. In this project, where the understanding of fractions and the meaningful use of them were emphasized, differences in the number of repetitions proved relatively unimportant.

Such experiments as these indicate that repetition alone is insufficient for learning; that its effectiveness depends on the simultaneous operation of other conditions of learning; and that, because of the greater importance of these other conditions, degree of mastery of a concept is sometimes unrelated to frequency of repetition.

Practice as Opportunity for Discovery. Observation of instances of effective learning reveals that practice rarely consists of mechanical, unchanged repetition of responses. What is repeated is the *attempt* to achieve goals—better goals and by more efficient procedures. Practice affords an opportunity to discover or to try out an idea and to test its correctness and value.

As an example of the role of discovery in practice, let us observe a high school student's attempts to illustrate in a drawing the concept of a child's interest in science. Beginning with an imprecisely structured goal and with only a vague idea of how to achieve it, she took 12 practice trials before achieving a satisfying picture! In trial 1, she drew a boy kneeling to examine a flower.

Then another idea occurred; trial 2 and, with some refinement of the same idea, trial 3 depicted the kneeling boy examining an insect under a reading glass. In trial 4, still another idea emerged; the boy, seated before a telescope, was making notes as he looked at the moon and a star. By trial 5, the concept changed again; and the boy was drawn standing with a long-handled butterfly net in his hand. In trial 6, the figure of the boy was improved and a sketch of a butterfly was added. Trial 7 consisted only of sketchy, rough outlines to suggest motion. Having created a satisfactory subject, the student developed the concept of the boy in action about to capture a butterfly in his net. In trials 8 to 12, the proportions, lines, and details were improved; in trial 11, only the boy's posture and head details were changed; and in trial 12, improvements were achieved in the positions of the boy, net, and butterfly. Finally, in drawing 13, with the elimination of all trial sketching, the accepted product was carefully reproduced in ink.

Practice in a Goal-Directed, Trial-and-Check Process. In the preceding chapter on structuring approaches to problems, it was suggested that the learner meets a problem by drawing upon his back-ground of experience or creative abilities for plausible hypotheses–assumptions of what will probably work. As a provisional trial, he may say, "I'll try this to see if it is correct." Perceiving the effect of a trial, he confirms or disconfirms his hunch. If he fails to achieve his goal or achieves it imperfectly, he tries again. At first he may think of no solutions at all or of only a few. Or many alternatives may appear plausible. But with experience–perception of the effects–the number of irrelevant hypotheses is reduced and more appropriate ones are discovered. Action without a hypothesis is useless, random movement. It rarely occurs. Even apparently irrelevant trial-and-error explorations are usually guided, at least groupingly, by hypotheses. And once the correct solution has been completely discovered and confirmed, further repetition of it without variation is unnecessary. From practicing a response in several varied situations, however, the individual learns further where the response is appropriate and where it is inappropriate.

If practice is to be effective it must, according to Jensen, be accompanied by *all* the other conditions of learning. Effective practice is well motivated, goal-directed, and exploratory. It yields knowledge of results of each provisional trial, is frequent enough for remembering discovered correct and incorrect solutions, and is varied to facilitate learning appropriate generalizations and discriminations. It is organized in sequences and interrelations to facilitate transfer and retention. Among these conditions of effective practice, *a plan for checking provisional trials is especially important.*

The Role of Perception of Effects in Learning

The crucial problem-solving process that produces the changes in experience and behavior which constitute learning is one of "approximation and correction," of "trial and check," of reacting to a "feedback" of information by correcting provisional solutions in the light of their perceived consequences.

In guiding effective learning, coaches, teachers, and learning theorists all become aware of the importance of checking provisional trials. Experts in such skills as bowling, golf, and baseball direct players to observe the results of each goal-directed trial–both their successes and failures—as a basis for improving subsequent trials. Shellenbach, the trainer of pitchers for the San Francisco Giants, says: "The biggest thing in learning control [the most important thing in pitching] is to keep track of how you do. It's like target practice. First you throw 10 or 12 fast balls and keep track of where they go. How many are strikes? Four or five maybe. Then you throw some curves and keep track of how many would be called strikes...If you do it regularly, keeping track of exactly what you're doing, you have to get better." Student nurses are directed to practice in pairs while learning to take accurate TPRs (temperature, pulse, and respiration records). Both nurses take TPRs independently on the same patients and compare their records. If there is a discrepancy, they repeat the process. If they agree, their accuracy is confirmed. Both experience and experiments support the importance in learning of such checking of provisional trials.

The Waste of Repeated Trials Without Checking. Imagine that you were one of Lashley's archery subjects. If your first arrow had struck the target on the outermost left edge, you would probably have tried to correct the error by shifting your aim toward the right in the next trial. In each successive trial, your approach would have been guided by your perception of the effects of preceding trials. But suppose you were blindfolded–that you had no information at all on the results of any trial. Would you–even from over a thousand trials–make any improvement? For an answer to our question, let us examine some experiments designed to test the hypothesis that perception of the effects of goal-directed trials is essential for learning.

In one such experiment which covered a period of 12 days, subject T drew 2,203 lines, each intended to be 4 inches long, without ever seeing any of them. The tabulation of the lengths of the lines revealed no appreciable progress toward a precise 4-inch line. The 175 lines drawn on the first day ranged from 4.5 to 6.1 inches, the median length being 5.23 inches. On each of the 12 practice days the 171 to 200 lines drawn showed similar variation, with no closer approximation to a 4-inch line. The 192 lines drawn on the last day ranged from 4.1 o 5.7 inches, with a median of 4.96. In a different but similar experiment, Thorndike instructed seven blindfolded adults to draw 4-inch lines. He gave them no information about their accuracy or improvement on repeated trials. Their errors averaged almost an inch at the beginning of the practice and, after 400 such trials, the extent of error remained practically the same.

Thorndike interprets these results as demonstrating that repetition alone is not a sufficient condition for learning. Perception of the effects is also necessary, as is implied by the statement: "*Had I opened my eyes* after each shove of the pencil during the second and later sittings, and *measured the lines* and *been desirous of accuracy* in the task, the connections leading to 3.8, 3.9, 4.0, 4.1 and 4.2 would have become more frequent until I reached my limit to skill in the task." Other experiments confirm Thorndike's results and his prediction.

Elwell and Grindley presented their ten 18- to 22-year-old subjects a complex coordination task requiring each subject to learn to guide bimanually (by manipulating levers) a spot of light from the outer edge to the center of a target marked by 10 concentric circles. Possible scores ranged from 0 (off the target) to 10 (in the center circle). The light was never visible while being moved. However, during the first 10 days of 20 trials per day, the learner observed the light in starting position and again (after manipulations) in the position to which he had moved it. Thus he was permitted to check how nearly he had come to the aimed-at bull's-eye. Then the subjects continued their 20 trials per day for an additional 5 days; but during this period no subject saw the outcome of his efforts. As figure 7.3 shows, with opportunity to perceive the result of each goal-directed trial, the subjects gradually learned to improve their accuracy in this motor coordination task. However, when the opportunity for checking the results of their goal-directed trials was withheld, their accuracy dropped almost immediately to the pretraining level.

Perception of the results of our efforts enables us to confirm the success of our approach or, in the event of failure, to restructure our approach. This fact is suggested by the spontaneous remarks of some of the subjects in the preceding experiment. Perceiving that he had achieved a bull's-eye, one subject said: "I must try to do exactly that movement again." After a failure, he said: "That means that I must pull farther with the left hand."

Experiments involving other kinds of tasks also confirm the need for checking in the trial-and-check process. Using the Seashore pitch-discrimination test, which requires the subject to tell whether the second of a pair of tones is higher or lower than the first, Wyatt had 24 college students make 500 such discriminations–100 per day for five successive days. Uninformed of the correctness or incorrectness of their judgments, these students made no appreciable improvement in the five days of practice. When, however, opportunities are provided for checking the correctness of each discrimination, both Wyatt and Connette have demonstrated that college students *are* able to achieve significant improvements in pitch discrimination.

These experiments demonstrate that practice produces improvement only when accompanied by provisions for checking the consequences of goal-directed trials. Let us now see how this checking may be done most effectively.

The Advantage of Precise Checking. In attempting to draw 4-inch lines, Thorndike's blindfolded subjects were not entirely without some knowledge of results. From their past experience, they had built up at least a vague concept of a 4-inch line. And they had, as they drew each line, some subjective, kinesthetic, nonvisual perception of their performance. From this admittedly inadequate feedback, however, they could make some slight improvement. Although subject T did not, as Thorndike reported, come any nearer to drawing a 4-inch line in 2,203 trials, his drawings *did* tend to approximate *slightly* more closely his own average of 5.01 inches. Other experimenters have shown that the effectiveness of knowledge of results depend upon its preciseness.

Comparing three degrees of completeness of feedback information, Trowbridge and Cason directed different groups of college students (15 students in each group) to draw, while blindfolded, one hundred 3-inch lines. Group I, like Thorndike's subjects, were given no information as to their accuracy. For Group II, the experimenter said, "Right," for every line drawn within one-eighth of an inch of a 3-inch line. This information, however, was provided infrequently because the subjects, especially in the early trials, rarely came within one-eighth of an inch of being correct. In Group III, the subject was informed precisely on each trial how many eighths of an inch his line was too long or too short. The average percentages of correctly drawn lines were as follows; for no information, 13.6; for the occasional confirmation of "right" responses, 22.6; and for precise information on the correctness of each trial, 54.8.

Reed, also using college students as his subjects, has verified the importance of precise perception of effects. His blindfolded subjects made no appreciable progress in drawing lines, rectangles, and circles of prescribed dimensions. With their eyes open and with the standard figures before them, they made *some* progress but soon reached their limits of accuracy. When permitted to measure every fifth figure drawn, however, the subjects, besides improving rapidly in the initial trials, continued to improve in later trials. The precise measurements of trial drawings yielded knowledge of otherwise imperceptible errors and provided guidance for correcting them.

The Need for Prompt Checking. Several experiments indicate that contiguity between trials and checking enhances the effectiveness of practice. For 48 adult subjects who practiced throwing small balls back over their shoulders at an invisible target of four concentric rings, Lorge and Thorndike provided information on the results of each throw–with delays of from zero up to six seconds. With the shorter delays, learning was more efficient.

In the trial-and-error discovery and mastery of complex clues for guiding multiple-choice selections among geometric patterns differing in color, form, number, size, orientation, and position, Bourne found that for 162 college students, concept mastery is directly related to the promptness of information on the correctness of each response. In still another experiment, Greenspoon and Foreman [22] varied the delay in supplying information on correctness of response as five groups of eight blindfolded college students practiced drawing fifty 3-inch lines. One group was given no information. Other groups–after no delay and after delays of 10, 20, and 30 seconds–were informed as to whether each line drawn was "short," "long," or "correct" (for lines between 2¾ and 3¼ inches). The results, which are typical for these experiments, are graphed in Figure 7.3.

Figure 7.3 reveals that without clear perception of the consequences of goal-directed trials, practice yields little or no improvement. With information, *immediate* feedback produces the most efficient learning. For this particular task, 10 seconds of delay between the response and perception of its effect reduces

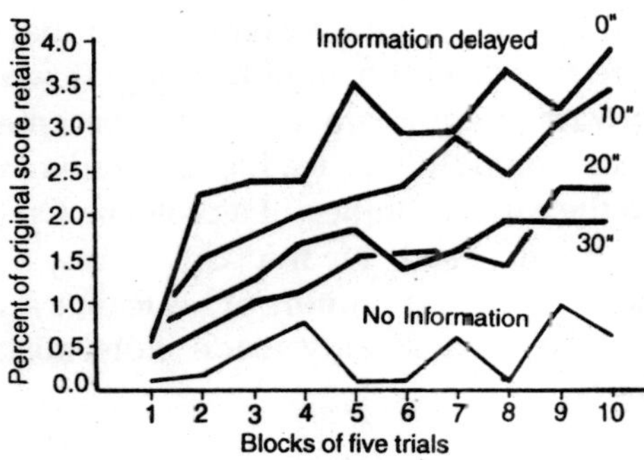

Figure 7.3. Promptness of Feedback Information Facilitates Learning to Draw 3-inch lines. Performance with Immediate Feedback is Compared with Delays of from 10 to 30 Seconds and with no Information. (From J. Greenspoon and Salley Foreman, J. Exp. Psychol., 1956, vol. 51, 227)

slightly the efficiency of learning. When the delays go up to 20 or 30 seconds, the learning is much less efficient.

Other studies indicate that the general implications of these experiments are applicable to learning such subjects as chemistry and psychology. Little compared the final test achievement in educational psychology of three groups of students who, during the school year, were given various opportunities to check the correctness of the concepts they were learning. Group I saw only the results of beginning and midterm tests. Groups II and III took 12 additional tests. For Group II, these tests were returned and discussed in class. For Group III, a special testing device permitted the student to discover immediately–by pressing from one to five keys–the correct answer for each item as he proceeded through each test. Both Groups II and III exceeded the achievement of Group I. And Group III, which experienced prompt feedback on each item of the tests, surpassed Group II, whose members learned only later the correctness of their response to the tests as a whole.

Learning From Mistakes. Since we have found that repetition alone is not an effective determinant of learning. It seems safe to assume that unrewarded errors are unlikely to become habitual. Unrewarded mistakes may, in fact, lead to alternative responses– and sometimes to the correct solution of a problem. On this possibility, Dr. Von Braun, head of the U.S. Army's scientific ballistic-missile team, speaking proudly of his team's accomplishments, remarked: "We have already made more mistakes than other people have."

Children and even monkeys learn early to be guided by their mistakes. Harlow has shown that both monkeys and two- to five-year-old children, who make an error in a two-choice discrimination problem learn to infer that the alternate choice will be correct. Moreover, as is shown in Figure 7.4, young children learn, from increasing amounts of problem-solving experience, to use the trial-and-check process more effectively.

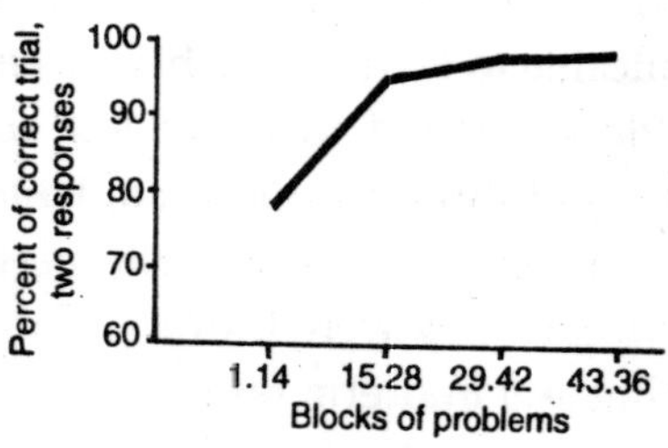

Figure 7.4. Perceiving that the First Choice on a Discrimination Problem is Wrong, two-to five-year-old Children Learn to Reverse Their Choices on a Second Trial. Percentages of Reversals on Trial 2 of Nine Children, After Solving Varying Numbers of Reversal Problems. (From H.F. Harlow, Psychol. Rev., 1949, vol. 56, p.59)

School children also learn from their mistakes. Sixth grade children do as well in mastering subtraction of fractions from detecting and correcting mistakes as they do from teacher guidance which minimizes experience with errors. Junior high school pupils who detect and correct language usage errors equal the achievement of students who do not see wrong forms but, with teacher guidance, practice completing sentences in correct form only. Spelling, however, was found to be improved more effectively by recognizing and correctly rewriting misspelled words than by merely recognizing correctly spelled words. Apparently, children can learn correct responses when either their errors or their right responses are signaled. However, as Holodnack discovered, in comparing signaling either correct or incorrect responses to six- to ten-year-old children who were learning a punchboard maze, young children learn more effectively "if the correct responses rather than the incorrect ones are pointed out and emphasized."

Perception of Effects and Reinforcement

Perception of the effects and motivational reinforcement of provisional trials are sometimes confused. Since they have different functions in learning, they need to be differentiated.

Information Versus Affect in Guiding Learning. Both informational feedback and motivational reinforcement function in the selection and elimination of correct and incorrect responses. Hitting the bull's-eye, for example, is both perceived as correct and experienced as satisfying. Because of these effects, the learner tries to repeat such performances. When the misses his target, the learner experiences dissatisfaction and also *perceives* that his arrow has struck, say, 20 inches to the left of the bulls-eye. In the next trial, he usually tries to avoid the dissatisfaction of another miss. The dissatisfaction alone does not, however, provide the needed *guidance* for better performance, except to indicate that something different is needed. It is his *perception* of the arrow 20 inches to the left of the bull's-eye which guides him in the next trial to aim much more toward the right. From observation of the effects of goal- directed provisional trials, the learner is informed of the consequences of alternative responses. Such information is crucial as a guide to better performance. Whether the learner uses such knowledge depends upon his motives. Typically, his behavior moves in the direction of greater motive satisfaction; that is, maximally reinforced trials tend to be repeated.

Reed has demonstrated that the pleasant or unpleasant effects of responses do not affect learning, except as they serve as clues for guiding the learner to his goal. He directed each of 78 college students to learn "as quickly and accurately as possible" a multiple T-maze by moving a finger along a wire threaded over a board on which the subjects could be electrically shocked at any given point. He advised them: "Should you experience an unpleasant feeling, you must decide what to do about it without further questioning." Despite the different effects for right and wrong responses provided for the different groups, all of them mastered the problem and with approximately equal efficiency. Group I, shocked for each error on the maze, required 7.18 trials. Group II, shocked for each correct response, required 6.82 trials. Group III, hearing "right" for errors, required 7.10 trials. Group IV, hearing "right" for correct responses, required 5.91 trials. And Group V, given neither "reward" nor "punishment," required 7.00 trials. Inappreciably influenced by variations in the verbal or electric reinforcements, each subject apparently discovered for himself kinesthetic clues indicative of the correct and incorrect pathways of the maze. Since the variations in pleasant or unpleasant effects did not effect the efficiency of learning significantly, Reed concluded that learning is "the result of the *interpretation* of these qualities." It is the *knowledge* of success or failure (however it is signaled) which enables the learner "to make up his mind what to do in the next trial to make a better performance."

Adjustment of Performance to Expected Reinforcement. As every fly-fisherman knows, a strike or hooked fish now and then is sufficient reinforcement to sustain his interest over hundreds or

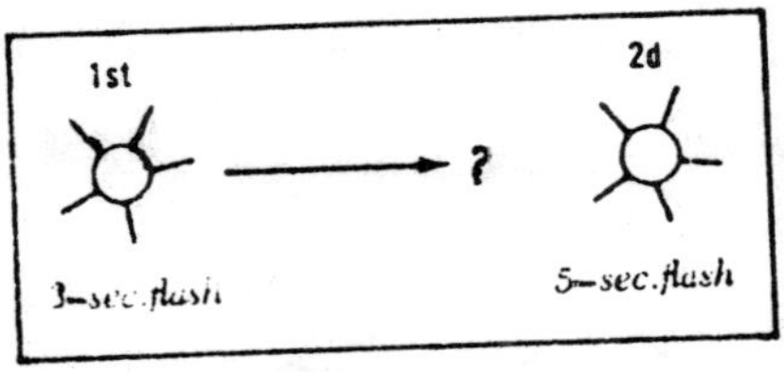

1st 2d

?

3—sec. flash 5—sec. flash

thousands of unrewarded casts. Experiments indicate that, although continuous reinforcement is better for learning, intermittent reinforcement is more effective in sustaining many learned behavior patterns over long periods of nonreinforcement. As one test of this hypothesis, Grant, Hake, and Hornseth [21] directed 185 college students (individually) to guess, for 60 learning and 30 extinction trials, whether or not following a 3- second flash of the first light the second light on a board would flash. For five different groups (17 in each group), he provided positive reinforcement (second light flashes) on 0, 25, 50, 75, and 100 per cent of 60 randomly arranged trials. Then on 30 extinction trials, reinforcement was completely stopped for *all* groups. For the five groups on different reinforcement schedules, the average percentage of guesses that the second light would flash are graphed in Figure 7.5.

As the figure shows, *all* the groups began responding positively (predicting that the second light would flash) on approximately 45 to 65 per cent of the trials. Gradually, however, each group adjusted its proportion of positive responses to the actual proportion of light flashes it experienced. The students adjusted their expectations to their checked experience. Guided by perception of the effects of their provisional trials, subjects in each group learned to expect the actual number of flashes given and to emit an approximately matched number of positive responses.

But what happens during extinction, when the second light ceases completely to flash? If each reinforcement added an increment of strength to a response, the group reinforced on 100 per cent of the learning trials should persist more tenaciously in guessing that the second light would continue to flash. Actually,

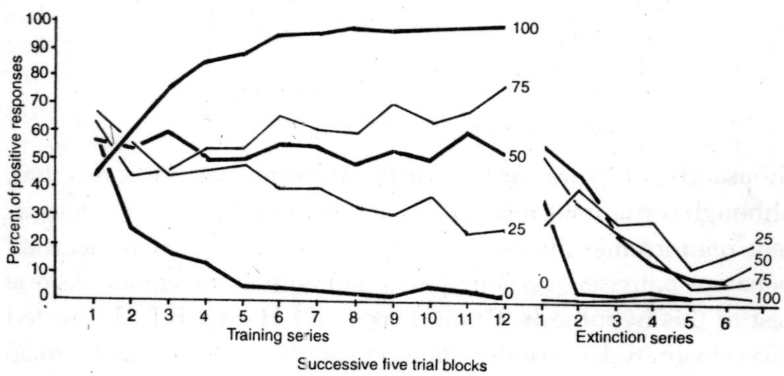

Figure 7.5. *College Students adjust Their Estimates that "a Second Light will Flash" to Frequency of Reinforcement, but they Cease Responding most Quickly after 100 per cent Reinforcement. (From D. A. Grant, H.W. Hake, and J. P. Hornseth, J. Exp. Psychol.., 1951. vol. 42, p. 2.)*

as Figure 7.6 shows, the intermittently (less frequently) reinforced groups persisted longer.

Although this paradox presents difficulties for the stimulus-response reinforcement theory, there is a plausible cognitive theory interpretation of it. In the 30 extinction trials, the change from 100 per cent to 0 per cent, being the most distinctive change, was most easily discriminated. Because of the sharp contrast in feedback, this group learned (inferred) from a single block of five trials not to expect a second flash. And, guided by this insight, they immediately adjusted their performance to it. Because it required more trials to discriminate between the less sharply contrasting *intermittent* and no reinforcement conditions, the intermittently reinforced groups took more trials to give up the expectation of eventual reinforcement.

In a similar experiment with fourth and fifth grade children, Rosenblum has indicated that the development and maintenance of such traits as selfconfidence is also affected by reinforcement schedules. Children continually praised for their efforts in copying geometrical designs become more sure of their proficiency in the task than children praised only *intermittently*. However, when approval ceased for both groups, the self-ratings on "confidence of succeeding" of the theretofore continuously approved group dropped below those of the intermittently reinforced group.

Providing for Perception of Effects in Learning

In the trial-and-check process of learning, effective checking of goal-directed provisional trials is essential for efficient learning.

Self–Checking. Fortunately, checking is an inherent feature of many learning activities. The correct solution to a problem is often identifiable immediately–because it works. In assembling a jigsaw puzzle, for example, when the correct solution is achieved, the blocks fit. For alternative patterns, they don't. Similarly, when a child who reads for meaning identifies an unfamiliar word by phonetic analysis and the word as identified fits the meaning, he usually knows he is right. If the word does not make sense, he tries and checks again. When the computed answer to an arithmetic problem matches approximately the estimated answer, a tentative assumption of its correctness is justified. The pitch of a note sung is recognized as right because it sounds right. After many unsuccessful attempts at drawing a bird in flight, an effective technique is finally discovered–because the bird now appears to be flying. In many other learning activities, whether or not a solution fits or works is a pragmatic test of its correctness. Such self-checking, however, is insufficient. For example, the pupil does not always recognize when he is singing off pitch.

Teacher Guidance in Checking. Teacher guidance in checking provisional trials is needed. Guidance, however, does not always mean telling students correct answers when they make mistakes. Guidance which motivates pupils to search for correct solutions and teaches them how to discover them is often more effective. But whether the teacher guidance is directive or pupil self-discovery-oriented, checking needs to be improved–in the information it gives, in its frequency, preciseness, and promptness.

The common procedure of returning a student's homework composition, exercises in mathematics, or research report in social studies or science several days after it was handed in and marking it only with a letter grade provides him little guidance on how to improve his next effort. Such inadequate teacher checking is unlikely to produce changes in subsequent assignments. On the contrary, it is likely to make pupil practice sheer repetition. Fortunately, as the several illustrations which follow suggest, there are better methods.

Tablle 7.1

Long–Division Errors and Symbols for Marking Them

Symbol	*Error*	*Symbol*	*Error*
z–om	Zero omitted	s	Error in subtraction,
w–q	Wrong quotient	p	Error in placement
w–c	Wrong carrying	bd	Error in number brought down
m	Error in multiplication	r	Error in remainder

Source: Holland, II. Elem, Sch, J., 1941–42, 42, 585–596. Reprinted by permission of the Univ. of Chicago Press.

Holland suggests an informative way of checking arithmetic papers. From a list of the errors most frequently made in long division, Table 7.1 is prepared and placed on the blackboard to call attention to the errors children are most likely to make and should try to avoid. The abbreviated symbol for each type of error provides the teacher a convenient device for marking specifically and informatively each child's exercises. For example, when a child sees on his problem No. 2 the symbol z-om and on problem No. 7 the symbol w-c, he is informed that he has made mistakes by omitting zero in a quotient and in carrying. He is thus guided to restudy these particular concepts. This device has general application in many phases of arithmetic, in language, handwriting, spelling, and in other subjects for ·vhich lists of commonly made errors have been inventoried or can be inventoried by a teacher for a particular purpose.

For checking high school and college students' compositions more informatively and precisely, Hook suggests using *Ideaform.* The student's composition paper provides spaces both for specific teacher comment and for checking ("Good," "Fair," or "Poor") on attainment of such objectives as "organization, development, sincerity of purpose and expression, sentence structure and punctuation, paraphrasing, usage, choice of words, spelling...and general appearance." Such teacher evaluations–especially when they are summarized for a succession of themes–guide the student toward needed improvement. Comments such as the following provide more specific suggestions: "Would *because* be a better world?" "By the details, you made me feel that I was climbing the mountain with you." Or, "Would this be better if you told us more about the Wright brothers themselves?"

Teachers can provide for informative, precise, and prompt feed- back of the result of provisional trials in a variety of ways. Elementary school children listen to tape recordings of their oral language—to check on pronunciation, voice quality, and effectiveness of composition. Then they try again and listen for improvements. In learning to speak a foreign language, students try to imitate, on certain segments of the tape, recordings of model speech interspersed on other segments. Then–to evaluate the quality of their efforts–they and their classmates listen to the playback of both the model's and the students' speech. Keller has found that students learn Morse code more effectively when they have the opportunity to confirm or disconfirm their reactions to each signal as it is made instead of waiting to check the correctness of an entire set of trials at the conclusion of a practice session.

Skinner has suggested that by effective application of this principle we can improve the teaching of arithmetic, spelling, reading, and many other learning tasks which can be analyzed into S–R sequences. He proposes that such sequences of problems be fed into machines which register the student's tentative solutions and then indicate to him immediately whether his responses are right or wrong.

Special Provisions for Checking. When the usual provision for perceiving the effects of learnings is not possible, the crucial importance of checking is brought more convincingly to our attention. This is illustrated by the great difficulty a deaf child has in learning to articulate words. Deprived of hearing–the usual cue for noting the correctness or incorrectness of our attempts to articulate words–the deaf child must find some other way of checking his speech efforts. The photograph presents a device, reported in *Life,* which shows a deaf child immediately and precisely how nearly his own provisional trial matches or approximates the teacher model or oral concept he is striving to reproduce. The teacher has said, "Shoe," into a microphone, and the sound is represented on a grid as a certain pattern of colored lights. As the child says, "Shoe," into another microphone, she can tell, by comparing the pattern of lights she produces with the pattern produced by the teacher, how near or how far away she is from the correct articulation. This precise and prompt feedback on the correctness of each goal-directed trial guides her toward improvement in each subsequent trial.

In some activities, normal individuals also need supplementary devices for checking the correctness of their learning efforts. Young children, for example, often have difficulty checking their speech. Since we do not hear our own voices very accurately and do not, of course, see our lip movements, a mirror and a sound recorder are excellent aids in approximating more closely the visual and auditory models of correct speech. Practicing before the mirror often aids the young violinist in matching the visualized, teacher-demonstrated good form for holding and bowing his violin.

In such loosely structured activities as participation in class discussion, self-observation needs some supplementation. Children like to think of themselves as contributing, but they often do not know how well they succeed. To improve their self-checking, a sixth grade class prepared the self-rating scale presented below. Such ratings made immediately after discussions–sometimes in conference with the teacher or another pupil–are more accurate than unaided impressions. Other more precise devices are described.

In a group, I:	(4) *Always*	(3) *Most of the time*	(2) *Half of the time*	(1) *Hardly ever*	(0) *Never*
—— take turns					
—— stick to the subject					
—— ask good questions					
—— pay attention					

Test as Effective Checks of Mastery. By a parallel teach-and-test process, teachers can facilitate the trial-and- check process required of pupils in mastering the sequences of the curriculum. Well-constructed tests–covering the objectives intended–are useful both in summarizing and in evaluating achievement in a unit of learning. As diagnostic appraisals of objectives already accomplished and of concepts of skills still to be mastered, tests indicate readiness and need for the next step in a sequence of learning activities. Such tests are effective learning devices. They should be used not only as midterm and final examinations but as checks on degree of mastery of each unit in a course. In preparation for a test, the learner practices his skills, and organizes principles for applying them. The test–at the appropriate time–affords an opportunity for checking his understanding and mastery of the skills and concepts. It yields the pupil information which confirms some of his provisionally tried hypotheses and disconfirms others—or indicates the need for revising them. The pupil must, however, see and use his corrected examination papers promptly.

The value of informing pupils on the correctness or incorrectness of their responses to examination questions has been demonstrated by Plowman and Stroud. These investigators had tenth and eleventh grade students, divided into two matched groups of 125 each, study textbook material on the history of bookmaking for 15 minutes. Both groups were then given a 30-item multiple-choice test on the material read. Afterward, one group was allowed to inspect the corrected test for five minutes–a learning opportunity not permitted the other group. After six days, without intervening warning, both groups took another test on the same content. Of these originally matched groups, the students given the learning opportunity of confirming or disconfirming their answers on the first test made significantly higher scores on the second.

Our separate analyses of these two aspects of practice–provisional trials and perception of the effects of these goal-directed trials–confirm the initially described close articulation of these essential conditions of learning. Oriented by this broad concept of practice–as a goal-directed trial-and-check process–let us explore it thoroughly in terms of children's needs.

Kinds of Learning Requiring Practice

The amount and kind of practice needed to acquire the numerous concepts and skills taught in the elementary and secondary school curriculum varies. While some concepts are mastered in a single trial, other concepts and most skills require a great many trials. Achieving a pleasing tone with vibrato on the violin, for example, may take thousands of trials. One obvious reason why such skills as reading, language, arithmetic, or musical performance require a great many practice sessions is that they are comprised of thousands of separate, though interrelated, subconcepts and subskills. Moreover, these numerous subconcepts and subskills must be differentiated and organized for appropriate functioning in many different situations.

As an illustration of a multiple-component skill, consider the major phases of computation arithmetic–adding, subtracting, multiplying, and dividing of integers, common fractions, and decimal numbers. Each of these processes is comprised of numerous variations. Division of decimals, for example, consists of 61 such variations as $4\overline{)8}$, $.7\overline{).49}$, and $103\overline{)6.375}$. Similarly, in art, the child learns to use variations of line, space, shape, texture, color, and lightness-darkness in composing a drawing. As these concepts and skills are mastered, they are applied, with refinements in skill, to numerous art designs. In science, the truth of such a concept as the interdependence of animal life may be verified by observing that woodpeckers eat insects, bears eat fish, owls eat rats, snakes eat frogs, etc. From such varied experiences, concepts are generalized.

Following Tilton's outline, we may classify the multiple element concepts and skills which children and youth learn according to several types of learning which require practice:

Generalizing Responses to Multiple Cues. The situations in which concepts and skills are needed are often different from the situations in which they were originally learned. Unless responses are generalized to multiple cues, they may fail in certain new situations. For example, it is said of John Locke, who had practiced waltzing by dancing around a trunk in his room, that when he tried his skill on the dance floor, he was unable to execute the steps he had practiced. The trunk was not there! Like John Locke, students often fail to apply in appropriate new situations those concepts on which they have had only narrow- range practice. The remedy, of course, is practice of varied applications in different situations. A football team, for example, is not easily caught unprepared by its opponents' surprise plays if its own plays are well executed and are the product of many different, adaptive rehearsals of them.

The inductive discovery of variations of the same concept or skill also produces generalized principles. For example, in reading such different words as *beat* and *laid* or *made* and *ride,* a child discovers (with teacher guidance) that the second vowel is always silent and determines the long sound of the first. He then applies the generalization in reading other words such as *straight* and *late.*

Making Discriminative Responses. While the individual is developing generalized responses to multiple cues, he also discovers the hazards of overgeneralizing. Mastery of such skills as reading, language, spelling, or mathematics requires discriminations between many competing responses. The same cue often requires a different response in only slightly different context. The child learns, for example, to double the e in *proceed* but not in *procedure.* If the beginning reader overrelies on the initial consonant in identifying unfamiliar words, he may read wanted as went, then as there, and several as seven. He needs, of course, to learn to respond differently when there are variations in the remainder of the world. Overcoming such faulty generalizations and learning to make such discriminations accurately and confidently requires practice.

The greater the number of competing alternatives among the associations to be learned, the greater will be the number of trials required to master the correct ones. As Beecroft has experimentally demonstrated, it is easier to associate (in respective pairs) 10 such words as *yearly, jolly,* and *fragrant* with 10 such different words as *gigantic,* drowsy, and *remote than* it is to associate them with 10 synonyms, such as *gigantic, massive,* and *immense.*

Automatization of Responses. The individual performs such frequently practiced skills as bicycling, piano playing, or rapid reading without conscious attention to the details of signals or processes. Such automatization of skills is achieved by learning to respond to reduced response-guiding cues. Woodworth has observed that when the inexperienced fielder is moving into position to catch a fly ball, he follows the ball's complete path of flight. The expert, however, is guided to the right position by seeing only the beginning of its trajectory.

In the initial stages of learning, the deaf child requires the visual representation of his speech for almost every sound, and the violin student needs a mirror to guide him in maintaining good form in holding and bowing his instrument. But as practice of such skills continues, fewer cues are needed. In a sequence of responses, each response becomes the conditioned cue for the next response in the chain.

As a classroom example of cue reduction, consider the automatization of skillful reading. In the early stages, the child attends both to the context and to a careful visual or phonetic analysis of words–their beginnings, roots and suffixes or prefixes, or each syllable. However, as a result of practice, the leaner comes to require fewer and fewer cues. Finally, when he has become a mature reader, he grasps the meaning of a passage from perceiving only parts of some words. In a familiar context, he achieves meaning by merely scanning a page. Many skills are automatized by such reductions in the cues needed to guide performance.

Organizing Patterns of Responses. Mastery of complex behaviour patterns–such as memorizing prose, poetry, a violin concerto, or assembling a complicated machine such as a carburetor or a watch–requires the sequential or integrated organization of several segments or components. Since all the associations and differentiated insights into the interrelations of segments or components are not achieved in one trial, a smooth performance requires practice. For example, in the early stages of memorizing a poem, the learner grasps the general scheme and some dominant details–with considerable inferred construction of how it "ought to go." At first, segments are correctly associated with adjacent segments or incorrectly associated with competing remote forward and backward segments. After a few trial-and-check practices, the components are better articulated, more appropriate details are differentiated, and misconstructions are eliminated. Finally, a literal reproduction is possible because each segment of the poem is differentially cued both to the central meaning and to the appropriate preceding part.

Variations of these processes also characterize the memorization and use of the facts in such subjects as mathematics, language, spelling, science, or social studies. The functional organization of these facts into various patterns for flexible, adaptive application requires practice in dealing with them in a variety of situations.

Refining Skills. The initial performance of a skill often involves helpful ancillary processes which, as practice continues, can be deleted in the interest of efficiency. For example, in achieving "meaningful habituation" in adding 26 + 7, a child may first count 26 objects and then count 7 more. With a little practice, he finds he can start with 26 and count only the 7 additional objects. Discovering a still more abstract level of functioning, to 26 he adds 4 and 3 (into which he has divided the 7). Finally, from such insight-yielding and confidence-building practice, he immediately recognizes that 26 + 7 = 33. Or a football player may learn to tackle in a series of steps, such as approach, contact, and follow through. He may at first verbalize the steps. After some practice, however, he eliminates the word guides and telescopes the steps into an integrated, smoothly functioning pattern. Many skills of the elementary and secondary curricula are friend by eliminating unnecessary elements, by telescoping sergeants, and by coordinating the parts into more efficient patterns. By such refinements, achieved through effective practice, skills are executed more rapidly, accurately, smoothly, comfortably, and confidently.

Imitating Complex Patterns. To improve their performance of complicated behaviour patterns, children and youth try to imitate a more expert classmate, the teacher, a motion-picture film or a sound recording. Successful imitation–of a serve in tennis, a new figure in skating, a chemistry laboratory test, the correct pronunciation of a French word, or a better-organized class report–often requires several trials because the complex model may be incompletely perceived in one trial. In observing the demonstration of the tennis serve, for example, the learner may not at first note every feature. The stance, the grip on the racket, the height to which the ball is tossed, the speed, or the attempt to curve the ball may escape him. In each repeated demonstration, a new aspect of the total performance may be grasped. Certain features may be very elusive, and may not be perceived until they are also explicitly verbalized or demonstrated in slow motion. In other cases–for example, in learning to pronounce a French word–provisional trials must be checked against the model before the learner can reproduce the pattern correctly. Learning from imitation usually requires several trials because the observed pattern must always be translated into independent self-activity.

Discovering Solutions. In such problem-solving activities as mathematics, science, social studies, creative writing, or art, where several alternative approaches or solutions may appear plausible, correct or satisfying solutions can often be reached only by several provisional self-discovery trials. The search for a solution is a process of repeated trial- and-check. We have all experienced this process in trying to solve a baffling problem.

When seven-year-old James was asked to name a flower that rhymes with "nose," he considered: "Not daffodil, not snap-dragon, not snowball, not tulip, not pansy." Then, restructuring the problem by slowly repronouncing "nose," he suddenly shouted "Rose!" A chemistry student was at the point of giving up after repeated failures in her effort to learn the laboratory technique of drawing fluid to a particular level in glass tube by means of suction. In another hour of homework practice on the task, however, she finally succeeded. She discovered that she had been trying too hard. As she said, "I hadn't realized before that you should go lightly." The route to the correct solution of a problem is often the roundabout one of first finding many ways that will not work. Each systematic trial-and-check practice, however, carries the learner nearer to his goal.

Because there is so much to learn and because so many of the concepts and skills elementary and secondary school children need require extensive amounts of practice, we need to use the practice time available to us efficiently. Therefore, in concluding this chapter, and in a more comprehensive study of the question in the next chapter, we shall look for guiding principles.

EFFICIENT USE OF PRACTICE OPPORTUNITIES

Children encounter the academic and personal-social concepts and skills which they need to learn not only in the classroom but in the school as a whole, at home and in excursions into the community. We must ask, however, whether such opportunities for learning provide sufficient practice for the mastery of concepts or skills, at what stage drill should be introduced. What should be the length and distribution of practice sessions? What is the role of a warm-up in practice? Is implicit practice effective? Answers to these questions can help us to use practice time more efficiently.

Both Functional and Systematic Practice. Such projects as "The Water Supply in Our Community," and the more comprehensive projects of the elementary school provide functional practice of a variety of concepts and skills. For example, in conducting a store which sold children the supplies needed in their school work, elementary school children–besides studying such economic concepts as wholesale, retail, and profit and loss–practiced arithmetic, language, writing, and spelling. Such school chores and social responsibilities as participating in lunch-menu making, writing letters of request and thanks, producing plays and operettas, and conducting pupil self-government provide additional opportunities for functional practice of curriculum concepts and skills. The practice connect with these activities is not confined to incidental use of the skills; it is also directed toward improvement of them.

The functional practice conducted in connection with a fifth grade experiment in nutrition illustrates the procedure. The children were required to write daily reports on the rats used in the experiment. When it proved difficult to tread their daily observations–because they failed to capitalize and punctuate correctly–it became apparent to the children that they needed to improve their skill in writing. The scheduled language lessons of the week were therefore coordinated with the nutrition experiment and devoted to the improvement of the needed writing skills. As the first lesson, the teacher wrote his own previous day's observation of the rats on the blackboard, leaving out the capitalization and punctuation. The children and teacher together correctly capitalized and punctuated his paragraph. From this problem-solving study–including both class discussion and textbook reading–they generalized the principles of capitalization and punctuation needed at their level of writing. Following this general exercise, the children corrected their own reports-with the teacher checking their efforts and guiding them individually when necessary. As in other instances of functional practice, the need for a skill grows out of an interest-motivated project; the skill is improved in teacher-guided practice sessions; and it is fed back into the original and other ongoing projects–with increased competency and satisfaction on the part of the children.

Several advantages are claimed for such functional practice. Child interest is high. The real problems make the study meaningful. The concepts are organized for effective application in problem solving. It provides varied opportunities for each child to participate in group problem solving according to his talents and interests. Because of these advantages, it is believed that such learning is easier, more permanent, and more likely to be applied in out-of-school situations than learning which takes place in isolated practice activities.

It would be difficult and unnecessary, however, to contrive arrangements for functional practice of all the concepts and skills which children need to develop to high levels of proficiency. Although projects and school activities provide valuable opportunities for practicing the skills of reading, language, writing, typewriting, spelling, arithmetic, drawing, crafts, and others, they need to be supplemented with systematically scheduled and teacher-guided practice. Otherwise the child fails to achieve the degree of proficiency he needs. Moreover, systematic, continued practice of a skill without immediate significant application is not necessarily poorly motivated. Knowledge of progress in language, science, or mathematical understandings or in academic craft, art, or music skills is self-enhancing and thus intrisically well motivated.

The Timing of Drills for Speed and Accuracy. Practice for refining skills, for automatizing responses, for increasing speed and accuracy should *follow* rather than *precede* the achievement of understanding and the discovery of efficient modes of attack. For children who still rely on inefficient or immature procedures, such as "counting" or indirect solutions in adding, drills produce gains only in speed and accuracy. From such drill, children do not discover more mature or efficient modes of attack; they merely learn to use more rapidly and accurately whatever procedures they have already found will work.

In the early stages of practice on skills–such as reading, arithmetic computation, typewriting, or tennis–teacher direction or guidance of self-discovery learning should emphasize understanding, discovery of efficient modes of attack, and cultivation of good form. When the timing of speed drills is adjusted to the accomplishment of these objectives, the long- range rate of progress and the ultimate level of proficiency attained are greater.

Distribution of Practice Time. How shall we answer the adolescent's questions about the most efficient distribution of time for practice and for lessons in violin playing or in other complex skills? Should he take a single one-hour lesson or two half-hour lessons per week? And should he spend his seven hours of practice per week in seven hourly practice periods, in twice that number of half-hour sessions, or in a couple of long periods on the weekends? For efficient learning of both verbal and motor skills, research results tend to favor several short practice periods rather than one or a few long ones.

In order to achieve a criterion of mastery of 100 successive catches in juggling, Knapp and Dixon compared the distributions of practice time for two equated groups of 35 college physical education students–both of which were taught the same systematic pattern of juggling. The group given 5 minutes of practice daily required, an average total time of 70 minutes to master the skill. The group practicing 15 minutes on each of alternate days required. on the average, 126 minutes. For this particular motor skill, 14 shorter periods proved more efficient than 8 longer periods. Other experiments have confirmed the advantage of shorter practice periods for high school students.

Reed found that college students gained more proficiency in addition from either three daily 20-minute periods or six daily

10-minute periods than from an hour of continuous practice. Oseas and Underwood, using very short intervals between practice periods, found that college students identified and remembered abstract concept associations more efficiently when practice trials were distributed rather than massed. Also using college students as subjects, Hormone and Miller obtained data on learning a complex perceptual-motor task (billiard set shots), which suggests that spacing practice periods with increasingly longer intervals between them is economical of the total practice time required.

Such experiments to not, of course, provide precise guidance on the most effective distribution of practice time for every school subject. They do, however, suggest that certain principles exist, and that efficient learners and teachers should try to discover optimum distributions of practice for the varied learning activities in which students engage.

Long practice periods on repetitive activities–studying spelling or language usage; memorizing arithmetic combinations, factual details in social studies, science, or a music composition; and practicing such skills as typewriting or free throws in basketball–lead to waning motivation, inattention to goal-directing ideas, fatigue, and to interference between the several only partially learned, competing responses. For such activities, shorter practice periods with rest intervals of an hour for a day between are likely to be more effective. The intervals between practice periods provide opportunities for implicit rehearsals, for achieving perspectives unencumbered with irrelevant details which tend to be forgotten between practice periods, and sometimes for freeing oneself from interfering mental sets.

For problem solving in science, social studies, or creative pursuits involving integration of many components, however, long practice periods are often needed. Relatively long periods are needed for the varied alternative approaches required to discover solutions to complex problems and for evaluating them before they are forgotten. In such projects, short practice periods would require the student to repeat preliminary preparations; they would interrupt his line of thought just at the moment when he had organized his work (such as his notes for writing a social studies or science report) and was ready to go on to the next step. Long periods would provide time for preparing, organizing, and carrying work through to a satisfying stage of completion. For the systematic practice of the skills related to such projects, however, distributed practice is more effective.

The Role of Warm-up in Practice. Virtuoso-level performers–such as musicians, dancers, athletes–expect to attain perfection only if they are in practice. And like reserve baseball pitchers, who warm up in the bull pen before trying to meet the crucial demands on the mound, they warm up on some preliminary exercises just before a performance. Several experiments have confirmed the validity of the assumption that there is a need for warming up before expecting high level proficiency.

In a sequence of equally difficult learning tasks, 60 college students learned to associated fifteen 10-items lists of pairs of unrelated adjectives. In four-second presentations of each pair, a subject was shown the stimulus adjective for two seconds; during the next two seconds, he was expected to say the associated adjective–after which time it was presented for checking. Learning three different lists per day in immediate succession, each subject was given 10 trials on each of the 15 lists. The average number of correct anticipations on the first trials of each list is graphed in Figure 7.6.

A stable learning-how-to-learn effect is demonstrated in the gradual attainment of higher levels of memorization skill on the initial list for each day, which is marked by the fine line connecting these initial list scores for each of the five days. The warm-up effect is indicated by the sharper increases in memorizing efficiency from the first to second lists on each day of practice. For example, after making only 8 correct anticipations on the first list of the first day, the subjects achieve mean scores of approximately 14 and 18, respectively, on equally difficult second and third lists. The relatively small increments in score from the second to the third lists, as compared to the larger gains from the

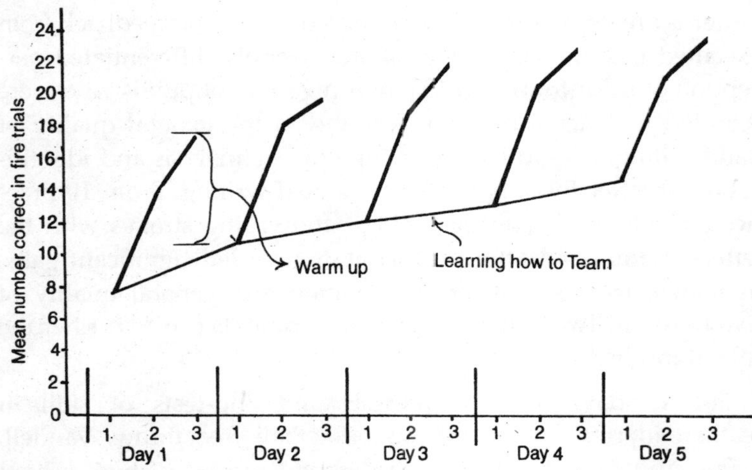

Figure 7.6. College Students, in Learning 15 Equally Difficult 10-item Lists of Unrelated Paired-Associate Adjectives, Demonstrated both "Warm-up" and "Learning-how-to-learn."
(From L.E. Thune, J. Exp. Psychol., 1951, Vol. 42, p. 252.)

first to the second, indicate that the warm-up in this particular task in accomplished mainly in the first trial. The warm-up gain is temporary, as is indicated in the drops in score from the third list of one day's practice to the first list of the next day. It takes a warm-up practice on the first list of each day to re-establish the proficiency attained on the last trial of the preceding day.

Implicit and Explicit Practice. One explanation of the advantage of distributed practice is the claimed added learning which accrues from mulling over or thinking about a task between periods of *actual* practice. Is such implicit practice actually helpful? According to cognitive-learning theory, it should aid in structuring approaches to problems—by formation of cognitive maps to be applied subsequently in actual practice. With some qualifications, experiments confirm the theory.

Handwriting is a perceptual-motor skill involving both perception of letter forms and their execution in patterns of motor behavior. These two aspects of handwriting are ordinarily learned simultaneously, as interrelated processes; the movement patterns are dependent on perception of form, and feedback from executed movements leads to more precisely differentiated perception of letter forms. To 15 junior high school pupils who were retarded in letter formation skill and in the general quality of handwriting, Leggitt gave training only in analysis and identification of letter formation–without actual writing. From 10 practice periods in visually matching handwriting strokes with the letters, before- and after practice tests revealed significant gains in both correctness of letter formation and general quality of handwriting. Two better-designed experiments clarify further the role of implicit practice.

For 19 days between pretests and end-tests of skill in feathereddart throwing and in basketball free throw, Vandell, Davis, and Clugston had three different groups of high school and college students engage in (1) no practice, (2) actual motor practice, and (3) "doing mentally that which they had actually done" on the pretest. While the no-practice group made no gain, both the explicit and implicit practice groups achieved significant and approximately equal improvement. At least in the initial stages of practice, it seems that merely imagining better modes of attack can produce improvement in such motor skills.

Eventually, however, gains from mental practice should diminish, since there is no effective feedback of the results of merely imagined provisional trials. This predicted outcome of implicit practice is confirmed by Twining's experiment. In 20 days between pretests and end tests of skill in tossing 6-inch rings over a peg 10 feet away, a group of 12 college students without any practice improved only 4.3 per cent. From twenty 15-minute daily practices of "mentlly throwing rope rings at imaginary targets," a similar group improved 36.2 per cent. Another comparable group, who-in the same number of practice periods–actually tossed rings, improved 137.3 per cent. Implicit practice is effective in structuring approaches to problems. In the long range, however, efficient practice requires the full trial-and-check process in which–as guides to improvement–each goal-directed, provisional trial can be confirmed or disconfirmed in, the light of perception of its effects.

Summary

Although repeated trials are necessary, they alone are not sufficient for mastering complex concepts or skills. Both repeated trials and perception of their effects (plus other conditions of learning) are required. Broadly interpreted, practice implies both making and checking provisional trials. It is more a matter of discovery than of repetition. Practice is a goal-directed trial-and-check process in which the learned tries out tentative hypotheses. On the basis of his perception of their effects, he confirms and consolidates responses or disconfirms and revises provisional trials.

In the trial-and-check process, perception of the effects of provisional trials is crucial. For effective learning, it should be pertinently informative, precise, and prompt. Moreover, it is important to distinguish between motivational reinforcement and *perception* of the effects of provisional trials. Both affect the selection and elimination of trial-and-error responses. However, it is perceived informational feedback which guides the learner in confirming or disconfirming responses and in revising subsequent efforts. According to cognitive theory, perception guides learning; motivational reinforcement determines performance.

Many learning activities provide inherent self-checking feedbacks; correct responses fit or work, incorrect ones do not. However, effective teaching—either as teacher direction or guidance of selfdiscovery learning-provides additional informative, frequent, precise and prompt checking of pupils' goal-directed trials.

A classification of the various types of learning which require practice helps us to understand why the numerous concepts and skills which elementary and secondary children learn require extensive practice:

1. They often need to generalize responses to multiple cues.
2. The same cue in different situations should elicit discriminative responses.

3. The automatization of responses requires learning to respond to reduced cues.

4. Effective performance often requires the organization of numerous specific responses into patterns of behavior.

5. The refinement of skills requires the elimination of unessential components and the integration of only the essential components into smoothly functioning patterns.

6. The successful imitation of complex models often requires multiple provisional trials.

7. A number of provisional trials are often needed to discover the solution to a problem.

Several principles determine the effective use of practice opportunities. There should be appropriate combinations of both functional and systematically guided and scheduled practice. The scope of effective practice opportunities extends beyond its center—a well-equipped classroom. It includes school-wide activities, homework, and the educational resources of the entire community. Drills for speed and accuracy should not be instituted until *after* the students have achieved an understanding of the skill or concept and have discovered efficient modes of attack. For different kinds of learning tasks, the teacher and students should try to discover the optimum length and distribution of practice periods. Before expecting top-level proficiency in the performance of complex skills, the need for a warm-up exercise should be recognized. Both implicit and explicit practice are effective–each in its place. In structuring approaches, preliminary, imaginary practice is sometimes helpful. However, in more advanced stages of learning and for checking goal-directed trials, actual practice is necessary.

Besides facilitating the mastery of concepts and skills, the thousands of practice activities in which children and youth engage should also produce more efficient learners. But this desired outcome is not automatic. In this chapter we have therefore considered some guides to the efficient use of practice opportunities. We shall continue this interest in the next chapter, where we shall consider the contribution which educational psychology has made and is making to the cultivation of *efficient models of attack* in learning.

8

Remembering and Forgetting

It has been said that "knowledge keeps like fish. Actually, we are" continually earning, remembering, and forgetting, and sometimes it seems tat the accumulation of knowledge is a process of taking two or three steps forward and one step backward. As students and as prospective teachers, we are concerned both with how efficiently we can learn and how well we can remember what we learn. It has perhaps occurred to each of us that the tasks of educating ourselves and of teaching children and youth would be very much easier if we remembered everything that we learn. If retention of learned facts concepts, and skills were perfect, consider how easy the examination in this course would be and how many things we should now know. Sometimes the net gain from a year's study of a subject is indeed small. Observe, for example, how much (or little) you presently remember of the foreign language you studied in high school but have not spoken or read since. Or try to recall from your biology course the phyla of the animal kingdom. When retention tests of specific facts—relatively isolated items of knowledge—are administered to elementary, high school, and college students a year or two after they completed courses in such subjects as history, Latin, chemistry, or botany, marked forgetting is often revealed. Average retention scores are sometimes as little as one-third of the end-of-course score.

Fortunately, not all the concepts and skills we learn are so quickly forgotten. Moreover, there are things we can do—as we shall discover in this chapter—to prevent forgetting and to enhance our effectiveness in the application of previously learned concepts and skills. Such principles, for example, as learning how to learn and transfer of training are just as effective in sustaining as they are in facilitating original learning. But before we begin a systematic study of the causes of forgetting and of ways to improve remembering, let us explore some informal illustrations of the factors involved.

Examples of Remembering and Forgetting

In her fifth grade geography class, a bright 10–year-old child barely succeeded in learning to associate the states of the United States with the names of their capital cities. When she was asked two years later to recite them, she recalled correctly only Salt Lake City (in her home state), Indianapolis (in the other state and in the state in which she had lived), Sacramento, Boise, Cheyenne, Phoenix, Santa Fe, Oklahoma City, and Austin. Since in her home state in which she lived temporarily the capitals are the largest cities, it probably seemed logical to reconstruct in her recall the capital of Nevada as Reno and of New York as New York City. Butte, Kansas City, and Miami intruded as capitals, possibly because they are frequently associated with their respective states. Mobile, Alabama, was perhaps incorrectly recalled for a similar reason. But for the remaining 32 states she could not make even a plausible guess.

Apparently, for such extrinsic associations, poorly mastered and rarely reviewed, retention is very limited and inaccurate. We note also in tnis illustration the operation of transfer (both positive and negative) in the child's assumption that the capitals are high big cities. The following illustration contain evidence of having learned how to learn and of effective transfer.

In an eleventh grade physics class, the same child was given a quiz on work and machanics which called for the names of the six simple machines. The child remembered that she had learned the names of the machines in the eighth grade. Now she needed to recall them. Thinking of the ways in which simple machines give the worker a mechanical advantage (their *general* function), she recalled first the *lever.* Then she recalled the *pulley* which provides a similar advantage, since both lever and the pulley lift. The idea of the pulley then suggested the *wheel* and axle. In another group, the *inclined plane* was remembered. The *wedge* was then recalled as a variation of the inclined plane. Finally, the screw was recalled as a combination of a wedge and an inclined plane wrapped around an axis. The better retention of the simple machines than of the state capitals suggests that meaningful, integrated concepts are easier to remember and to recall than detached details.

The factors of mental set, interference, transfer, and saving in relearning are all illustrated in Janet's recall of some piano pieces she had memorized for recitals tow or three years earlier but had not reviewed since. Asked to play "Soldier's Chorus", she at first thought she could not recall it. Then, as she re-established an appropriate mental set in thinking about it, the general natur eof the melody came to her. In a few trial-and-error attempts, she reconstructed it. She recalled the gay mood of "Playful Rondo", but she could recall only bits of the melody. As she worked at its reconstruction, she observed: "I don't know whether all these parts are from 'Playful Rondo' or from the 'The Doll's Dream." Actually, when the music was checked, she discovered that she had been confusing bits of "Playful Rondo" with parts from "The Music Box" rather then from "The Doll's Dream." Both of them, she said, "have gay things in them." Since these two pieces are alike in mood and in pattern, and had been learned in close succession, bits from "The Music Box" intruded to interfere with accurate recall of "Playful Rondo."

But the relearning of these pieces now revealed that more was retained then seemed apparent from the recall efforts alone. Originally, it had required approximately 50 trials to memorize "Playful Rondo" for the recital. Now, when Janet practiced to relearn "Playful Rondo", it required only 11 trials, or 39 fewer than were originally needed. In other words, because of the original learning three years earlier, she was now saved 78 per cent of the trials which would otherwise have been required. This may be an overestimate, however, of the degree of her retention. In her continued study of other pieces following original mastery of the recital pieces, she probably had learned something about how to learn music which she was able to transfer in relearning "Playful Rondo." Such a transfer effect plus the warm-up effect were clearly demonstrated in the relearning of "The Music Box", which she undertook immediately after relearning "Playful Rondo." Relearning "The Music Box"—similar to "Playful Rondo" in key, mood, and pattern—required only six trials.

The role of active reconstruction in memory is suggested in all these illustrations. It is more explicitly revealed, however, in testing seven-year-old Brant's immediate recall of the items of the following story which was read to him:

THE WET FALL

Once there was a little girl named Betty. She lived on a farm with her brother Dick. One day their father gave them a Shetland pony. They had lot of fun with it. One day, when Dick was riding on it, the pony became frightened and ran away. Poor Dick fell into a ditch. How Betty laughed when she saw him! He was covered with mud from head to foot.

Anxious and easily distracted by his worries, Brant had unusual difficulty in answering questions about the story. Asked, "What is the name of the story?" he constructed the plausible little "Ràin, or something." Asked, "What was Betty's brother's name?" he reasoned: "Could be Tom." For, "Who gave the pony to them?" he also imagined a credible response: "A man—should be, or one of their friends... or their father." On the most dramatic parts of the story, however, he reproduced the items correctly with only slight elaboration. For "What did the pony do?" and "What happened?" he said: "It ran away", and "The boy fell into a puddle of water—a big puddle."

These informal observations reveal that learning, forgetting, remembering, and transfer are interrelated process. They also indicate that remembering is not a passive process of reproduction, but an active process of reconstruction. Some of the factors affecting both forgetting and remembering have been suggested. We now turn to some of the experiments which psychologists have conducted and the theories they have proposed with respect to these processes.

General Patterns of Retention

The things we learn are not equally well remembered: studies show that what has been learned my be forgotten rapidly and almost completely; it may be retained without appreciable loss; or it may be recalled more efficiently after an interval of time has lapsed than it was immediately after learning. For example, Elder found that, over the summer vacation, 27 per cent of 203 pupils in grades 3 to 6 sustained losses of knowledge, 15 per cent of them had neither gains nor losses, and 59 per cent showed gains [20]. For primary grade pupils; whose skill in reading is less mature, slight losses often occur over the sum. Largest losses are usually reported in arithmetic—varying, however, from inappreciable to considerable. At the intermediate grade levels, where the majority of pupils have developed greater mastery and interest in reading, average gains in reading skills over the summer are quite uniformly reported. In these simply designed experiments, the specific factors causing losses, sustained retention, or gains are not clearly indicated. Other experiments, however, reveal the factors more clearly.

Rapid Forgetting. In his historically important study of the retention of nonsense syllables, Ebbinghaus found that forgetting of such meaningless material is extensive and rapid, especially immediately after learning. A schematic representation of his results is shown in the bottom curve of Figure 8.1. Relatively meaningless lists of associations, such as the states and their capitals, and the detached facts of many school subjects are forgotten almost as quickly and completely as are nonsense syllables. As the middle curve of Figure 8.1 shows, 3 months after completing a course in botany, college students had forgotten almost half of the numerous facts they had learned. After 27 months, they remembered only 24 per cent of these fact.

Sustained Retention. The retention of interesting and meaningful concepts, such as the six machines which give man a mechanical advantage, is often much better. As the top curve of Figure 8.1 shows, under conditions favorable to retention, certain kinds of school content are retained very well over long intervals of time. This curve represents junior high school students' retention of material learned in a world history course, as reflected in their answers to such questions as the following: "Alfred improved his kingdom by (a) gathering all the best laws into one book, (b) fighting the Huns, (c) going on a crusade, (d) teaching

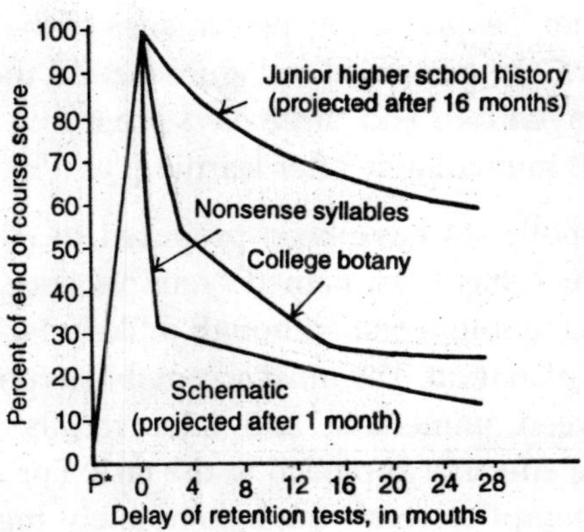

Figure 8.1 *Retention Varies for Different Materials: Understanding of Junior High School History (7), Top Curve; Specific Facts in College Botany (30), Middle Curve Curve; and nonsense Syllables (23), Bottom Curve. P* Designates the Pretest, for Batany only, Prior to the Learning Experience.*

the French language." Continued study, after the world history course, of the social studies in the seventh and eighth grades and the added practice afforded in retaking the test in a sequence of four 4-month intervals also probably facilitated retention of these facts.

Augmented Retention. Under certain especially favorable conditions the performance on delayed-retention tests may exceed that on tests taken immediately after the original learning. Two different kinds of experiments suggest that if, after original learning, the individual achieves an attitude more favorable to effective recall or enhances his understanding of pertinent general principles, his recall of the related specific content may be augmented.

For school children who memorized long selections of poetry under time limits *insufficient for mastery,* Ballard discovered that the score on retention tests taken two or three days later often exceeded the immediate-recall score [5]. To different subgroups of his 5, 192 subjects, he gave recall tests immediately and again, without prior notice, one, two, three, four, five, six, or seven days later. The immediate and delayed average recall scores on "The ancient Mariner", expressed as percentages of the mean immediate-recall score, are presented in Figure 8.2. As the figure shows, the recall delayed two and three days are 6 to 9 per cent better than the recall immediately after learning.

Several hypotheses have been proposed to explain this phenomenon, which has been named "reminiscence." The effect of practice from the initial test, although a likely factor, is probably not the full explanation. The most acceptable hypothesis seems to be that between immediate and later recalls the individual adopts a more effective approach to the task. For example, in the immediate attempt to recall the incompletely memorized selection, the individual may strive to recall it as a maze of details—a situation in which "the trees obscure the forest." Later, when his attention is returned to the recall task, the learnery may consider the selection as a more integrated whole. Having first recalled it as a whole, he may then in the reconstruction process, which we

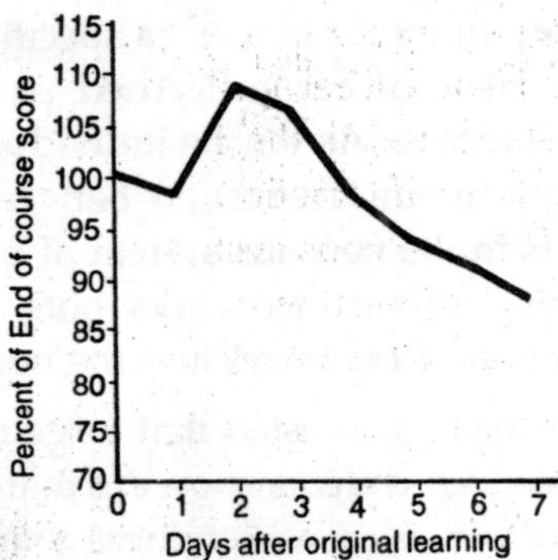

Figure 8.2 Reminiscence Curve of 12-year-old Children's Recall of "The Ancient Mariner," Tested Immediately and After Varying Delay Intervals. (From P.B. Ballard, Br. J. Psychol., Monogr. Suppl., 1911, Vols. 1–4, No. 2)

observed in our introductory examples, fit in the specific details more efficiently than he could have done initially.

In another kind of study of longer-delayed retention, Tyler discovered that college students applied certain of the concepts they had learned more effectively 15 months after completing a course in zoology, then they had in the end-of-course test. In the part of the test concerned with interpretations of new experiments in zoology, the delayed-retention score was 25 per cent higher then the end-of-course score. Although in the meantime these students had not taken additional courses in zoology, they had—through the study of other science courses—enhanced their understanding of the scientific principles of experimentation. In the delayed-retention test, they transferred this enhanced understanding to zoology, with improved interpretation of the experiments [59].

The Causes of Forgetting

Our illustration of the child's recall of the several piano recital pieces suggest that forgetting is not merely the fading away in time of memory traces (hypothetical residues of experience) in the nervous system. In trying to recall a specific piece, she found that bits of other later- or earlier-learned pieces intruded and interfered with accurate recall. As the individual remembers and learns, there is continuous interaction between memory traces (the retained effects in the nervous system of prior learning) and new learning. This "interaction works both ways, modifying both" the organization of the traces and the new learning [62].

Our illustrations have suggested that forgetting, like learning, is an active process. Experiments showing that forgotten is more rapid during the activities of wakefulness than during the relative inactivity of sleep also indicate that forgetting is an active process. It is a process in which new experiences interact with the trace systems from prior learning to interfere with accurate recall of them. As is shown in Figure 8.3. Jenkins and Dallenbach's subjects forgot the nonsense syllables they had just learned more rapidly while they were awake then when they were asleep. But let us explore the problem further. What are the kinds of activities and situations which cause forgetting? In answering this question, Deese lists six causes.

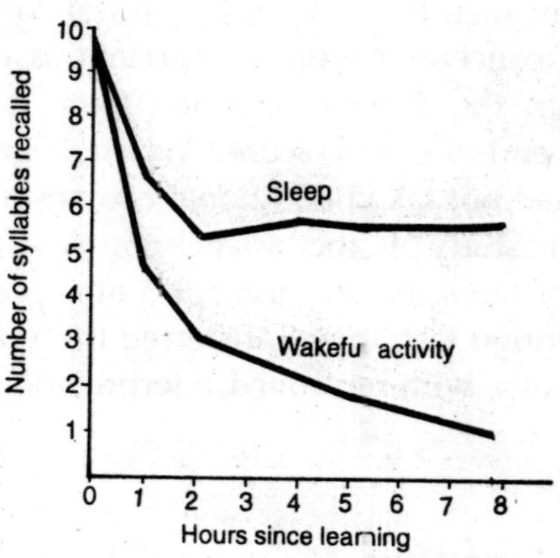

Figure 8.3 The Comparison of Retention of Nonsense Syllables After Sleep with That After Equal Periods of Wakeful Activity Suggests that Forgetting is an Active Process. (From J.G. Jenkins and K.M. Dallenbach, Amer. J. Psychol., 1924, Vol. 35, p. 610.)

1. Interactive Inhibition. At the recall of either of two sets of facts or concepts which have been learned in succession, there is the likelihood of competition between them. At the recall of the first set, intrusions from the second set may occur (retroactive inhibition). And when the second set is recalled, elements from the first set may interfere (proactive inhibition). Such interactive inhibition is probably the single most important cause of forgetting. In the child's recall of the state-capital associations, later-learned pairs inhibited accurate recall of earlier-learned pairs. And the accumulating earlier-learned associations interfered with memorization and recall of the later-learned associations. On experiencing such interference, a student in a college course, Theories of Personality, recently remarked: "The more different theories we study, the more difficult it is to remember and to distinguish between them. I grasped and differentiated the theories of Freud, Jung, and Adler. But now as we take up the theories of Fromm, Horney, and Sullivan, I am becoming confused. For example, I believe it was Adler who proposed the concept of 'inborn social interest', but I am not sure; it might have been Jung."

These observations of the effects of retroactive and proactive inhibition have been confirmed by several experiments. Following their study of the meanings of 25 French words, 94 high school students were divided into two equal groups. One group was directed to study a second list of French words, while the other group rested. Jenkins and Sparks report that retention of the initial list was significantly better among the students not subjected to the retroactive effect of learning a second list [29]. Another study shows that the extent of loss in retention of unmeaningful content varies with the amount of similar learning interpolated between initial and delayed recall.

Underwood believes that proactive inhibition from previously learned content is even more important as a cause of forgetting than retroactive inhibition. His review of several studies indicates that "the greater the number of previous lists [leaned], the greater the proactive interference". As is indicated in Figure 8.4, retention-test scores, after 48 hours, on lists of pairs of associated adjectives become increasingly poorer as the number of pre-

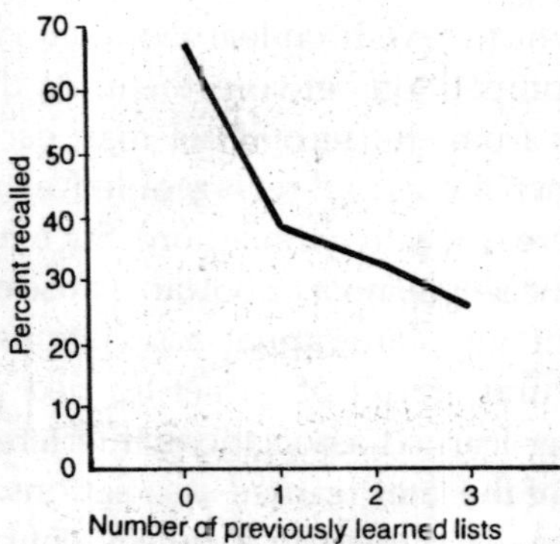

Figure 8.4 Because of Proactive Inhibition, the Recall of Subsequently Learned Lists of Paired Adjectives Becomes Less Efficient as the Number of Previously Learned Lists is Increased. (from B J. Underwood [cited from B.J. Underwood and R. Greenberg], Psychol. Rev., 1957, Vol. 64, p.51)

viously learned lists is increased from none to three. Both the drop in mean score–from 69 per cent on the first list to 25 per cent on the fourth list—and the intrusions of adjectives from the previously learned lists demonstrate that proactive inhibition is a major cause of forgetting.

2. Changes in Cognitive Structure, Attitudes, and Interests. The delayed recall of learned concepts or of observed events depends both upon the original experience and upon the cognitive structure, attitudes, and interests of the person at the time of recall. If, between initial learning and delayed recall, children acquire different ways of thinking and reasoning, different beliefs, attitudes, or interests, the traces from these intervening learnings can be expected to modify their recall of the originally learned concepts or observed events.

Such forgetting, or distortion of memory, is illustrated in Bartlett's report on his subjects' long-delayed recall of stories read to them [6]. In one of the stories Bartlett read to his subjects there were references to a young man who joined some ghosts in a war party. The structure of the story as a whole was not very logical or coherent. In succeeding recalls of this story, Bartlett's subjects—in order to make it conform to their naturalistic beliefs and logic—often deleted the ghosts and constructed the story more logically. Another study shows that if we feel competent, successful, and satisfied with ourselves as adults, we tend to recall our high school experiences as constructive and as contributing to our needs. On the other hand, if we presently feel unsuccessful and inadequate, we tend to look back critically on our high school experiences and to recall them as unsatisfactory and unsuited to our needs.

3. Changes in the Recall Situation. concepts and skills learned in a particular setting are sometimes unrecallable in a different situation. When some of the cues guiding the original learning are absent, or when distracting cues are introduced, the once-remembered concepts or skills seem to be forgotten. A variety of illustrations of this cause of forgetting are at hand.

At home, a six-year-old had successfully rehearsed a song to sing at a PTA meeting. When the child suddenly found himself perched on a high stool facing his audience, however, he could no longer remember the beginning line. The radically changed situation presented too many distracting cues. Another child sometimes, although not always, confused the reading of *then* and *there, boy* and *dog*, and pig and big. In the original piece in which he had leaned to recognize *then, boy,* and *pig.*, the accompanying pictures and other cues supported perfect recognition of these words. His recall of them was faulty only in different situation in which some of the original cues for recall were absent and in which new and distracting cues were present. A high school orchestra demonstrated the same phenomenon. After coming to rely on the cues of the regular orchestra conductor during rehearsals for the school operetta, the orchestra was unable to perform at its best when the choral conductor (who was more concerned with signaling the chorus than the orchestra) took over the conducting role at the presentation of the operetta. Grossnickle's experiment, which we discussed earlier, also illustrates this point. In division problems his pupils were unable to use the multiplication facts which they had previously used only in the multiplication situation.

4. Incompatible Mental Set. As an individual learns concepts or skills, he develops a functionally effective mental set for the activity, including the needed confidence and ready availability of appropriate responses. If intervening activities cause the mental set to change during the time between original learning and the retention test, recall will be more difficult. Bartlett's subjects failed to recall the role of the ghosts in the story he read to them because belief in the existence of ghosts was incompatible with their naturalistic training. We have all experienced such examples of forgetting as that of a student who intended to ask her English teacher whether to hyphenate "blue" and "green" in the phrase "blue-green lake." Once in the classroom, she forgot to ask the question because ongoing activities distracted her from her original set. She remembered the question again only when she returned to her incomplete composition and needed the answer.

An experiment by Carmichael, Hogan, and Walter demonstrates how different mental sets can alter remembered reproductions of the same perceived objects. As three groups of subjects viewed a list of 12 drawn figures, such as those in the middle column of Figure 8.5, Group I heard them named with the words in the left-hand column and Group II heard them named with the words in the right-hand column. For the third group, the objects were unnamed. Directed to reproduce all 12 patterns, the subjects in all three groups reproduced many of them correctly. However, of the poorest drawings of Groups I and II, about three-fourths of the distorted reproductions tended to resemble the forms each group had heard named, in the ways indicated in the left- and right-hand drawings of Figure 8.5. The different names heard by Groups I and II had created mental sets, and many of the reproductions conformed to those sets rather than to the original drawings. For the third group, distorted reproductions and did not take either of these particular directions.

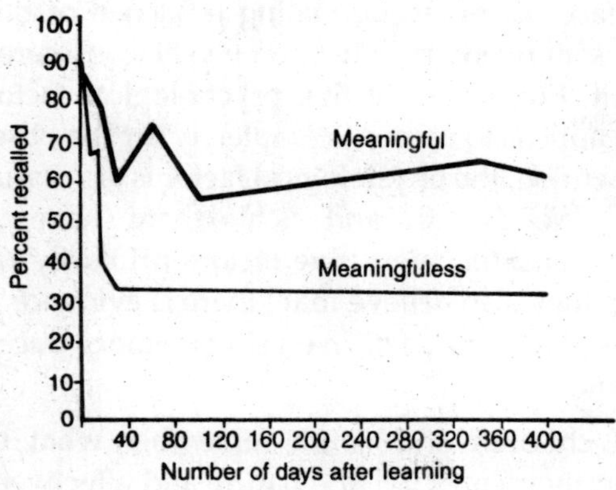

***Figure 8.5** Composite Retention Curves for 18 Studies of meaningless Material and 24 Studies of Meaningful Material [17]. (From R. A. Davis, Psychology of Learning, McGraw-Hill, New York, 1935, p.211.)*

5. Repression. As a protective device for avoiding anxiety, an individual may fail to recall certain emotionally disturbing ideas. Because they are repressed, embarrassing or threatening concepts are forgotten more readily then satisfying concepts. For example, Levine and Murphy discovered that students forget more rapidly propaganda which is contrary to their biases than that which is in agreement with them. There is also the example of Helen, who could not remember the content of a unit on health in her science course because to do so would re-arouse earlier-established anxiety. As a child she had responded to hospitalization with anxiety. In adolescence, when the health unit content reminded her of the painful, anxiety-provoking treatments and of what she had interpreted as abandonment by her parents, she avoided the full recurrence of the anxiety by repressing or forgetting ideas which would remind her of the earlier conditioning experience.

6. Disuse and Metabolic Changes in the Nervous System. It seems plausible to assume that the residual traces imprinted in the nervous system by experience should fade with time. Indeed, this factor was at one time believed to be the primary cause of forgetting. In the face of the accumulating evidence of other active interferences with retention, it has come to be considered less and less important. But since the five psychological factors named above do not appear to account completely for the observed decrements in retention, the physiological factor is also assumed to be a possibility. Woodworth and Schlossberg have said that, although they consider interactive factors primarily responsible for forgetting, they also believe that "there is evidence that metabolic activities play some part" in erasing memory traces from the nervous system.

How well children and youth remember what they learn depends upon their curricula, the nature and effectiveness of the conditions of learning, the degree of degree of mastery attained and individual differences in their interests, other motives, and talents.

1. Meaningfulness of Content and Approach. Meaningful content and a meaningful rather than a rote approach to learning facilitate both original learning and retention. As out introductory examples illustrate, meaningful concepts—especially those related to general principles—are retained much better then rote-learned detached details or nonsense syllables. This difference was clearly indicated in the child's perfect retention of the functionally interrelated six simple machines and her marked forgetting of the detached state-capital associations.

The better retention of meaningful content than of meaningless content is demonstrated in the composite of experimental findings collected by Davis and Moore, In their review of these studies, Davis and Moore point out that the retention curves for both kinds of material are similar—they show rapid early loss and then a leveling off; but, as the curves also show, the retention of meaningful prose and poetry is maintained at a much higher level than the retention of nonsense syllables.

Several studies of school learning show that meaningful, organized content is better remembered than are isolated details. Pressey, Robinson, and Horrocks have summarized studies indicating that as much as two-thirds of the detailed facts students acquire in high school and college courses is forgotten within two years. In contrast with these reports of extensive forgetting of unrelated facts, there are also several reports of generalizations and meaningful principles which have been retained over long periods of time. Schrepel and Laslett have reported that, although junior high school pupils lose some computational skill over the summer vacation, their ability to apply general principles of arithmetic is retained. Frutchey with high school students and Tyler with college students, confirm the findings on rapid and extensive forgetting of isolated details, but show that general principles and the ability to apply them are well retained a year or more later.

As a consequence of our discoveries of the kinds of content students retain, we are learning how to make better achievement tests. For example, recent studies show good delayed retention of the general concepts students learn both in general and in educational psychology. Delayed-retention scores on tests given four to eight months after completion of the courses ranged from 71 to 79 per cent on such items as "Accepting pupil diagnosis as a major function of testing, which of the following is the best test: (a) a comprehensive achievement battery at the end of high school, (b) an achievement battery given early in the year, (c) an intelligence test, (d) a series of tests used to determine a student's grade."

In order to enhance the retention of meaningful content, teachers should also see that the *learning approach is meaningful.* Many children do not approach a retention task so meaningfully as did the child who based her recall of the six simple machines on the observed functional interrelations between them. Some students try to recall such concepts as separate, unrelated facts. In rote fashion, they memorize numerous geometry theorems or chemical formulas as relatively meaningless facts rather than as differentiated elaborations of a few meaningful principles. Both our experience and experiments, however, demonstrate the advantage of the meaningful approach.

Steele found, with equated groups of fifth and sixth grade pupils, that the group which was taught fraction with emphasis upon understanding and the inductive discovery of principles did better both on end-of-course tests and on retention tests seven months later than did the group whose emphasis was on verbatim mastery by repetitive drill. Using two groups of 35 college students as his subjects, Carpenter directed them in learning to classify blocks-differing in color, size, and shape—into four categories: *cevs, biks, lags,* and *murs.* For example, in successive teacher demonstrations, the group taught by rote memorization, observed that the *mur* class included a white hexagon, a white circle, a blue circle, a yellow square, and a yellow triangle. The group instructed in a meaningful approach observed that *murs* were "tall and small, that *cevs* were short and small" and so on. On a retention test one week later, in which the subjects were given a block of each class and required to pick out the remaining members, the rote-memorization group correctly identified only 29 per cent of the blocks while the meaningful-approach group correctly identified 77 per cent of them.

One of the important aspects of meaningfulness, as a factor favoring learning and retention, is organization of the material to be learned.

2. Organization. Retention of the thousands of facts concepts, and skills—in language, science, mathematics, social studies, and other subjects—which elementary and secondary school children learn is greatly facilitated by effective, functional organization. Especially over long intervals, organizational categories for classifying or interpreting separate details determine the number and quality of ides students retain. Postman has experimentally demonstrated that "learned rules of organization can systematically influence both the amount and quality of retention." When his subjects were given explicit verbal formulations of principles governing the content to be remembered, they improved their retention.

Let us illustrate the role of organization on recall in some recent experiments. In recalling a radomly arranged list of 40 words—such as *collie, lance, Belgium, Wallace, Panther, Brazil, husky, Susan, revolver, bayonet, Homer, musket, Rumania, leopard, Chile, Elaine*—college students tended to group them into classes and subclasses. For example, there were ten animals divided into two classes: canine—collie, husky, etc., and feline—leopard, panther, etc. According to Cohen and Bousefield, the greater use students make of organizational concepts, the more effectively they recall words read to them. In explaining the process of clustering items in recall, and its facilitation effect upon recall, Sakoda says that the individual "naturally" tends to organize the miscellaneous ideas he has learned into meaningful categories or under general concepts. In such an approach, an item suggests its classes; the class concept then generates its members. Retention is thus facilitated by transfer of previously achieved generalizations.

In another recent study, Hall has shown that meaningful, well-organized verbal content is quite resistant to retroactive inhibition. Forty-five college students, subdivided into three groups, studied for three minutes a story about the customs and characteristics of a hypothetical primitive tribe. The story consisted of

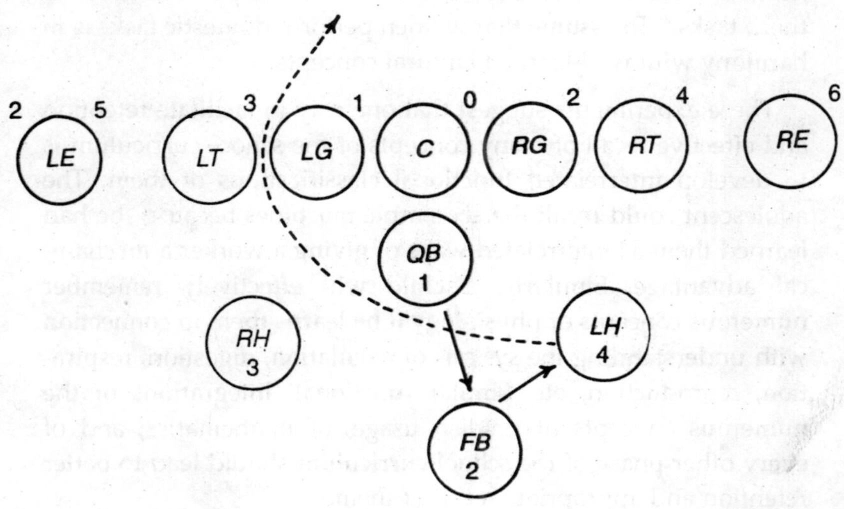

an introductory statement and 30 sentences, such as: "Women perform most of the *domestic* tasks." Immediately following the study, all three groups were given recall tests. Before a delayed-retention test, given 45 minutes later, Group I, the control group, took mechanical aptitude tests whose content had no relation to the original content but prevented them from rehearsing the story. Group II studied a quite different story about another hypothetical tribe. And Group III studied a story similar to the original story. It was anticipated, of course, that in the process of trying to recall the original story, items, especially from similar sentences in the interpolated stores studied by Groups II and III might intrude. Despite the possibilities of retroactive effects, however, the percentages of items recalled by all three groups ranged form 91 to 101 per cent of the immediate-recall score. Even after 21 days, these retention scores ranged from 81 to 83 per cent. These short, fairly well-learned, coherent paragraphs probably left as a trace a unitary impression from which the details could be logically reconstructed. Because of their mental set to recall customs about a primitive tribe, and because of their ability to transfer generalizations about their own culture to the test situation, the students might very logically have inferred the missing word in such a sentence as: "Women perform most of the... tasks." To assume that women perform domestic tasks is in harmony with well-learned cultural concepts.

These experiments suggest that one way to facilitate retention and effective recall of many concepts of the school curriculum is to develop interrelated functional classifications of them. The adolescent could recall the six simple machines because she had learned them as interrelated ways of giving a worker a mechanical advantage. Similarly, a child will effectively remember numerous concepts of physiology if he learns them in connection with understanding the *systems* of circulation, digestion, respiration, reproduction, etc. Similar functional! integrations of the numerous concepts of English usage, of mathematics, and of every other phase of the school curriculum should lead to better retention and appropriate recall of them.

As a specific illustration of the advantage of good organization, consider how it enables high school football players to remember the 100 to 200 differently signaled plays they learn in a single short season. How do they remember for example, the particular one signaled by the call "four-three—on two".

The players instantly recognize the play because the *system* they have learned gives the call meaning. For example, one system is organized in the following way: (1) All even-numbered plays go to the right and odd-numbered plays go to left; (2) signals beginning with 1 are quarterback plays, those beginning with 2 are right halfback plays; (3) a running play begins with a number; a passing play begins with the word "green"; (4) the first number called indicates the player to carry the ball, the second number is the hole number (over the right hip of the offensive players), the third number is the flanker, and a fourth number is the charging signal. If it were not for such organizational patterns, the signals would be a confusing jumble for both the quarterback and his teammates.

3. Thorough Mastery. Poorly or barely mastered concepts and skills are soon forgotten. "Material that one wishes to retain for long periods to be studied and restudied." As Krueger has demonstrated, the additional practice beyond that required for minimal or uncertain performance of a skill pays dividends in sustained retention. After his three groups of subjects had taken the minimum number of trials needed to be able to trace a finger maze correctly, he gave one group 50 per cent more practice and a second group 100 per cent more. The added overlearning trials were not merely perfunctory repetitions, but were active efforts to improve proficiency and confidence on the maze. As the curves of Figure 8.7 show, the more thoroughly the material is mastered, the better it is retained. Other experimental studies indicate that on recall there is less interference of retroactive inhibition if there has been thorough mastery, both of the material originally learned and of the material interpolated before the retention tests.

The role of original mastery in sustaining retention is also indicated in delayed retention studies of school subjects. For pri-

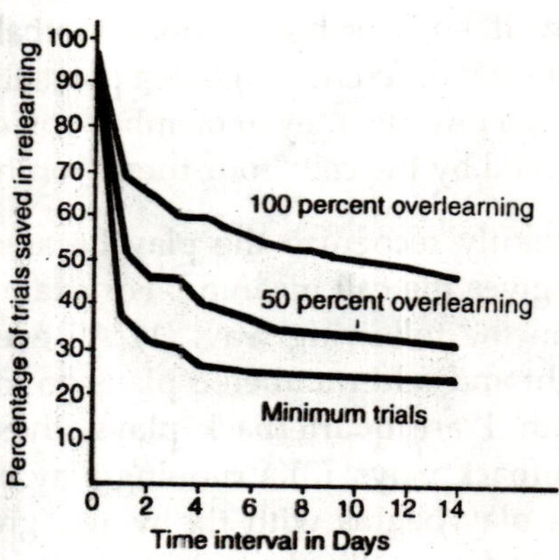

Figure 8.7 Comparison of The Retention Curves on Finger-Maze Performance of Groups Given (a) the Minimum Trials for Mastery; (b) 50 per cent Added Trials; (c) 100 per cent Added Trials Shows that Overlearning Sustains Retention. (Data From W.C.F. Krueger, J. Exp. Psychol., 1930, vol. 13, p. 155.)

mary grade pupils, whose skills in reading, spelling, and arithmetic are developed to only minimal levels of proficiency, slight losses often occur over the summer vacation. For the intermediate grade levels, however, where the majority of pupils have developed higher degrees of mastery and interest in reading, average gains over the summer are quite uniformly reported. Ashbaugh found that third grade children sustained net losses in spelling over the summer, but that fifth and sixth grade children, who had accumulated a greater background of spelling generalizations and skill in learning how to spell, experienced gains. Brueckner found that second grade children retain, over the summer, the relatively well-learned easy addition and subtraction facts, whereas they tend to forget the harder, less well-learned subtraction facts. On retention of American history, Kolberg reports that seventh grade pupils retain familiar, well-learned information items better than they do new, less well-learned facts.

Two studies, similar in design to Krueger's, show the effects of added amounts of practice on sustained retention. During the spring semester, Morgan gave his experimental group of sixth grade pupils two weeks of intensive remedial teaching in reading and arithmetic based on the diagnostic-test-discovered needs of individual children. An equated control group was given no special attention. It was found that the pupils whose spring achievement levels were raised by the remedial teaching maintained the higher levels without loss over the summer vacation. The control group, who ended the spring term at lower achievement levels, sustained a loss in computation skill and maintained only their lower levels in arithmetic reasoning and in reading. Brueckner and Distad compared the summer-retention of first grade children who had had 12, 24 and 36 weeks of reading instruction, and who attained corresponding levels of proficiency. For the children given only 12 weeks of instruction in reading, a significant loss occurred. For the children given 24 or 36 weeks of instruction, there were no appreciable losses.

Added practice is not, of course, the only way to facilitate mastery or retention of concepts and skills. Giving proper attention to *all* the conditions of effective learning-readiness, motivation, appropriate guidance of the trial-and-check process, emphasis on transfer principles, and the cultivation of mental health—will enhance both original learning and retention.

4. Reviewing. Interactive inhibition and other causes of forgetting take their toll of even well-mastered, meaningful concepts and skills unless they are reviewed. For example, without further instruction or review, ninth grade students in one year forgot two-thirds of the knowledge they had mastered in elementary algebra. However, effective review, systematically scheduled review sessions, periodic retests, continued use of concepts, or expansion of previously accumulated concepts and their integration with new concepts can prevent such forgetting.

By means of relearning reviews in the fall, school children soon recover the losses sustained in some subjects over the summer vacation. In an experimental demonstration of the role of review in recovering losses from forgetting, Stroud and Johnson had about six hundred pupils in grades 7 to 9 read a 1,750-word article on paper making. Preceding the retention tests taken by different experimental and control groups after 1, 15, and 29 days, the experimental groups were permitted a 12-minute rereading review of the material. Control groups were denied this opportunity. Groups permitted the review earned retention scores 15 to 60 per cent higher then the control groups. As these data show, the need for review increases as the retention interval is lengthened. After only 1 day, the review produces an advantage of 15 per cents; after 29 days, the advantage is 60 per cent.

In order to prevent the losses which would otherwise occur from forgetting, the reviews need to be systematically spaced in a way to take into account the findings from curves of forgetting. To prevent the typical rapid forgetting which follows shortly after initial learning, a thorough review should be given early. Then comprehensive reviews, but with smaller samplings, can be spaced at longer and longer intervals. In spelling, for example, the words learned during the week are reviewed on Friday. Those missed on Friday are included in the next week's lesson. Other comprehensive reviews may be spaced at the end of the month, at the end of the term, and at the beginning of the following school year.

Periodic retesting of earlier-learned concepts and skills is in effective reviewing device. When children have opportunities to confirm or to revise concepts by study of their corrected test papers, they not only sustain retention but often achieve improvement. For example, of the addition problems which children missed on the second test after having correctly solved them on the first—Davis and Rood found that 82.5 per cent were corrected on the third test, 8.8 per cent more were corrected on the fourth test, and an additional 2.9 per cent were finally corrected on the fifth test. The five successive tests, given at intervals of four to seven months, resulted in the eventual recovery of 94.2 per cent of concepts initially forgotten. Studies by Tiedeman, with fifth grade pupils, and by Spitzer, with sixth grade pupils, show that multiple-choice review tests, given immediately after learning and spaced appropriately over the retention interval, aid in sustaining retention. As a comparison of the curves in Figure 8.8 shows, retention aided by intervening tests is superior to unaided retention. The advantage of the test-aided recall could have been greater, however, if the corrected tests had been utilized more effectively in confirming correct test responses and in revising incorrect ones. Unless wrong answers are corrected, they tend to be repeated.

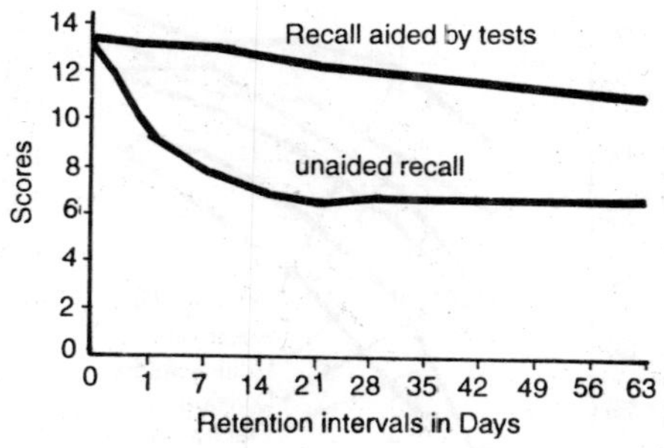

Figure 8.8 *Test - Aided Retention of Geography Facts is Superior to Unaided Recall of Such Content. (From H. F. Spitzer, J. Educ. Psychol., 1939, Vol., 30, p. 647.)*

Although systematic reviews and appropriately spaced retention tests help children to remember school content, perhaps the best way to promote retention and to improve understanding of earlier-learned concepts and skills is to provide opportunities for their continuing use. Davis and Rood demonstrated that junior high school pupils who were given such opportunities improve in rather then forget the computation and problem-solving skills they learn in the elementary grades. During the four-to seven-month intervals between retention tests, their continued study of arithmetic required them to use the previously learned concepts and skills. For example, during the first semester of the seventh grade, they reviewed the four fundamental processes in studying decimals and fractions. In the eighth grade, they reviewed percentages by applying the concepts to interest, insurance, and other problems. In the succession of retention tests given over a two-year period, each child was encouraged to try to better his previous record. As is revealed in Figure 8.9 such continued and extended application of concepts not only prevents their loss but increases understanding of them. The orderly arrangement of sequences of topics so that new problems provide for functional applications of significant facts and principles will ensure both their retention and expanded development.

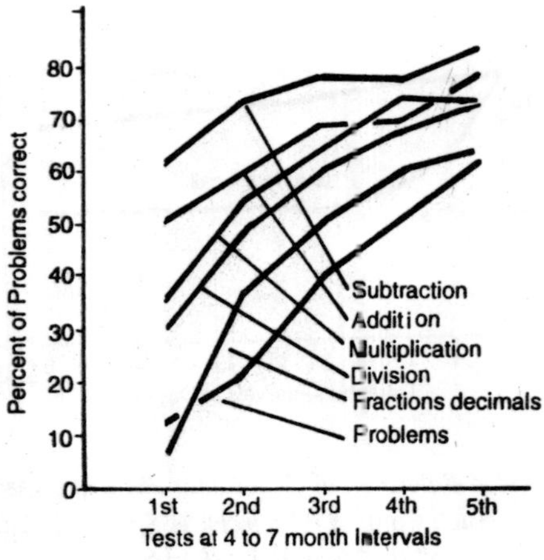

Figure 8.9 ***Retention and Improvement of Concepts and Skills Occur When Review, need, and use of them are Provided.*** *(From data by R. A. Davis and E. J. Rood, J. Educ. Psychol., 1947, Vol. 38, pp. 216-222)*

5. Integration. Two studies point out especially clearly how retention can be improved by the integration of topics in a sequence. When pupils study a sequence of topics—as in science, social studies, or literature—each new topic should be related to or developed as an extension of the organized accumulation of preceding topics. With such integration of topics in a sequence, studies show that the kind of interactive inhibition complained of by the student in the previously mentioned course in theories of personality does not occur.

In a study of seventh grade science pupils, Word and Davis demonstrated the role of integration in retention of general science concepts. As review devices, they employed repeated testing, continued use of previously learned facts, and attempts to interrelate or integrate new concepts with previously accumulated and organized concepts. At the conclusion of each two-week assignment, the pupils were tested both on the newly acquired content and on retention of content from the preceding two-week assignment. Their accumulated scores on both the old and the newly acquired concepts, recorded biweekly over a period of 18 weeks, are presented in Figure 8.10. The figure shows that the integration of new concepts into the student's functionally organized background of concepts not only keeps the background facts alive but probably gives them broader and enriched meaning. As a consequence, the possibilities of both retention and transfer are enhanced.

In another study of the effect of integration on the retention of social studies content, Ausubel, Robbins, and Blaeke had 188 college students first study for 25 minutes a 1,700-word passage

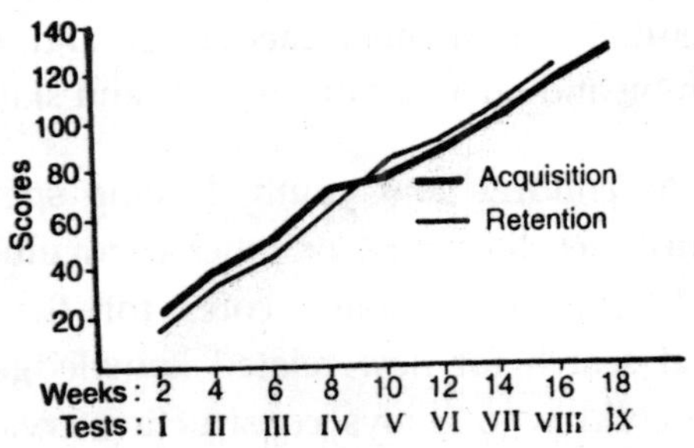

Figure 8.10 Receiving Sustains Retention and Facilitates New Learning, as is shown by Acquisition and Retention Scores Plotted Cumulatively. (From A. H. Word and R. A. Davis, J. Educ. Psychol., 1939, Vol. 30, p. 121.)

on Buddhism (its history, sacred literature, doctrine, and ethical teachings). Immediately after this initial study, the students took a multiple-choice test on the content of the passage. Twenty-four hours later, different subgroups of the 188 students studied different interpolate materials. A nonintegrative group read a new 1,700-word passage on Christianity (its history, sacred literature, doctrine, and ethical teachings). An integrative group read a comparative 2,100-word essay on Buddhism *and* Christianity, recapitulation the content on Buddhism and pointing out the similarities and differences between it and Christianity. Eight days later both groups took a delayed-retention test on the content of the original passage on Buddhism. For the nonintegrative group who studied the passage on Christianity without relating it to Buddhism, retroactive effects reduced the mean score on Buddhism to 82.3 per cent of the original score. However, for the integrative group who compared Buddhism and Christianity, the delayed-retention score on Buddhism was 107.7 per cent of the original score. Instead of experiencing interference from study of the second topic, the students who integrated their study of the two religions enhanced their understanding of Buddhism.

6. Dynamic Factors in Retention. Such dynamic factors as interests, intention to remember, mental set, and attitudes affect both the learning and retention of concepts and skills.

Interests. As children and youth develop specialized interests—in science, art, literature, or other curriculum activities—these interests become dynamic cores for the organization, extension, and search for new related knowledge or skill. For example, the child who enjoys constructing crystal, tube, and transistor radio sets becomes preoccupied with his creative interest. In extending his insights into the principles of radio and the general field of electronics, he is continuously reorganizing his accumulation background of concepts for more effective use. Such highly motivated learning and *use* of concepts reinforce them for permanent retention.

Intention to Remember. The interest-motivated child learns concepts with intention to remember them, and, as experiments show, intention to remember facilitates retention. Karen directed two groups of students to look over long lists of words and nonsense syllables; one group was told to draw a line through 30 of them, and the other group was told to "study and remember" these 30 words and syllables. In a retention test requiring the subjects to recognize the 30 items when mixed with 30 other words and syllables, the group which had *intended* to remember them recognized 9.47 of the items while the *incidental-learning* group recognized only 5.70. Another experiment indicates that for "intention to remember" to be effective, it must operate during, not after, learning. These experiments remind us that effective learning is goal-directed; and that anticipation of using the concepts and skills we learn enhances our retention of them.

Set to Recall. Retention depends upon intention to remember during learning and upon an appropriate mental set at the time of recall. Often before earlier-learned concepts and skills can be recalled, the individual must "warm up" to the specific task. Suddenly confronted with a request to play the piano-recital pieces she had not practiced for two or three years, the child of our easier example was at first baffled. She seemed completely unable to remember "Soldiers' Chorus", but as she persisted in her efforts to recall it, an idea of the melody occurred. Then, in a goal-directed trial-and-check process, she reconstructed the piece-first the melody and then even the accompaniment. As the warm-up proceeded, she became able to recall pieces which had seemed completely forgotten. In re-establishing an appropriate mental set for playing these pieces, traces from general musical concepts and related clue traces were reactivated and attention was diverted from distracting traces and cues.

Unless children come to understand the role of mental set in recall, they may assume that it is useless to try to recall partially forgotten concepts or skills. It often seems futile to attempt some recall tasks because they seem too difficult, and they *are* difficult until one gets into them. Children need, therefore, to learn to make trial efforts. By encouraging resourcefulness generally, we may aid children in getting through the warm-up period. If we can develop in out pupils a mental set to remember and to apply, to transfer general concepts and skills, we shall also aid the development of their retentive power.

Beliefs, Attitudes, and Self-concept. A motivational bias in harmony with the concepts being learned tends to facilities both the learning and retention of such material. In testing this hypothesis, Garber found that students who believed and approved the concepts in a passage they read twice in *Russia Today* retained more of the essential ideas than a group who disbelieved and disapproved them. In another study, Levine and Murphy had pro-Communist and anti-Communist college students read and recall, in five weekly practice periods, both pro-Soviet and anti-Soviet prose selections. Then, in five weekly delayed-retention tests, they measured the number of ideas which the students could correctly reproduce from the earlier-read selections. As Figure 8.11 shows, each group learned more and forgot fewer of the concepts with which they could agree. The anti-Communist students retained more of the anti-Soviet ideas; and, as a similar graph in Levine and Murphy's article shows, the pro-Communist students retained more of the pro-Soviet ideas.

One's self-concept is another dynamic factor which affects retention. In demonstrating the role of this factor, Cartwright read to 80 adults lists of adjectives and names of objects, both consistent and inconsistent with their self-concepts. Self-consistent or self-inconsistent adjectives and names had previously been sorted by the subjects as "most like [or least like] me" and as "most like [or most unlike] me to own", respectively. On immediate-retention tests, the subjects recalled significantly more of the self-consistent items. Adjectives inconsistent with the self-concept were sometimes distorted in the direction of greater self-consistency. For example, *satisfied* was misrecalled as *dissatisfied*, *hopeless* as *hopeful*, and *hostile* as *hospitable*.

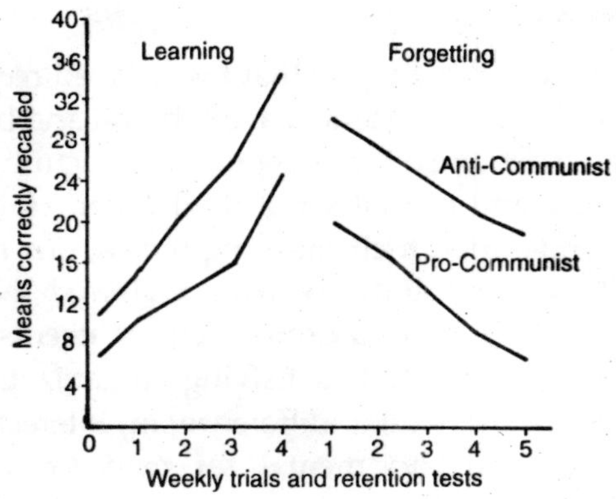

Figure 8.11 Students with anti-Comunistsm Attitudes Surpass Those with Pro-Communist Attitudes in the Learning and Retention of Anti-Soviet Material. (From J. M. Levine and G. Murphy, J. Abnorm. and Soc. Psychol., 1943, Vol. 38, p. 513)

A General Theory of Remembering

The introductory examples of remembering and the experiments both on the causes of forgetting and on the factors which facilitate retention all indicate that remembering is not a passive reproduction of previous experience. On the contrary, they indicate that remembering is a complex creative process. In the specific acts of remembering described—recalling the capitals of the states, the six simple machines, the events in "The Wet Fall", and the piano pieces—the roles of both past experience and current problem solving are evident. From past experience, there are the residue of the events to be recalled, transferable beliefs and generalizations, and conditioned attitudes and interests. Operating at the moment of recall are the present mental set and the goal-directed trial-and-check process of problem solving. For example, in remembering a story children often recall the story's general outline and some especially significant details from the original learning experience. But in the process of recalling it—by additions, deletions, substitutions, and distortions—they tend to mold the original story into a form in harmony with their present concepts, beliefs, and attitudes.

We have learned in this chapter that the delayed recall of concepts or skills is affected by interactive inhibition and by changes in both the situation and in the cognitive structure, attitudes emotions, interests, and mental set of the learner. How well we recall them depends upon their meaningfulness, our mastery of them, and on how thoroughly we have reviewed them in the meantime. In recalling miscellaneous facts or events, we give them more economical and satisfying organization. Such dynamic factors as individual difference in interests, beliefs, attitudes, self-concepts, and mental set tend to shape each individual's recall to suit his needs.

Other data are in agreement with these findings. Morris reports that as each of six children reproduced in a succession of retellings a story read to the first child, the story became shortened. Details were deleted. The titles and names of persons and places were either changed or omitted. Events were transposed. And complex sentences were simplified and put into more child-like language. Talland found that when college students from different nations, working in teams of four, retold in serial reproduction essays from various areas of interest, there was some tendency to restructure the concepts in terms of the student's different cultural attitudes. For example, Americans misinterpreted cricket scores as baseball scores, and then marveled at a player's 95 consecutive runs. British students reproduced "the difference goes deep" with "the cleavage goes deep." Tiernan found that in delayed reproductions—at intervals of 11, 46, and 120 days—children aged 7 to 14 tended to complete such uncompleted figures as hearts, circles, or diamonds. Their reproductions tended to conform more nearly than the uncompleted drawings to their concepts of these figures. Williams and Knox, in summarizing some of the dynamic factors affecting memory, note that (1) reproductions are affected by naming objects; (2) they tend toward symmetry, simplicity, and completeness; and (3) their traces are affected by organizational process, by interaction with other traces, and by attitudes.

As a concrete illustration of these tendencies, let us examine a nine-year-old child's reproduction of the left-hand pattern. After observing the stimulus figure for 10 seconds, with intent to remember it, he was asked to reproduce if from memory. His drawing shows that it is partly a reproduction and partly a logical reconstruction. He first reproduced the larger rectangular pattern and, with some variation, included a smaller enclosed rectangle. Next, he drew the enclosed triangle on the left side. Instead of the right-hand enclosed triangle, however, he first drew the dotted line, which he immediately erased. Then, apparently to make the whole more symmetrical, he completed the drawing with the other self-contributed triangle.

Our review of the experiments on remembering and our observations of particular examples, such as those above, indicate that remembering is more a process of construction than of reproduction. According to Bartlett, whose theory has guided us in this discussion, "Remembering is an imaginative reconstruction, or construction, built out of the relation of our attitude towards a whole active mass of organized past reactions [traces], and to a little outstanding detail which commonly appears in image or in language form."

An act or remembering involves the trace left by the experience to be remembered, interaction of this trace with the integrated organization of traces from the individual's entire background of experience, and the creative process of reconstruction. As Bartlett says, "Remembering obviously involves determination by the past." From past experience the individual develops an active organization of traces, which Bartlett calls "schemata." In remembering however, the individual, at least in part, *infers* the past from his present cognitive structure—of hypotheses, assumptions, interests, and attitudes. It is as though the individual said to himself: "This and this and this must have occurred in order that my present state should be what it is." In remembering something, often the first thing to emerge is an attitude. The constructed recall justifies the attitude. The original trace probably determines the attitude, the general form of the event, and some vivid detail. From these the individual "constructs the probable detail."

Summary

Accumulating knowledge for both present and lifetime goals is a complex function involving the interrelated process of learning, remembering, and forgetting. In the elementary and secondary school, children do not simply march forward, mastering the sequences of concepts and skills as they are presented. Earlier-learned concepts and skills can either interfere with or facilitate their mastery. And later-learned concepts and skills can either impair or facilitate their retention and application. As teachers, we are concerned with efficient learning, sustained retention, and effective application of the concepts and skills children learn. Hence we need to understand and to control the complex of factors involved.

Delayed tests have revealed that retention depends upon the nature of what is learned and upon the opportunities for review and applications. There is often rapid and extensive forgetting of unrelated details. But meaningful, well-mastered, and frequently reviewed or applied concepts are retained for long periods of time. And when conditions are such that transfer can operate, delayed retention and application of concepts and skills may be better then immediate recall.

Forgetting, like learning, is an active process. It does not consist merely of the fading of memory traces in the nervous system. On the contrary, several factors cause us to forget the concepts and skills we learn. Because of proactive inhibition, our accumulating stores of knowledge sometimes make it more difficult to memorize and to recall subsequently placed material. And later-learned concepts sometimes retroact to inhibit accurate recall of earlier-learned content. The changes an individual undergoes—changes in his way of thinking and reasoning, and in his beliefs, attitudes, and interests—are likely to modify his recall of earlier-learned concepts. Changes in the original leaning and the recall situations, such as the elimination of certain relevant cues and the addition of distracting ones, can also prevent accurate recall of once-remembered concepts or skills. Moreover, an incompatible mental set at the moment of recall can divert an individual from accurate recall of an earlier-learned behavior pattern. And sometimes our need to avoid anxiety can cause us to repress recall of a painful experience. In addition to these active causes of forgetting on going metabolic activities play some part in erasing memory traces from the nervous system.

In the light of our understanding of the causes of forgetting and of other conditions which favor retention, we can suggest several ways of facilitating retention of the concepts and skills children and youth need to remember. The curriculum should be comprised of meaningful material organized for the discovery, developmental expansion, and continuous application of significant principles. The approach to learning should emphasize understating and the inductive discovery of principles rather then rote memorization. By conscientiously providing for the conditions of effective learning, teachers can guide children to the attainment of high levels of mastery and effective functional organizations of the concepts they learn. Even meaningful, organized, and well-mastered concepts and skills are forgotten, however, unless they are reviewed. Review is essential for sustained retention. It should consist of systematically scheduled periods of the relearning of test-discovered forgotten concepts, of the integration of new concepts into functional organizations of accumulating knowledge, and of provisions for continuous and extended applications of the expanding systems of principles being learned. Retention is also facilitated by relating the curriculum to children's interests; by appropriate consideration of and guidance in the development of their beliefs, attitudes, and self-concepts; by establishing intentions to remember useful concepts; and by developing mental sets for the recall and application of them in an ever-increasing variety of problem situations.

As integration of all the facts we have reviewed, both on the causes of forgetting and on the ways of facilitating retention, suggests that remembering is not a passive reproduction of previous experience. Our review supports Bartlett's theory that remembering involves both reproduction and creative reconstruction. In remembering an experience, the individual often reproduces only its general form and some of the vivid details and then constructs the probable details in harmony with his present cognitive structure. The condensations, elaborations, substitutions, and inventions characteristic of memory are contribute from the individual's general system of traces—to suit his present logical assumptions, beliefs, interests, and attitudes.

At any particular moment in the individual's sequence of learnings, his present cognitive structure provides a probable solution in both the learning and memory problems he meets. Each new learning experience, however, leaves a residual trace in the nervous system which interacts with the organization of trace systems previously established from his entire background of prior experiences. Thus new experiences are constantly changing the organization of trace systems. When a learned behavior pattern is recalled, the reproduction is affected both by the residual trace from the specific experience to be recalled and by the individual's total organization of trace systems, with which the original trace and traces from all intervening experiences have integrated. It is more correct, therefore, to think of learning as a *reorganization* than an addition to the individual's cognitive structure. And in this manner of thinking, it is more accurate to think of memory as a process of reconstruction than of reproduction.

In previous Chapters. we have presented the functions, supporting experiments, and varied applications of six essential conditions of effective learning: readiness, motivation, guidance in structuring approaches to learning tasks, repeated trials and perception of the effects in the trial-and-check process, and transfer. In the present chapter we have discovered that these same conditions facilitate sustained retention. They are pervasive factors in the acquisition, retention, and application of the concepts and skills we learn. Transfer, for example, is both an essential condition of effective learning and retention and an effective test of retention. But as we learned in previous Chapter, there is a seventh condition of effective learning. Like readiness, it is supplementary, although nonetheless essential, condition.

For effective operation of the first six conditions of learning, the learner also needs confidence, a self-concept of competency, and healthy relations with his classmates—with whom he achieves both academic and personal-social-development objectives. Otherwise, anxiety, feelings of inferiority, and social maladjustment may produce self-protective defenses which impair his intellectual efficiency. In the next three chapters we shall consider this condition of effective learning—mental health social adjustment.

9

Teaching of Chemistry

In any discipline, whether in the physical sciences, the life sciences, or the humanities, the first, or introductory, course offered the student is the one assuming the greatest responsibility. The manner in which it is presented may attract or repel our young student, who at this point in his educational career may not appreciate the worth of knowledge in any area. We, as teachers, must honestly present the basic fundamentals without overwhelming him with rigor. The physical sciences in general, and chemistry in particular, face the dilemma of establishing the limits of arithmetical rigor.

There have been changes over the decades not only in the depth of understanding of the forces operating in our physical universe but also in ways of presenting even the more esoteric aspects of chemistry, so that now much can be presented in a fashion comprehensible to the student taking his first course.

I should like to express a few personal convictions concerning this first course under several arbitrarily chosen subheadings: to whom the course should be addressed—that is, just who our clientele is; what kinds of individuals are best suited to assume this teaching responsibility; and what might be the content if, for instance, this is the only science course included in a student's curriculum. With the content suggested, what are the expectations from this course? Can it be a true learning experience, or is it only to be a line item on a transcript showing that a "group requirement" has been fulfilled?

FOR WHOM AND WHY?

I am fully aware of the point of view, both expressed and in some institutions put into practice, that what is good for the major in the first is good for everyone—a sort of "What's good for General Bullmoose..." philosophy. Certain of our elite technical schools have indeed functioned successfully on this principle. Many of us have followed such courses with great interest, stealing liberally from them, but most teachers have responsibilities to a student body chosen from other than the small percentage of high school graduates who desire a technical or engineering education. On the other hand, the introductory course may be in danger of overfragmentation, a situation that in the past occurred in my own institution. To begin with, there were special sections for the chemistry majors, others for the students of premedicine, predentistry, prepharmacy, prenursing, agriculture (with its subdivisions), engineering, *ad nauseam.* To further complicate the issue, each of the subdivisions was later split into two sections—one for students with, and another for students without, a secondary-school chemistry course. Still another kind of subsection added in more recent years and adding to the woes of staffing and logistics was the course for those who had received one of the special secondary courses such as CHEMS (Chemical Education Materials Study), CBA (Chemical Bond Approach), or some other accelerated course, or who had more than one year of high school chemistry. Few colleges or universities can afford the luxury of staffing such a multitude of courses or sections, even if they serve a pedagogic purpose.

A number of years of experience has convinced me that there is indeed a need for certain subdivisions in the introductory course. The student who will take additional work in chemistry deserves different content from the student who may never take another science course in his academic life. One would think that all the problems inherent in the science course for the non-science-oriented student would have been solved, in view of the number of sponsored conferences, symposia, and papers on the subject; but it is obvious that a general solution has not yet been found, nor can I hope to offer one within the next few pages.

The number of introductory courses that should be offered, as well as the content of each, can be in part determined by keeping open lines of communication with other colleges of a university or with departments within a college. This is a sound, but often ignored, policy. It is not unusual to find a college or department expressing concern that its students must compete with students from some other college or department where a more extensive background is required in a particular subject. While this might seem to provide some justification for offering different introductory courses to students from different fields, the number of courses must be kept at a minimum. The size of the staff will be a major consideration in establishing the total number of courses to be scheduled. One plan, that of dividing the students into four categories, has operated with some success in my own institution. In this suggested grouping it has still been possible to make modifications and improvements in course content as well as in methodology.

Group I consists of students who have elected to major in the subject (though in a substantial number of cases the decision may have been ill-advised). These students will, of course, receive exhaustive treatment of the subject matter in subsequent years of training.

Group II comprises the preprofessional students in a related field (such as premedical or paramedical) who will take one or more courses in chemistry in addition to the introductory one, having found enough appeal in that course to attract them to science. This group is often categorized as the "science major group."

Group III consists of students of technology and engineering, most of whom have a high proficiency in mathematics and have taken, or are taking concurrently, physics, mathematics, and various technical courses required for their curricula. Experience has proved that such students may find the usual introductory course insufficiently satisfying or challenging because of the low level of aptitude in math expected.

Group IV is made up of the large, important, and heterogeneous body of students who will take no additional science courses and who may well be taking this particular chemistry course only to satisfy a graduation "group requirement."

All the students in these four categories—even students in Groups I and II, whose curricula for the most part will include additional courses in chemistry—deserve an introductory course that is more than a "prerequisite." I have not been satisfied with the generally accepted definition of a prerequisite course. Such a course is too often considered as one including only material that is essential to the understanding of the next course in the sequence. In my opinion, a prerequisite course should offer information, concepts of general interest, subject content, and intellectual tools—material that will stand on its own merit and perhaps will not be repeated or even elaborated upon in any later course.

Even though, in a university structure, the students in Group III, technology students, usually all come from a college of engineering, they are not especially homogeneous in their background, interests, or needs. The engineer preparing himself, for instance, for a career in waste and sewage disposal will need far more in the way of bio-chemistry than could ever be given in any introductory chemistry course. His requirements obviously would be different from those of the mechanical or electrical engineer. Yet all students of engineering, like students in any other discipline, should learn about the "chemically oriented" problems facing our society.

The students in group IV represent not only the greatest challenge but also the greatest opportunity. In this group we are likely to find that student attitudes vary from great interest and curiosity to outright rebellion against science. We often encounter a student who desires open dialogue with the teacher. Many of the students may even wonder, "Why must I learn this crap?" And some students want to know, with some justification, how a one-term course in chemistry can possibly prepare them adequately to understand the complex environmental and production problems facing us today. The subject matter orientation, especially the laboratory, is in special need of relating to current problems—energy obviously high on the list—as they affect our societal problems.

TAUGHT BY WHOM?

Unfortunately, in teaching there *are* no uniform prerequisites or universally accepted qualifications that could be guaranteed to produce optimum results in any course. The success or failure of a course—especially for students such as those in Group IV—depends on the genuineness, skill, and enthusiasm of the instructor. These attributes are not necessarily found only in the teacher with many years of experience. In fact, in nearly thirty years of teaching and assigning duties, I have found that some of the most imaginative, enthusiastic, and effective teaching has been done by young, newly appointed staff members. They often try new techniques, unencumbered with the bias that they "won't work." Occasionally, the teacher with a great research background and international reputation in his field, but experienced only in teaching upper-level and graduate courses, finds that teaching an introductory course is filled with frustrations. Many of these frustrations stem from a need for the teacher to develop from "scratch" the students' scientific vocabulary. The further removed the teacher is from the time when he himself was developing this vocabulary, the more difficult he may find it to lecture, to demonstrate and discuss subject matter requiring it.

The instructor of any introductory course is not likely to be effective over the years unless he is sufficiently interested in both subject matter and methodology to involve himself in research programs, which may cover a wide range. Thus, it is not necessary for him to be the leader of, or even a part of, a research empire involving expensive instruments and large expenditures from granting agencies, though quality teaching often does indeed come from such persons. The research may involve innovative teaching experiments or scholarly writing based upon experiences in anything from examination procedures to laboratory experiments.

Graduate and undergraduate teaching assistants can make important contributions. A new staff member fresh from his graduate or postdoctoral work may, with proper supervision, bring this freshness to the introductory course. However, new assistants should be given some orientation to cover such items as the level of the course and what can be expected of the students, the operation of and techniques used in recitation sections, preparation of quiz material, logistics and operation of the laboratory, preparation of grades, conduct of tutorial sessions, and safety operations in the laboratory. The interest and efficiency of his new assistants should enhance the experienced professor's own teaching effectiveness.

CONTENT AND PRESENTATION

The content of the introductory course should change—and in most institutions has changed—as research provides us with new and better explanations of natural phenomena. There is also a need for flexibility as departments and colleges served by the chemistry department change their own course offerings and credit values and as new emphases are placed within their own disciplines. In the sixties and seventies long-overdue modifications in curricula have brought about changes that require the student to have a better understanding of his environment and especially ways of healing and improving it. The chemistry courses at all levels must reflect these attitudes. The ways in which it is best accomplished are not easily defined.

The content of the courses for majors continues to change in keeping with the ever-increasing depth and complexity of the subject. The holder of a baccalaureate degree is expected to have some mastery of a myriad of topics. To present them all, it is necessary to increase the number and depth of upper-level courses, with an unfortunate concomitant—condensing or eliminating a foundation introductory course. It is assumed, without pedagogic justification, that all secondary school preparatory courses are identical and are sufficient to allow a student to plunge into a rigorous treatment of the subject with little or no review of "general" principles. However, I feel strongly that even science majors with a strong secondary school background in mathematics and chemistry can benefit from a good introductory course. The course can present a survey of factual information that will be treated later in greater depth in more advanced courses and can cover many topics as well—such as certain aspects of analytical chemistry—which have been abbreviated or even avoided in upper-level courses.

A few generalities concerning content and methodology in teaching the introductory course, based on my own experience, are presented below. Most of them have been found applicable to any of our four student groupings.

No theoretical concept should be presented without demonstrating its practical application. This approach does not imply that "backyard and kitchen chemistry" should fill each hour of every day of instruction. It does mean that the very important and all-too-often neglected concepts of descriptive chemistry can be developed concurrently with theory and not relegated to specific sections of the course or gleaned from specific chapters of a text. The instructor can strengthen his points and make his discussion more interesting by injecting "real life" observations relevant to the subject under discussion. The examples he cites should be related, if possible, to the geographic area of the institution or touch upon topics that appeal to the interests of the majority of the students. Obviously, this kind of approach is easier for the more experienced teacher to undertake than for the novice. However, there are literature sources that can be tapped for use by the less experienced teacher.

The lecture experiment should be used more often than the classical lecture demonstration. The former is designed to be more of a challenge to the student's power of observation. Data are derived from a lecture table experiment, which the student is expected to analyze rather than simply observe. If discussion sections are provided as part of the course structure—as they should be—the data can be further evaluated as a class project. (The student will, of course, be tested at the next hour exam on the principles that are part of the experiment.) These lecture experiments are not intended as a substitute for the individually performed laboratory experiments, but they do provide the student an opportunity to observe chemical phenomena that in some instances might not be possible for him to produce in the laboratory because of insufficient time, inadequate equipment, or logistic limitations. The student entering any introductory course is entitled to see, feel, and smell chemistry early in his course career.

The nonscience major (Group IV) can be easily overwhelmed and even discouraged when his first confrontation in a chemistry course is entirely arithmetical. My first class meeting is generally devoted to a series of simple (noninstrumental) experiments that are reasonably spectacular from the visual and auditory standpoint. All instructors may well not choose identical experiments, for there are many demonstrations involving elemental combinations, some of which require energy of activation and some of which do not, that are satisfactory. The "whys" of the reactions demonstrated may be explained to the class in detail at the *end* of the course, after the concepts have been mastered. As principles are developed, it is possible to apply most of them either to this set of lecture experiments or to others which are incorporated into the course as it progresses.

Variation in degree of mathematical rigor in the introductory course is one of the major points differentiating the four categories of students from one another. For instance, the technologically oriented student (Group III) finds no special pain in adapting himself to the logic and mathematics of a reaction rate study, though he may be troubled considerably by the difference between the chemical behavior of an iodine ion and an iodine atom. A more significant point is whether this student really needs or benefits from the usual treatment of the subject of reaction rates. Perhaps a lecture or laboratory experiment more directly related to that which he will encounter later in his professional career would serve better. Instead of one of the classical rate studies, the engineering student might find a corrosion rate of more interest, treated more qualitatively than quantitatively. Although different experiments cannot be designed of every conceivable curriculum, it is possible, even for larger numbers of students, to design experiments with interests and arithmetical rigor in keeping with the students' previous training and future needs.

It is possible for even the most elementary course in science to be "derivation-happy." The purist never uses an equation or a principle without starting, so to speak, from ground zero, or at least with the First and Second Laws. Time and common sense tell us that many relationships—equations included—can be treated as intellectual tools, which serve a specific purpose in providing information about nature without being dissected, probed, integrated, and differentiated. However, there are times when the student gains much from showing how an equation can be derived starting with experimentally determined data.

Sometimes, too, mathematical rigor can be sacrificed for practicality, as long as in so doing chemical fallacies are not introduced. It is effective and necessary at times to deal with less than "the whole truth." A one- or two-term introductory course in any discipline, especially chemistry, neither can nor should be a mere "packet" covering all of the major topics that are part of that discipline. I have suffered through many nationally convened conferences, as well as intra- and interdepartmental committee sessions, considering lists of topics as long as your arm and promising that a certain number of hours will be devoted to each one, regardless of how the topics seem to mesh into an integrated whole. There must be a better way of "teaching school" than by instruction via a "hamburgerized cafeteria line." Of course, it is possible to be boxed in by the above philosophy, since there must always be topical coverage. But the basic question is: What is the best way to wave subject matter concerning these topics into a homogeneous whole, covering as few topics as possible, yet providing enough scientific thought and reasoning?

If time and satisfactory reference sources permit, one approach is to use an already established and accepted technique of, first, developing the major structural concepts of matter (nuclear, atomic, and molecular); second, discussing the moving or dynamic forces of nature; and third, using considered judgment upon a select body of synthetic aspects of matter, stressing those that will best relate to the student's own experiences in his daily life. The gross inadequacies of text material were made clear to me when I searched a score or more of introductory texts to see whether any of them suggested, for instance, dangers in the production of chlorine and caustic by mercury cells. I had hoped that at least one text might suggest that good housekeeping operations should be used in waste disposal, yet none did. Neither did any of the texts examined suggest the possible aftereffects (pollution potential) of herbicides, insecticides, and pesticides. Up to the years bordering the decade of the seventies, no author seemed concerned with the chemistry of biodegradability at a level that might be understood by the nonscience major. More recently such material is given its due and more, but it has taken ecological disaster to goad the authors. No one seemed to think it important to tell something of the biochemistry of sulfides, fluorides, azides, or cyanides as poisons, though all did mention the chemistry of carbon monoxide poisoning. Obviously, enough of the basic principles—theory—should be provided to allow understanding, but the introductory course would be "meatless" if it were designed only as a recitation of descriptive facts, no matter how "relevant," without the challenge of "why."

If the course is so abbreviated (perhaps a ten-week or one-quarter course) that this three-pronged approach is not possible, the core theme may be used. Many institutions have presented courses with a variety of such core themes. Still another approach is the use of the case history. I prefer the core theme, using the concepts of structure as that core. It is obvious that structure is also too broad a topic to do more than chip away at the edges, but more can be done with it that will be both directly and indirectly useful to the student than with many other common themes.

No two teachers need stress the same structural concepts, but a common framework of nomenclature should be developed and the nature of both organic and inorganic matter explored. A current theme, and a workable one, is "energy," emphasizing the interfacing of the materials of science with the problems of energy production and consumption.

Technology has provided the teacher with a myriad of teaching devices and aids. Given enough money, we can use an increasing number of technological teaching aids.

Closed circuit television, quality films, loops, projection devices of many kinds, armchair lab kits, computer devices, model systems of virtually as many variations as there are teachers, and teaching machines for self-evaluation—all of these can be used with varying degrees of success.

Over the years I have incorporated these aids into my teaching, although I am convinced that every device that removes the teacher from the student has some deleterious effect. Even in large classes a teacher should be able to project himself and his subject without a large number of mechanical aids. A chemical principle developed, albeit laboriously, on a good, well-illuminated blackboard in a good lecture auditorium, even with occasional errors of omission and commission (which the students delight in catching), by a teacher available for after-class consultation is a very effective way of diminishing, if not eliminating, the student-teacher gap.

Certainly it is easier to flash on a screen in the darkened lecture hall predawn or copied material of great perfection, but most of such material is already available to the student in a rather good teaching aid known as the textbook. (This relatively primitive device has an "information retrieval" system, can be read at any speed (within bounds), and possesses many other qualities that technology has only recently matched—"slow motion," "stop action," and even "instant playback.")

The teacher can close, bridge, and eventually eliminate the student-teacher gap mentioned above with a concurrent sharing of the facts of our discipline in a way both acceptable to and digestible by the students.

10

Teaching of Theater Arts

Acting, and participation in theater, can foster the development of the whole personality, strengthening self-confidence and independent action in a setting that encourages communal relationships and sensitivity to others. Drama involves us with man-kind, helps us escape from egocentricity, develops our capacity for intimacy. The anxiety that accompanies learning is handled within the work, as part of the problem of performing. Flexibility and openness to change are rewarded. Performing is a high-risk activity, but it brings both immediate and long-range rewards. The actor's ability to make choices and to act decisively is an essential ingredient of his success as a performer. The play is an integrated moral, emotional, intellectual, and sensual universe; it demands of all those who work with it a commensurate integrity of body, mind, and soul.

There are dangers in theater, of course. Performing can be selfish, analysis can be lifeless, competition can be fierce. However, the rewards of successful theater can contribute directly to the goals articulated in this book—the types of challenging, flexible, mature learning that are truly responsive to the varied needs of a changing society and its diverse members.

The wide range of disciplines represented in theatrical activity makes drama an ideal subject for imparting a general education, enhancing artistic sensibility, and fostering the capacity to work as a member of a team. However, in a society such as ours, in which theatrical activity is rather limited (compared, for example, with the theater in countries like Germany, the Scandinavian countries, France, or England), the practical applicability of theater studies is still somewhat questionable. There are, accordingly, considerable differences in the objectives and attitudes of different drama or theater departments—and not a little confusion about the definition of such objectives.

In some cases, theater studies are pursued as a vocational type of training and aim at producing professional directors, actors, designers, and theater technicians. In others, the objective is to produce theater scholars, highly versed in the analysis and interpretation of dramatic texts and in the history and sociology of the theater. Both lines of training can lead to posts in other theater departments teaching theater skills to further generations of students. But theater training can also be part of the training of elementary and high school teachers specializing in the use of drama as a teaching aid and educational method. In addition, theater departments regard their activity as simply part of a wider general humanistic education for undergraduates, who, by participating in productions and taking survey courses of theater history and dramatic literature, will be better able to enjoy drama as theatergoers. And, finally, theater departments also fulfill the function of supply theater to their communities and therefore provide a vital cultural service to the colleges and universities of which they are a part. All these objective are desirable and wholly legitimate, provided that theater departments design separate programs to fulfill each, rather than leaving the distinctions undefined and offering a compromise program that covers all the objectives only superficially.

THEATER STUDIES

In order to evaluate the place of theater in the American college of the future, we should first consider the scope of theater studies and the skills that such studies are designed to develop. As suggested earlier, one of the special characteristics of theater or drama training is its interweaving of theoretical and practical knowledge from a variety of different fields.

Theoretical Studies: On the theoretical plane, the study of theater overlaps with the wider field of general *literary history*—the study of texts within their historical context. This includes textual criticism—for example, to establish a valid text for the plays of Shakespeare—and the study of the historical and social background of the great drama of the past, which in turn includes social, intellectual, and religious history. For example, to understand the masterpieces of Athenian tragedy of the fifth century B.C., one needs to understand the religious myths of the ancient Greeks and the organization of Greek city-states as well as the political history of the times—for instance, the relationship between certain thematic concerns in the plays of Aeschylus or Euripides and the events of the Persian and Peloponnesian wars of their time. As drama mirrors life, an understanding of the drama of any period requires familiarity with the social and political conditions of that time.

But the study of drama does not merely call for an understanding of the *content* of theatrical masterpieces; of equal importance is a grasp of the *formal* aspects—that is, the esthetics of drama as they have changed through the centuries. This implies a study of the general principles of literary form, the methodology of the analysis and interpretation of texts, and a knowledge of the development of the critical vocabulary of drama from Aristotle to the theorists of our own time. As drama is an eminently social form of art, this again leads toward social history and, as drama overlaps with so many of the other arts (architecture, painting, music), toward the history of art in general. For example, no understanding of drama is possible without a knowledge of the evolution of theater architecture or the development of the use of perspective in painting.

An awareness of the historical, literary, and social context of drama must, however, also be linked with the ability of analyze and discuss its technical and esthetic aspects. This leads to a study of the methodology of *criticism* and its vocabulary. The techniques of criticism are essential for all who work in the theater, not only for those who specialize in writing about the theater for newspapers, periodicals, or scholarly journals. The director will not be able to communicate with action or designers, and the latter will not be able to understand the director, if they are not skilled in the techniques of discourse about drama. Hence drama is a field in which the methodology of criticism is of the utmost practical importance.

Another practical application of the skills just described is in the teaching of creative writing in the theater. It is from the analysis of great texts of the past and a comprehension of the esthetic theories on which they were based, as well as from the ability to think an talk about the principles of their own creative process, that budding play-wrights can acquire those elements of their craft which *can* be taught, although it is clear that creative talent itself, the imaginative power of genius, lies outside the field of academic study.

Finally, there is the study of the performance aspects of theater—the history of theatrical performance and its techniques, as distinct from the literary history of drama. Theater history is a fascinating field, which straddles a great number of subjects: the social position of actors, their techniques of speaking and movement, the history of costume, the history of directing, and a multitude of others.

From the above it will be seen that the *theoretical* study of drama opens up access to what, if it is properly structured, would give the student a good general education in the humanities: the drama of the past cannot be understood without an awareness of history, philosophy, and sociology. Moreover, the study of drama also involves the development of *practical* skills, which are no less important and in many ways complement the theoretical side.

Acting: The art of acting is central to theater studies. Acting requires a unique combination of intellectual, emotional, and physical aptitudes. The actor uses his own body as his expressive instrument, and hence the training of the body—its movement and flexibility, the strength and modulational range of the voice, the expressiveness of the features—is of utmost importance. But these physical factors are at the service of a creative imagination and an analytical mind. The actor or actress has to understand the motivations of the character he or she portrays. He must develop an imaginative grasp of his character's psychology. And, to do so, he must also understand the character's social background, mode of dress, and the whole intellectual and social universe he inhabits. In addition, the actor, as an interpretative artist called upon to infuse life into the text provided by an author, must understand the structural principles upon which the play as a whole is build. He must grasp its rhythm, its inherent poetic pattern and style. There is also, of course, improvisational acting, in which the actor is, as it were, his own poet.

Acting is in fact the paradigmatic theatrical activity, for theater primarily exists in the performance of texts, and from the performers spring those qualities that are unique to theater. It is worth pausing to consider the kind of person an actor must be, what skills he needs to acquire, and how this actor "personality" fits into the university environment.

What does the actor do? While it is commonly assumed that the actor's central skill is the ability to imitate other people's actions, and to imaginatively enter their lives, actors in fact are good only insofar as they can find the character's emotions within themselves. If the actor is emotionally agile—"loose," in the terms of the profession—he can summon up almost any feeling at will from his own experience. Carefully assembling these feelings, he develops or suggests the "character" demanded by the text. Thus, the actor must confront, within himself, many feelings, impulses, and desires he may consciously dislike, find foreign or forbidden. In order to deal with such "taboo" experiences, he must free himself from prejudice and develop a certain playful and tentative relationship to his own feelings; he must be willing to dissolve the normal boundaries of his ego. The ability to take emotional risks, to delight in strange experiences, and to refrain from overcontrolling his reactions is the mark of a fine actor. It is clear from many statements in Part One of this book, such as Weathersby's chapter on ego development and Douvan's chapter on intimacy, that these qualities are important for learning and change in any area.

What further complicates the actor's task is the communal nature of theater. Unlike much of the learning in the academy, acting is done with other people, to other people, in front of other people. In fact, plays are primarily concerned with relationships. An actor's attention is centered on his fellow actors' feelings and gestures. his performance is dependent to a great extent on others: on the technical and artistic staff as well as on his fellow actors. If he is not a deeply "empathetic" personality, capable of swift and accurate responses to changes in other people's attitudes, he cannot perform. The actor works out of an intuitive sense of interpersonal demands. His very body must change, subtly but exactly, in response to the needs and pressures generated by others. Acting thus trains us to be responsive to others, and further, to accept the influence of others on our lives and thought. As such, it offers a way to lead all students, especially those who have withdrawn from the complexities of community, into an awareness of the fundamental interdependence of human beings.

Acting not only demands new kinds of empathy, interpersonal competence, and the capacity for intimacy. It asks the actor to think in special ways. In a play, thought is always concrete, embodied in an action or event, in a gesture, tone, or word. One cannot act a concept, one can only perform those actions which reveal or evoke thought. The actor is forced to connect the conceptual and physical realms, and find ways to move easily from one to the other. He learns the limitations of thought: he cannot perform everything he thinks or imagines. Indeed, the nature of the theatrical script reinforces this qualification and criticism of pure thought. Thus, Kolb's experiential learning cycle underlies the creation of every character.

In a play, no person knows or embodies the "truth" of the work. All characters live in a "contextual" and "relativistic" world such as that discussed by Gilligan in her chapter on moral development. Each character displays or encounters his versions of "truth" through his confrontation with other characters' assertions of their own truths. Ideologies grow out of human needs and feelings. The actor must discover the connections between what a character wants and how he thinks. Consider, for example, how the concept of action is presented in *Hamlet;* we understand the concept by watching very different people enact their own conceptions of action within the specific circumstances of their lives. For Claudius, action is plotting, for Laertes it is impulsiveness, for Ophelia it is a retreat from thought into unrestrained feeling, or madness. The play's "thought" arises from the confrontation of these concrete modes of behavior, from a rhythmic, dynamic, complex meeting and opposition of wills. Generally, the academy tends to suffer from an imperialism of the intellect, a one-sided evaluation of the nature and quality of thought-in-the-world. Theater can do much to humanize and refine our understanding of the place and power of ideas. For those students who come late to the academy, rich in experience but with little training in abstract thought, it can offer a bridge from the familiar flow of events they know to the abstract world of knowledge.

Finally, the actor must accept himself as a limited and conditioned being, tied through sympathy and need to other beings more or less like himself. He must not judge himself or others as he performs; he must accept his feelings and those of his fellow actors. He must forgo the temptation to control events, remembering that his first task is to make his character, as drawn in the script, come alive. True, for others his performance will have meaning and resonance, but if the actor attempts to predetermine this meaning and his effect on an audience, he destroys his character's believability.

To summarize: Acting introduces the student to modes of thought and feeling not common in the university. Above all, it asks from the student an organic, unified response to life. The performer's actions resonate through the three psychic tiers of his reason, will, and passion. He conspires with his opposites, he finds himself in self-forgetfulness and discipline, he achieves wholeness through conflict. Acting combines the traditional academic good of withdrawal, observation, and understanding with a passionate involvement in what is immediate, sensual, and changing.

Directing: The director, as the coordinator of the whole performance, must obviously be well versed and fully trained in the craft of acting. In addition he or she must possess the critical and analytical skill to grasp the meaning and structure of the play, as well as the expressive power and the vocabulary to communicate these insights to the actors and the other members of the company: the set designer, the costume designer, the lighting designer, the stage manager, and the other technicians. But these skills are only the technical basis for the director's work. In addition, she must possess—and training must try to impart—the full gamut of leadership qualities associated with the field of management. The director must be able to inspire confidence in her cast and crew; she must have the charisma that induces people to work hard and give of their best. And she must display the organizational capabilities needed to assure the smooth flow of the production process, which involves difficult problems of logistics and the accomplishment of an intricate structure of interdependent tasks within a narrowly defined time schedule. A successful director must thus posses a multitude of talents, some of which dearly are inherent in her given personality, but many of which can be greatly enhanced by a well-designed course of intellectual and practical training.

Technical Skills. The design functions (set, costumes, lighting) clearly derive from their own special fields: set design from painting and architecture, costume design from dress design and fashion, and lighting design from electrical engineering. But in order for these skills to be applied in the theater, the *designers* must be able to understand the nature and requirements of drama. They must be capable of reading a text with a clear understanding of how their contribution can enhance the totality of the dramatic experience. They must therefore be highly familiar with the techniques of acting: placing a door in the right area of the stage, for example, might greatly enhance the expressive power of an actor's entrance or exit, the cut of a costume might help an actor tremendously in giving effect to his gestures, and the details of the costume provide important clues to characterization; the lighting of the play might be important in enhancing mood and focusing attention on the aspects of the action the director wants to emphasize. The *theater technicians,* too—scene painters, carpenters, stagehands, and the rest—all contribute to a theatrical event and must be fully aware of the part their work plays in the total production. For example, a scene change that lasts only a few minutes longer than the rhythm of the play demands might destroy the effect of a whole act or even the entire play.

The coordination of the technical flow of the production is the task of the *stage manager.* Stage management is an important and highly specialized skill, which is also part of the training provided by theater and drama departments. This, too, demands complete familiarity with all processes involved, a grasp of the intellectual and artistic implications of the play as well as strong organizational and leadership abilities.

Some theater departments also provide courses in *theater administration,* an area where theater studies overlap with general management and business training. Here a thorough knowledge of the vast field of union rules and regulations, fund-raising techniques, publicity, and public relations is as essential as complete familiarity with techniques of selling tickets, accounting, and tax law.

What unites and integrates all these extremely diverse functions is the need, for every member of the highly diversified team, to be fully conversant with the dramatic and theatrical qualities of the end product of their efforts, the finished play. The box office manager as well as the stage carpenter and the musical director must be able to read and analyze a text and he aware of its potentialities and requirement. The box office manager must recognize its potential attractiveness to audiences; the carpenter must solve the technical problems required for optimum realization of the text's potential; the musical director must understand the type and amount of music the play will require—and so on through all the different functions involved in producing a play.

THE WORK OF DRAMA DEPARTMENTS

There is, over and above these multiple specialized skills, a central core of purely theatrical, dramatic knowledge that everyone who works in theater must possess, or at least understand in its essentials. It is this general core of theatrical knowledge that integrates the work of theater or drama departments. And it is this central subject that must form the basis of all instruction. Essentially, this amounts to imparting the skills required to read a dramatic text in such a way that the performance can be fully and graphically imagined in all its aspects. This entails training in the analysis of texts, which, by their very nature, require careful decoding to determine the relationships of the characters, the style of performance required, and the theatrical effects envisioned by the author. To achieve mastery of this skill, *all* members of the theatrical team, the humblest as well as the most creative, must at one time or another have been involved in all aspects of the production process. The actors should have worked as stagehands or box office managers and the stagehands as actors.

If these considerations inform the educational practices of theater departments, theater training will become a veritable character training process. Each member of the theatrical team must learn the need for discipline, the virtues and necessity of cooperation, regard for the contributions of other members of the collective, and respect for the importance of each element and specialized skill that goes into creating the total effect. Training in the analysis of texts will sharpen the capacity to think clearly and logically, to analyze human character, and to understand the social conditions and manners of distant periods or different civilizations. Involvement in acting will strengthen powers of observation, concentration, body and voice control, and the art of being relaxed while being intensely self-aware. and this is all over and above the specialized technical requirements of each theatrical specialty.

In view of all this, there can be little doubt that well-conceived drama training has much to offer students, whether or not they aspire to careers in theater. Drama training can clearly promote general personality development as well as teach a number of skills that can be used outside the theatrical context. The analytical techniques learned in the process of reading and understanding complex texts will enhance the individual's ability to read and reason. The improvisational techniques and theater games used in the training of actors develop the imagination and sharpen the individual's ability to react quickly and effectively to unexpected situations. The development of voice and body control will inevitably enhance one's capacity to express oneself and to present oneself to one's best advantage in any life situation.

DRAMA TRAINING IN THE FUTURE

Drama training and theatrical activity would thus appear to be ideal educational instruments for the college populations of the next decades. Drama is the most accessible of all literary forms, particularly in a society that, through the mass medium of television, is exposed to enormous amounts of dramatic material, however, inferior in artistic and intellectual quality it might be. The study of drama is particularly well suited to bringing middle-aged people who have hitherto not been exposed to high art and serious intellectual activity into contact with these fields. Drama opens a way into poetry, history, social problems, and philosophical speculation, and it does so in an amusing and exciting manner. At the same time, it provides a rich opportunity for human contact, as well as the opportunity to be noticed and admired, applauded and recognized. Nor does the fitting of older students into existing patterns of drama training present any difficulties. Indeed, drama and theater departments have tended to be hampered in their production activities by the absence of middle-aged and older students who could take on the parts of parents and character roles in plays requiring older persons. The professional skills that such older students would bring to the mounting of plays should be equally welcome and immediately appreciated, whether it is a housewife's skill in sewing, an electrician's ability to wire the lighting system, or a businessman's training in selling tickets or keeping the accounts. There is hardly one professional aptitude of this kind that could not be put to excellent use in the collective effort of theater production.

Depending upon the specific nature of student populations in different areas, special programs could be initiated to meet the needs of particular socioeconomic, ethnic, or age groups. Thus, for example, the production program could highlight certain types of drama whose subject matter would appeal to such groups: proletarian plays for people with a working-class background, plays from different ethnic cultures for Blacks, Armenians, Hungarians, Latvians, and so on. Plays could also be selected to deal with the problems of old age, the unemployed, or specific psychological problems of women at different life stages.

The therapeutic aspect of acting training and the socializing influence of teamwork could also be put to good use. A production team is, during the rehearsal process, a social unit of considerable cohesion and usually develops into a kind of ad hoc family group. Integration into such groups might well be of considerable benefit to people who feel lonely, isolated, or unfamiliar with the college and its mores. For such individuals, participation in the cooperative work of a drama project might well help to develop social allegiance and a sense of belonging. The therapeutic aspects of acting training have already been stressed. For elderly people or the middle-aged adjusting to a new environment, it could bring such benefits as enhanced emotional and physical flexibility, relaxation of body and mind, and increased concentration. Close physical and emotional contact with other people during the rehearsal process would also widen horizons, and participation in a variety of plays might well open up possibilities for new lifestyles and broaden social horizons.

Theater is particularly useful in restructuring the university because it involves learning through clearly defined projects. These projects have clear goals (performances, for example), clear time limits, and precise conditions. Moreover, dramatic projects, as we have indicated, are extremely flexible in choice of materials, in emphasis and approach, and in levels of competence demanded of the participants. A play can be performed casually, script in hand, or in full production; by amateurs or by would-be professionals; in classrooms or in hospitals or on street corners. People of very differing abilities, backgrounds, and age can work together, contributing skills their varying backgrounds have supplied. For example, older people can contribute expertise in carpentry or sewing or management without ever having previously acted. Acting projects can be tailored to the needs of a group; one may choose to use the project to develop literary or philosophical skills, or to enhance bodily awareness, to free feelings, or to create community. As long as the leader and the group agree on the aim, any dramatic project can be a complete and valuable experience.

DRAMA AND THE COMMUNITY

The increasing enrollment in drama and theater courses of older students from ethnically diverse backgrounds has significant implications for the community. In an age when the working week is likely to be progressively reduced, the increased leisure time at the disposal of the working population will present an ever more acute social problem. The training given by drama and theater departments to mature students who come directly from the working community will provide the expertise needed to organize community theater and amateur dramatic activities, which can provide valuable enrichment of leisure both for those who are active within them as performers and production auxiliaries and for the larger number who will attend as spectators.

The college or university can thus become a focal point and powerhouse for the cultural life of the community.

Through this link with the community and amateur dramatic activities, the university or college can become more closely involved in local activities. The people trained in the college who have become active in such theatrical undertakings can always return to the college for advice and help in tackling difficult conceptual problems, choosing or interpreting plays, or solving practical problems. These activities can, in turn, be integrated with the wider study projects of the university or college. For example, the college's theater department could work with community theaters to mount a cycle of related plays illustrating a theme such as race relations, local history, or the work of a specific playwright, such as Shakespeare or O'Neill, or to mount a community arts festival.

With the increasing employment of married women in jobs outside the home, older relatives are increasingly called upon to provide supervision for children. Here theater training might also be of considerable value, as it imparts skills specifically designed to create entertainment of educational value in and out of the context of formal schooling. The growth of children's' theater sections in university and college drama departments emphasizes this very important new application of theater studies. Training of both teachers and lay drama group leaders for children might therefore assume considerable social importance.

Another social development that may well call for drama training is the increasing use of drama as a method of communication, most obvious in the onslaught of television. A high proportion of television programming, from major drama productions to serials right down to television commercials (which are typically skillfully constructed minidramas), is in dramatic form. Hence an ability to criticize and evaluate this material and to recognize its formal esthetics and subliminal influences is vital if a responsible democracy is to be maintained in an age of manipulation of the masses through the media. The creation of a well-informed, critical public, able to judge the quality of the material as art and as social comment, is thus a pressing social need in our time. Training in the critical analysis of drama and in an evaluation of its practical aspects would go a long way toward meeting this need.

As a separate academic subject, the study of the theater arts—that is, dramatic art in theory and practice, including actual performance—is a relative newcomer to higher education in America.

The variously named Theater Arts, Drama, or Speech and drama Departments gradually evolved as extensions either of the study of rhetoric in speech departments or of English, when it was realized that at least some knowledge of the practice of performance might be helpful in the understanding of the texts of Shakespeare and other great playwrights.

As theater and drama departments evolved between the wars, and especially after World War II, impressive theater complexes arose in many American colleges and universities. The regular performance of plays, ranging from the classics of Greek drama to modern musicals, became an important cultural asset to the colleges and universities themselves as well as to their surrounding communities in areas otherwise lacking professional theater.

Theater, as an activity that involves intricately structured teamwork and the cooperation of people versed in a multitude of skills, from scene painting and electrical engineering to the highest forms of scholarly analysis or creative talent, naturally straddles a large range of disciplines, not all of which at first sight might appear to be in themselves academic subjects—for example, voice training, fencing, ballroom dancing, carpentry, tailoring, millinery, or the construction of property swords.

While this hybrid and somewhat amorphous nature of the subject has created a not inconsiderable number of problems and confusions in the definition of the purpose and methodology of drama and theater departments, it also presents tremendous advantages to any educational philosophy that stresses the need for development of the whole human personality. Theatrical activity can be seen as a microcosm of society itself, in which activities of the humblest physical kind are subtly orchestrated and blended with those of the highest intellectual and artistically creative nature to produce a harmoniously balanced whole, each part of which is interdependent with every other part of the final result, which is itself not a dead object but an ongoing, living process.

11

Teaching of Anthropology

Anthropology contributes to developmental education for adult development by—to paraphrase Kluckhohn's (1949) classic image–serving as a mirror for humankind in which it can see itself in its infinite variety. But that mirror also shows us certain patterns of uniformity. Are there implications here for developmentally oriented higher education such as that proposed in Part One?

As a discipline, anthropology is holistic–seeing humankind in both its biological and cultural dimensions, and studying cultures in their totality. It is also comparative, relativistic, eclectic, and strongly rooted in intensive fieldwork. In the United States, anthropology traditionally includes four subdisciplines: (1) physical anthropology, (2) archaeology, (3) cultural and social anthropology, and (4) anthropological linguistics. This makes anthropology the only discipline that is simultaneously a science, a social science, and a member of the humanities, giving it extraordinary potential as a tool for developmental education.

Within the academy, anthropology often has served as a gadfly. When other disciplines have constructed generalizations based on their research, we often have pointed out that the "generalizations" were based on observations made only in one culture or in one kind of culture, usually a European or

European-derived culture or a modern, industrial culture. "It may be true in Switzerland," we are fond of saying, "but not among the Puka Bora," We can assume this familiar stance regarding the findings of developmental education. Many of the generalizations about the nature of intellectual, personal, and moral development are based on studies limited to a very small range of the earth's peoples. We cannot yet be at all sure that the developmental "steps" and "stages" hypothesized by such writers as Piaget (1928), Erikson (1950), or Perry (1970) are universal or nearly so. One of our tasks as anthropologists is to help subject such schemes to further cross–cultural testing and verification.

After further cross–cultural testing, the findings and implications of education for adult development undoubtedly will be revised and modified. As they stand, however, they have implications for the teaching and learning of anthropology. This is true for the teaching and learning of anthropology at every level. However, in this chapter I will draw examples from the teaching of introductory college–level anthropology.

Most anthropologists feel that anthropology has an important place in the liberal arts curriculum and that underclass students should be exposed to the introductory course because it is "good for them." We rarely spell out how and why, preferring to view that as somehow self-evident. Even the classic work in the field. *The Teaching of Anthropology* (Mandelbaum, Lasker, and Albert, 1963), left many of these assumptions largely implicit. A partial exception was the paper by Bennett, "A Course in Comparative Civilizations," which listed some of the traits of freshmen thinking that this course was designed to correct or, at least, adapt itself to: concreteness, bipolar thinking, pragmatic bias, limited time perspective, ethnocentric attitudes, confusion, hesitance, and basic seriousness (Bennett, 1963). Most anthropologists who teach an introductory course in general anthropology or one of the four subfields have in their heads some such template characterizing their students, notions of changes they would like the course to make on that template, and some conception of the process by which those changes can be made to occur. In this chapter I try to make some of those assumptions explicit and relate them to the material in Part One of this volume.

ANTHROPOLOGY AND INTELLECTUAL DEVELOPMENT: TOWARD RELATIVISTIC THINKING

Intellectual development of traditional–age students is an important instructional goal in undergraduate anthropology courses. But, particularly in introductory courses, instructors have given equal weight to the humanistic concern of developing tolerance of other cultures. Sometimes the intellectual anthropological skills developed by the student are seen as a *means* to this humanistic end (see Bruner and Spindler, 1963). Under this model, anthropological study involves increasing one's tolerance of other cultures by learning about the cultural context of behavior and the relativity of cultural. However, following these steps usually brings about simultaneous achievement of another intellectual goal—shifting from absolutistic thinking to relativistic thinking (see Perry, 1970 and in this volume). The paradigms of intellectual and ethical development (Perry, 1970) show that this is the key intellectual task in undergraduate education. Implicitly or explicitly, we anthropologists recognize this as an outcome of effective teaching in our discipline. However, the attainment of parallel outcomes in moral and personal development is seen by many anthropologists as our discipline's unique mission in liberal education. I will say more about this later.

The Comparative Inductive Method: How do undergraduate anthropology courses facilitate the shift from absolutistic to relativistic thought? Introductory courses in general anthropology or in cultural and social anthropology always include some exposure to ethnographic descriptions of a sample of the varying forms of social and cultural institutions. The traditional–age beginning student thus learns of the existence of variation in patterns of basic aspects of culture that, up to now, he or she had taken for granted. The lesson is not completely a new one for most beginning students today. But even television exposure to other cultures and knowledge of self-conscious alternative "counter–culture" variants in our society do not prepare them for everything they will learn in an introductory course.

For reasons that Part One of this volume makes clear, the inductive method of teaching is particularly appropriate for presenting comparative material from other cultures in an introductory course. By immersing their students in materials about a *few*, carefully selected cultures, anthropology instructors strengthen the possibility that the student will reason from the particular to the general, inferring regularities for himself or herself. This helps to reinforce the shift in student perception of the locus of intellectual authority from external to internal (see Weathersby, this volume). However, this method requires exceptionally careful planning on the part of the instructor and considerable tolerance for ambiguity on his or her part. In the inductive method, outcomes do not follow a script.

The immersion-in-few-cultures method heavy use of discussion and dialogue, not all of which need be oral. The assignment of frequent papers is a way of enhancing the dialogue for those students whose learning styles are more oriented to written expression. Skilful instructors steer the dialogue to discussion of students' direct experience of their own culture or of cultures in which they have travelled in order to bring this dimension into the learning equation. Heavy use of written and oral dialogue with the students enables the instructor to shape the learning experience more to the varying cognitive styles that characterize different adult age groups (see Schaie and Parr, this volume). Then too, students learn in various ways from the discussion contributions of persons in different phases of life experience or with different cognitive styles (see Schaie and Parr, this volume).

Depending on the problem at hand, the learning environment in which this comparative and inductive approach is employed is perceptually complex or symbolically complex or both as Kolb reminds us in Part One.

It is for both intellectual and developmental reasons that the exotic and therefore engaging inventory of humankind's cultural variations are an attractive starting point for students and instructors in anthropology courses. For example, traditional–age undergraduates are particularly captivated by puberty rites and varied customs of betrothal and marriage such as infant betrothal and polygyny. Not surprisingly, older students are intrigued more by parent-in-law/child-in-law relations in unilineal extended families or by culturally institutionalized senilicide. And all students are fascinated by cultural institutions like ritualized warfare, blood brotherhood, or trial by ordeal. Harris' (1974, 1977) best-selling writings have demonstrated anew the appeal of such hoary exotica as potlatches and sacred cows.

Of course, understanding of adult development informs us of some of the reasons for the appeal to students of a given age of studying particular exotic cultural institutions: the participants in those institutions are of the same age or stage as the students and face similar personal questions and dilemmas. By studying institutions of other cultures and their impact on individuals of their own age, students can gain help in comprehending the changes in their own behavior that reflect maturation and aging (see Schaie and Parr, this volume). As for the instructors, some of the exotic material is relevant to *their* own present or past (not to mention future) age and stage. Then, too, what instructor would not prefer to teach with pedagogically engaging and relevant material?

The shift away from absolutistic thinking that can occur in undergraduate introductory courses in cultural and social anthropology results not form mere exposure to descriptions of a range of cultures, cultural institutions, and cultural practices, such as those just mentioned, but from the understanding of the *meaning* of those cultural forms as revealed in the ethnological explanations and analyses that usually are a part of those descriptions. Most of those explanations center on the concept of function and related concepts such as adaptation.

Students are introduced first to the apparent function of cultural forms. For example, they readily grasp the fact that the levirate, a form of marriage in which a deceased husband is replaced as a marriage partner by a kinsman culturally defined as a brother, is a way of providing for the care of the widow and her children. They learn that assumption of this responsibility can be critical in a society whose habitat and state of technology dictate a strong division of labor by sex, which makes economic contributions by adults of both sexes essential. Next, students are introduced to the idea that the levirate as a "secondary" or "continuation" marriage is a way of giving expression to the notion of marriage as linking two groups of kin and to the idea of the conceptual equivalence of siblings, or both. They learn, too, that conceptions like the continuity of marriage beyond the biological life of a partner and the equivalence of siblings may be given symbolic expression in a culture. They will be taught than an anthropologist may check his or her hypothesis that such conceptions underlie the levirate by looking for their reflection in symbolic beliefs and behavior.

The instructor, sometimes prodded by students' observations and comments, must move to the observation that "function" is not always *eu*function and may include *dys*function. He or she must raise the question of how one properly defines the consequences by which one attempts to determine function and deal with the pitfalls of circular reasoning and teleology.

Thus, in an introductory anthropology course the student learns something of the context of behavior, especially of how behavior is rooted in cultural norms. He or she comes to see how these norms reflect cultural values and adaptation to the possibilities (and more often the limitations) of habitat. Finally, the student learns that each culture has its own explanation of the reasons for cultural practices and of their meaning and that these stated reasons may or may not coincide with the reasons or consequences posited by the anthropologist. Before long, the student discovers that a custom abhorrent to one society may be not only highly valued in another society but eufunctional in that society–

in short, he or she is introduced to the concept of cultural relativity.

Introduction to Cultural Relativity: Mere exposure to the fact of significant variation in basic aspects of culture such as forms of marriage will shake the hold of absolutistic thinking on the student (see Perry, 1970, and in this volume). But introduction to the concept of cultural relativity and repeated examples of it speed the shift to relativistic thinking. This has long been understood as a major contribution of anthropology to liberal education. Time and time again, the student learns that what at first blush seemed superstitious and primitive has a logic of its own an consequences that are understandable. For example, not to have a completely free choice of spouse may not be inherently bad. Once the student recognizes the fact, the existence of so-called "freedom of choice" of spouse in our own society may be more closely examined and seen to be limited in highly patterned ways. Thus, old "truths" dissolve or are transformed into new ones.

Disengaging from the truths that one has been handed by Authority (including one's culture) may be very difficult for the student. Anthropologists ease this disengagement and facilitate the shift to relativistic thinking by use of the comparative method and the inductive approach, both of which have been partially implicit in the discussion so far.

Let me make this classical pedagogical strategy of anthropology explicit. The basic idea is to have the student study an institution or problem first in the literature about another culture. Reading about, say, infant betrothal, secondary marriage, or culturally permitted killing in another culture, the student is more likely to be able to be "objective," or, more precisely, to have less interference from early traumas, current intergenerational conflicts, community prejudices, religious training, and so on. Then, under the rubric of the comparative method, the instructor moves closer and closer to the student's own culture and subculture. For example, one moves from consideration of infant betrothal in premodern Nigeria to arranged marriages of young adults in traditional China and then to arranged marriages in some American subcultures. The pattern of limited freedom of choice of spouse in American culture that our exemplary student discovered earlier under his or her nose can now be examined more dispassionately than it otherwise would have been—in terms of functional pros and cons, like the more explicitly limited choices he or she examined in other cultures. It is to be hoped that the student will draw the inference that arranged marriages function to promote marital stability partly because physical attraction and romantic love are played down in favor of other attributes that may be more important over the life of the marriage. Attention then can be turned from benefits of arranged marriages to the matter of the correlated "costs" of both arranged marriages and those of "free choice" and to an assessment of the circumstances under which either form of marriage choice may be advantageous.

This pedagogical method capitalizes on both the exotic and comparative aspects of anthropology. First the institution in question is examined in another, distant culture to which the students bring little or no cultural "baggage." With the knowledge and relatively objective stance gained through that distantiation, the students can then be brought to examine the same institution or its functional equivalent in our own culture. The aim is for the students to see our own cultural institution in perspective. Often, they will perceive something about that institution that they had not noticed before approaching it with a comparative perspective. In performing this kind of exercise, the instructor tries to help the students to examine the role of an institution from the perspective of various actors and groups and from the point of view of "society" or "culture," while avoiding the twin pitfalls of reification and teleology.

The attempt to assay the net worth or effectiveness of a cultural institution can boomerang. Asked to attempt such an assessment, the student may raise the question of relativity and ask how such a judgment can be anything other than ethnocentric. In short, while the concept of the relativity of culture can help to speed the shift from absolutistic thinking, it can also reinforce the student in moral relativism, thereby slowing or blurring his or her moral development (Perry, 1970). I will return to this point in a later section of the chapter. For now, however, let me return to the issue of how the study of anthropology reinforces the conception that truth is not absolute.

Linguistics and Value Studies: The study of anthropological linguistics can reinforce the notion of relative truth. One of the most important concepts of linguistics is the Sapir–Whorf hypothesis, the view that the grammatical categories of a language have some effect on the perceptions and characteristic ways of thinking of the speakers of that language. Linguists, psychologists, and psycholinguists agree that grammar does not *determine* perception or thought, and the extent to which it shapes or guides them is a matter of contention. Understanding of this hypothesis is more profound for the student who has studied a foreign language long enough to see the applicability of the hypothesis to the speakers of that language and their behavior.

I have found that a particularly compelling way to present the Sapir–Whorf concept is to screen the Navajo-made films produced as part of a study by Sol Worth and John Adair (1972) aimed at understanding Navajo thought from an "inside" view, what anthropologists have come to call an "emic" view. More precisely, the goal of the Worth and Adair research was to determine the degree to which motion picture film as a medium of communication would be shaped by the categories of Navajo language and by other aspects of the Navajo world view. I have the students read Worth and Adair's lively yet germinal monograph documenting how the format and visual language of the films reflect grammatical categories of Navajo language as well as Navajo conventions of myth telling. The monograph is a fine supplement to another assigned reading that is part of the unit, Dorothy Lee's well-known paper "Lineal and non-lineal Codifications of Reality" (1950), which traces out some contrasts between the basic world views of the Trobrianders and of the West. The Navajo, like the Trobriand Islanders, have a nonlineal view of reality. The West, of course, has a rather pervasive lineal view of action and causality.

The students (sometimes with some guidance from the instructor) should come away asking: "To what extent are Anglo and other Western–made ethnographic films shaped by a basic world view about causality and connectedness between events and by the linguistic patterns of the filmmakers?" At a more personal level they should ask themselves: "To what extent are *my* thoughts or assumptions about the world shaped by the fact that I am a native speaker of English (or whatever)?" And so, the student is introduced to another dimension or relativity, of meaning varying with context.

Another perspective on the relativity of truth can be gained through the study of values as an underlying and determinative attribute of culture. A now classic example is the Harvard Values Study, which researched values in five American subcultures all occupying the same southwestern habitat: the Navajo, Zuni, Mormons, Texans, and Sapanish–Americans (Vogt and Albert, 1966). The basic hypothesis of the study was that since habitat was a constant, intercultural variation in adaptation to the ecological setting would not be due to ecology but to differences in values and the resulting cultural traditions. A piece of research that makes a similar point is the UCLA study of four East African societies, each of which has both an agricultural and a pastoral component. The research notes the role of values in shaping the differential adaptation to the same habitat by pastoralists, on the one hand, and agriculturalists, on the other (Edgerton, 1971). Because they use the method of controlled comparison (Eggan, 1954), utilizing habitat as a constant, these studies highlight sharply the role of values as a significant determinant of thoughts, attitudes, and actions. Again, students should ask themselves: "How much are my thoughts and those of others determined by the handed–down values of our culture?"

Meta–Thought: Discussion of the role of values is a good place for the anthropology instructor to stress the role of meta–thought, thought about thought. Traditional–aged college students should be particularly receptive to learning about meta–thought, for, as Gilligan notes in this volume, it is in adolescence that one acquires the capacity for reflective thought, the ability to think about thought itself. But training in meta–thought should be equally relevant for the middle adult stage of cognitive functions, which, according to Schaie, is characterized by the importance of organizational, in integrative, and interpretive intellectual skills.

A major joy in teaching introductory cultural anthropology is seeing the sense of discovery that even many contemporary students have when they are exposed to the concept of ethnocentrism, a concept and label based on meta–thought. Research in anthropological linguistics and on values shows how world view and values (as cultural conceptions of the desirable) shape behavior and morality (or which more later). The Harvard Values Study and the Edgerton study mentioned earlier are but two among many studies that can be used effectively to introduce the notion of ethnocentrism and make students aware that their values, like those of the Zuni, the Kamba, or the whomever, are strongly shaped by culture. The label *ethnocentrism* makes it easier for students to perceive that fact and to see that they are likely to judge the institutions and behavior of other cultures by the values of their own. Ethnographic examples can be used to show how values vary not only with culture or ethnicity but with caste, class, age, sex, and so on.

Once introduced to the question of ethnocentrism, students who are more mature intellectually raise the question of whether the assumptions and methodology of anthropology itself are not ethnocentric—one more product of the anthropologist's culture. They are in good company. As Cora DuBois notes, "the prime importance of relativism in perspective of the undergraduate student is that it places Western thought within rather than above the rest of the human scene...[for it] can raise the question of the degree to which our Western scientific treatment of sociocultural data is itself a patterned and partial phenomenon" (DuBois, 1963, p. 33). Since DuBois' comment, the whole question of the ethnocentrism and intellectual imperialism of anthropology has become a more conscious and widespread concern within our discipline, especially among the proponents of "radical anthropology." There is a rich and growing literature in this area about which to center class discussion (see Hymes, 1969).

Discussion about meta–thought is most likely to occur in the context of discussion about anthropological methods of analysis, including making inferences from data and constructing and testing hypotheses. Case studies that one can use as a basis for such discussion abound in anthropology, two such being Obeyesekere's study of pregnancy cravings among Sri Lankan women and my own study of a therapeutic dispute settlement process among the Kpelle of Liberia (Gibbs, 1963). The Sri Lankan research suggests questions like "How do you differentiate a manifest function from a latent one?" and "How do you verify a latent function?" My own paper suggests the question "When are two therapeutic processes—in this case, a Western and an African one —enough alike to be called 'similar'?" This approach is usually thought of as training the student in "critical analysis" and has been touted as an important benefit of undergraduate training in anthropology. But the recent critiques of anthropology I mentioned earlier (for example, Hymes, 1969) suggest that we might move closer to the approach of philosophy by making our fundamental assumptions and biases more explicit.

The Archaeological Perspective: Exposure to some of the anthropological subdiscipline of archaeology is still another way in which anthropology can assist a student's development of relativistic thinking. Because archaeological study of the past includes prehistory, it treats larger time periods than does history. Archaeology shows how over very long periods of time human knowledge and actions were shaped by many forces—with human intelligence and purpose being only one among them. Especially in the archaeological record of early times, whose material nature necessarily emphasizes technology and economic patterns more than, say, religion and kinship, we can see the role of shifting climates, resulting migration, diffusion, and technological change. These processes, in turn, over time changed and still change humankind's biological makeup. Through archaeology, students are introduced to more than historical reconstruction. They become aware of cultural evolution. With some data from physical anthropology they can also perceive biological evolution and the relationship between it and cultural evolution. From archaeology comes the humbling view that early human culture everywhere developed in broadly similar ways, following the laws of cultural evolution. The role of individuals stressed so much by history as a discipline (see Chickering, 1976) is muted in the prehistoric records. Archaeology puts individual choice and individual will in perspective as subject to the limitations of biology, habitat, and pre-existing cultural technology.

Anthropological study of the past also facilitates students' development of tolerance for intellectual ambiguity, a concept closely linked to developing relativistic thinking. Tolerance for intellectual ambiguity refers to the fact that there are some areas of knowledge where one can never "know" the "truth" or even delude oneself into thinking that one does (Perry, 1970). A case in point would be "knowing" what primate form was the first "human." Even an introductory course in physical anthropology will teach students that that particular "truth" changes quite regularly. (Older students whose knowledge of early human evolution comes primarily from the popular press will realize that they have read press releases about the "first human" with increasing frequency over the years.) More important, it will teach them that what form one counts even temporarily as the first human depends on how one defines *human* and on the phenomenal chanciness of which few individuals survived in fossil form and which (probably very few) of those have been discovered. Some instructors have brought the point home in a compelling way by assigning a science fiction novel that turns on the question of whether or not a particular primate individual can be classed as human.

The Self–Skeptical Mind: The culmination of the several kinds of exposure to anthropology that I have mentioned should be the self–critical mind. As I have said elsewhere (Gibbs, 1976), the mind that has been exposed to anthropology—that has learned something of other cultures and of cultural and of cultural relativity, of the role of values, of the influence of language, and of evolutionary processes—should begin to understand better how to evaluate knowledge itself. That mind will begin to understand how it—and all minds—are shaped by the structure of language, values, and historical circumstances—including the state of knowledge of its own times. As a result, one should become capable of informed skepticism about one's own thinking and pronouncements as well as those of other individuals. One will have learned that knowledge is not absolute but relative, that knowledge is both complex and limited.

In working to bring this about, the anthropology instructor must bear one caution in mind. Changes in cognitive development bring personality changes in their wake (see Weathersby, this volume), and the instructor must be prepared to cope with these ego changes in the role of mentor and advisor.

ANTHROPOLOGY, EGO DEVELOPMENT, AND STAGES OF LIFE

The study of anthropology can enhance the adult's ego development as well as his or her intellect. Ego, in much of the literature on ego development (see the chapter by Weathersby in this volume), is used in the Adlerian sense of "style of life." It refers to the unity of personality, its "individuality, method of facing problems, opinion about oneself and the problems of life, one's whole attitude to life and the schema of life" (Loevinger, 1976, p. 9). It is, then, a global term, encompassing much that characterizes the individual, including the structural notion of "stages" that flow in a logical sequence, each of which is marked by characteristic dilemmas and concerns. The study of anthropology can help the student to work through and solve some of the dilemmas and conflicts that characterize particular stages of ego development.

Let us turn first to the stage of adolescence. Erikson (1950) has noted that the development of identity is a major psychosexual or developmental task of adolescence. Helping the adolescent define his or her identity has traditionally been recognized as a goal of liberal education, although most often it has been considered an intellectual goal rather than a developmental one. Thus, Lyman (1971) observes: "a principal objective of education [is] to find out, to the limits of one's ability, where one stands in relation to the rest of the human race, the long sweep of human history, and—for that matter—the universe." Anthropology strives to achieve this end in ways I described earlier, by first helping individual students to understand something of the institutions and conventions that have shaped their own characters and values, to see how and to what extent they are creatures of culture. This is one function of the study of dominant American culture and of our subcultures, including—but not exclusively—one's own.

But in order to provide students with perspectives that will help them define their own identities, we must go beyond exposing them to variants of American culture. Reading an ethnography or monograph about an exotic culture inevitably leads to implicit, and often explicit, comparison with one's own culture. Each such cross–cultural exposure provides another point of triangulation from which the nature of one's own culture and hence one's self can be plotted. For example, a traditionally reared, somewhat sheltered young woman from a small town in Utah and a peer from Manhattan who read an ethnography on village life in Pakistan both gain perspective on the "restrictions" of their society and on themselves on a continuum of compliance versus assertiveness. Of course, such perspective does not convey automatic insights; the guidance of a developmentally oriented instructor is helpful.

Study of cultures contrasting with one's own can help one to see those features that distinguish one's own culture and shape some of one's life tasks. Thus, through exposure to even a small range of other cultures the American student becomes aware of the relative distinctiveness and pervasiveness of the rapid technological and culture change characteristic of contemporary societies (see Schaie and Parr, this volume).

One reason why skilful ethnographic studies of other cultures sharpens awareness of one's own identity is that a sensitive ethnographer builds his or her writing around the questions that the reader from an outside culture will bring to the material. Fifty years ago, in writing her classic study *Coming of Age in Samoa* (1928), Margaret Mead asked, in effect, "What makes a Samoan?" She hoped that her readers would ask "How would I feel to be a Samoan? How would a Samoan feel to be me? Do the same factors operate on a Samoan to make him or her a Samoan operate on me to make me an American, or a particular type of hyphenated American? Or there different factors that operate in American culture? Both similar and different factors? Or similar factors operating in *different* ways?" Mead would also want her readers to ask if there are circumstances unique to individual Samoans or Americans that shape them, for she did not really see culture as the only force that molds individual character. By working through these questions first for a Samoan or a member of another culture and then for himself or herself, a student sharpens his or her sense of identify, of—if you will—roots.

Developing or strengthening a sense of being rooted in a culture—an identity—usually is particularly important for minority group students because their cultures so often are viewed as "subcultures" in the pejorative sense. As the various ethnic pride movements of the 1960s and 1970s have stressed, study of the culture of one's homeland and full treatment of the American variant of that culture enhance a sense of identity and self-esteem.

For older students of either majority or minority background, immersion in knowledge of other cultures usually does not develop a sense of identity, but it may crystallize, affirm or enlarge the sense of identity.

Chickering and Havighurst, citing Levinson, note that a developmental task of the middle-aged is to reduce some of the illusions or assumptions and beliefs about oneself and the world that are not true. But some illusions serve a purpose, and distinguishing between the helpful ones and the harmful ones is not always easy. The anthropological study of myth and symbolism, following the classic approach of beginning with distant cultures and then moving closer to one's own, would help adult students to externalize and intellectualize this task. Here the writings of Lévi–Strauss and Victor Turner would be relevant (for example, Lévi–Strauss, 1969, and Turner, 1969, 1977).

As I have observed elsewhere (Gibbs, 1976) and others have noted too (for example, Chickering, 1976), the study of literature can help foster personal awareness by enabling the student to try on other identities and live them vicariously. Reading autobiographies of persons from other cultures or their life histories as written by anthropologists can have the same result. In contrast to these other vividly experienced lives and identities, one's own may come into sharper focus. One can ask of anthropological life histories the same questions that Chickering (1977) sets for literature: What are the pressures which force those persons (characters) toward one level of development or another? What internal strengths, from what sources, provide leverage against those external forces? The popularity of Oscar Lewis' (1959, 1961, 1964, 1965, 1966) documentary life histories of Latino individuals and families shows that many readers undoubtedly recognize—at least subconsciously—their usefulness in fostering self–awareness.

Developing a capacity for empathy and intimacy is one aspect of ego development (see Douvan, this volume). In late adolescence this is connected with acquiring friends and relating to them. This developmental task can be related to intellectual ones, although this may not be obvious to students. As Douvan notes in this volume, the idea that friendship or family relationships or love relationships can be thought about and analyzed systematically is probably as alien to many freshmen as are concepts like the black hole or the quark. But anthropological study of friendship can move the traditional–age student beyond the ethnocentric, idealistic view that friendship is solely affective or that it is exploitative or manipulative to value the pragmatic, instrumental aspects of friendship.

Let me flesh out this suggestion with an example. Studying the anthropological literature on blood brotherhood, the student might see aspects of ordinary friendship projected in bold relief in this ritualized form of friendship. In most cultures blood brotherhood places very high value on both intimacy and utility (see Gibbs, 1962). Here, again, we see the heuristic value of our pedagogical paradigm that compares the far with the near. Armed with this insight from the anthropological literature, the student might re-examine friendship in our culture and see more clearly that instrumentality is a significant part of it. The student might now see that the strong normative primacy that our society gives to the dimension of intimacy in characterizing friendship reflects more the values and ideals of our society than the actuality or friendship. The payoff for ego development would come when the student could acknowledge that admitting the coexistence of instrumentality and intimacy in friendship is neither cynical or manipulative. In the student's own friendship, he or she would be more able to accept less than complete intimacy and to view instrumentality in friendship as a legitimate goal rather than as an intrusion or subversion. The student would have moved closer to achieving realistic intimacy in friendship. Again, the developmentally related insights do not emerge spontaneously. Skilful Socratic questioning by an instructor helps to elicit them.

For the traditional–age student, the developmental issues concerning empathy and intimacy are linked to the task of resolving the tension between autonomy and interdependence. Douvan, in this volume, notes that the latter issue is a developmental task for older women students, too. They may be helped in resolving the tension between autonomy and interdependence by intellectualizing it and externalizing it. Following reasoning parallel to that I have used earlier in this chapter, she observes that by formal study of social systems they can learn of the inevitability of interdependence and, thus, to accept it in their own lives. Of course, the same strategy is applicable to traditional–age students, whose problems with autonomy versus interdependence come at an earlier developmental stage.

Older students, having lived longer and encountered a greater variety of people—and, perhaps, cultures—than traditional-age students, seem to find much of the excitement and applicability of anthropology in exploring the universals or similarities of cultures. Because of their life experience, they tend to take the differences among cultures more for granted. More than with younger students, there is an understanding and appreciation of, say, what is universal in fatherhood—or grandmotherhood. This makes possible another developmental application of the study of anthropology. Again, by externalization and intellectualization, the study of other cultures can help these students to accept their need for generativity, to be nurturant and supportive of oncoming generations—not just of their own children and kinsmen but of other persons as well (Erikson, 1959, and Chickering and Havighurst, this volume).

A good case in point is Guttmann's (1974) research on passivity in older men. Guttmann's paper uses the Druze of Syria and Israel to show that the disengagement that is reported as characteristic of old age in many societies is not true of old men in that society. Using comparative data, Guttmann suggests that passivity is characteristic of old age, but that it need not take the form of disengagement.

The literature on both cognitive and ego development shows that formal study may have the effect of shifting a student to the next cognitive or ego stage (see Perry and Weathersby, this volume). Careful research probably would demonstrate that exposing older students to the notion of generativity as it is expressed in the allocation of roles in differing social structures and kinship systems may prompt individuals poised on the edge of accepting their generative needs to cross the boundary to this next ego stage.

Let me conclude this section with a caution. In using anthropology for strengthening ego development, we must beware of unwittingly encouraging students' acquiescence to the *status quo* (see the criticism of pre-1970s anthropology in Hymes, 1969). As in my example of the young women from Utah and Manhattan, cross-cultural exposure may be used to provide persons with "realistic" perspective on their current situation. But sometimes the change must be made "out there" rather than inside the person. At times cross-cultural exposure suggests that a situational change is necessary and appropriate to handle the developmental issue of a particular life stage. Cross-cultural exposure may even suggest what form that situational change might take. As Weathersby notes in her chapter, individuals at the higher stages of ego development are able not only to cope with the complexities of society but also to view society's rules with a critical eye.

Anthropology and Moral Development

Discussing moral development during the college years, Gilligan notes in this volume that the educational experiences that foster moral development will be those which enhance the capacity to shift perspectives. She observes that history and literature can make important contributions to moral development by extending students' experience through the study of other lives, both past and present. Chapters Fifteen and Eighteen develop Gilligan's point well. Obviously, the same claim can be made for anthropology. However, anthropology fosters moral development not only through the study of individual *lives* of other times and places but also through the experience of other *cultures* via the writings of anthropologists and the direct experience of fieldwork.

The same material the anthropologists use to foster the student's intellectual development—by speeding and guiding the shift from absolutistic thinking–and ego development also can be used to foster the student's moral development. Here, again, we see the possibility of promoting several developmental objectives simultaneously. This, of course, is one of the most important implications of part One of this volume. For example, in attempting to stimulate moral development, the anthropology instructor can return students to Obeyesekere's study of pregnancy carvings among Sri Lankan women cited earlier, keeping in mind Gilligan's suggestion that knowledge of the causes and consequences of human suffering is a source of the moral capacity to respond actively to social experience. With their initial naiveté and particular cultural set, most tradition–age American students exposed to the description of the Sri Lankan institutionalized practice would probably see the young married women suffering at the hands of their in-laws, especially the husband and his mother. The young wife would be seen as giving up her "autonomy to move into the joint family household of her husband—partly because autonomy versus dependence is a salient life stage issue for most traditional–age students. (Older students would be more apt to identify with the joint family upon which she is "intruding.") But Obeyesekere's analysis helps the student to see that the "cause" of the suffering is equally the woman's natal family, specifically the way in which they reared her. In short, the contrast between her childhood life and her married life creates a situation of relative deprivation. The pregnancy cravings and the household's response to them function partly to alleviate the sense of deprivation. Obeyesekere's analysis also suggests other factors that can be labelled "causes."

The point to be emphasized is the that Obeyesekere's paper, which ostensibly does not focus primarily on moral issues, *can* be used to show a class not only that determining cause and consequence is not easy but the judging the morality of an act is equally difficult because ascribing "blame" requires prior ascertainment of cause. Determining cause and blame or moral fault is certainly risky if the observer brings to the situation simply his or her own unexamined perspective.

Other examples can be cited to show the complexity of the causes of human suffering and the related moral and ethical issues. Thus, drought is the result of complex interaction between people and habitat. High value placed on the use of cattle for bride-wealth may lead to overgrazing, which results in erosion, exacerbated by shifts in the pattern of the rains. Of course, the ethical consequences of interrupting this cycle at any point also are very complicated.

I use the Sri Lankan example to show how the same ethnographic description and analysis can be used to stimulate both intellectual and moral development. However, for fostering moral development, more apt examples would involve cultural patterns in which moral issues are more explicit and more central. The classic example, and one that is relevant to older students even more than traditional–age ones, is the conventional Eskimo practice of senilicide. In this custom, elderly persons whose feeble condition endangered the mobility and, hence, the lives of the nomadic group, would commit suicide or be killed by a designated member of the group. A vigorous discussion can be stimulated by questions such as: "Is it moral?" "By what standards?" "Suppose a particular old person protested, should he or she have the right to live?" and so on.

In discussing the role of anthropology in nurturing intellectual development, I observed that introducing the students to the concept of cultural relativity has implications for their moral development. Let me return to that issue. Gilligan, in reviewing the literature on moral development, cites the work of Kohlberg on the phenomenon of moral relativism—notably, the claim made by students that, in the face of individual difference and cultural heterogeneity, moral judgment was impossible and therefore that one "should" do what one wanted to do. Not surprisingly, students' familiarity with the concept of cultural relativity and with data from other cultures tends to reinforce this tendency. After all, from anthropology one learns to take the perspective of the other cultures. One's own moral standards are revealed to be largely an artifact of one's culture–a culture shaped by many forces, of which the conception of morality is only one. So how can there be a way of making absolute moral judgments except possibly within a single culture? Even anthropology itself has no easy answer to that question. This leaves the anthropology instructor interested in education for adult development with a moral obligation of his or her own to help the student move beyond the moral relativism that his instruction may have aggravated. But how? One way is to link the issue of the relativity or absoluteness of morality to field experience.

Fieldwork and Moral Development: Doing fieldwok often pushes anthropologists themselves beyond absolute relativism. Participation in fieldwork can have the same effect on students. Even hearing of or reading about field experiences and subjective responses to them may achieve this result. I can make my point best by recounting some relevant personal experiences.

At the end of my senior year in college, when I was completing my major in sociology and anthropology, I was a finalist for a national Woodrow Wilson Fellowship, which subsequently, I was awarded. As part of the selection procedure I was interviewed by two professors at Princeton. The conversation turned to the topic of cultural relativity. One of them, a historian, probed to see if I was as committed to the concept as I seemed to be. *Suppose,* he said, "you were an anthropologists doing fieldwork in India and you saw a widow about to be thrown on her husband's funeral pyre in the custom of suttee. What would you do?" Hesitating only briefly, I said that I would not do anything "because anthropologists could not interfere with the customs of the people we study, nor pass judgment on them." I knew that my response seemed callous, but saw no way out of the dilemma. The professor smiled slightly (with hindsight I suspect it was indulgently) and said that in time I might arrive at a different point of view. Gilligan's label of *moral relativism* would surely have applied to my stage of moral development at the time.

Five years later, the same issue arose during my doctoral fieldwork, this time in still more dramatic form. The powerful paramount chief in the town where I was doing my fieldwork, my "father of the stranger," suspected some of his many wives of adultery. He had administered to them a "medicine" that would cause any of them who had committed unconfessed adultery to become ill and, perhaps, to die. One of them, a young woman whom I shall call Nowai, became ill. The mother of three very young children, she was not an informant for me or my wife, but she was a frequent casual visitor at our house. She lay on a mat in front of her house in the paramount chief's compound, shunned by most of her co-wives, berated by the chief, and becoming progressively weaker and losing weight. Two weeks went by the she was so sick that she could no longer nurse her youngest child. The illness, with symptoms of dysentery and malaria, was attributed to the effect of the "medicine," which "caught" her for unconfessed adultery. Her husband, the chief, declined to call the medicine man to counter the effect of the combined pharmaceutical and fetish.

My wife and I both called on Nowai as we made our daily rounds of the town, and my wife, who became increasingly concerned about her, asked me if I would give Nowai some Western medicine for her symptoms. We discussed the pros and cons heatedly and at length. In contrast to five years before, I could see more shades of gray, including contextual complications. But I thought we should not risk treating her and incurring the chief's wrath. "After all," I argued, "*he's* her husband. Even her co-wives won't help her. If we interfere, the chief could force us to leave the village. And Nowai has refused to give you any interviews about childrearing, something she could easily have done." The continuation of the fieldwork deserved the highest priority in determining the course of action, I thought, even though I felt great anger at the chief for the way in which he was treating his wife. I did go so far as to ask him if he did not think it was time to relent. Had not Nowai been punished. His answer was "no."

Nowai's condition worsened and, unbeknown to me, my wife gave her medicine for dysentery and malaria from our kit, reasoning that either or both would do some good. In a very few days, Nowai was better and soon was walking about town. My wife revealed to me her hand in the dramatic recovery. It was, of course, already known to Nowai's co-wives and to the chief. I waited for the chief's reaction. Much to my surprise, he commended my wife for her actions. "That's how women are," he confined to me, "they stand together against us men." I should be proud, he observed, that my wife had reached out to help another person in distress.

I had learned a valuable lesson. The townspeople were not going to judge us morally or ethically by the canons of anthropological works on methodology or field methods that stress "objectivity," "noninterference," and preserving access to the data for the enlightment of future generations and the enrichment of anthropological knowledge. No, they judged us as human beings in the broadest sense. The standard of humanitarian concern (see White in this volume) was to be the prevailing one. I could have done what seemed right and natural to me personally and not only been understood but even admired. I had assumed far too little transmutability between our culture and morality and that of the Kpelle.

Eleven years later, on a third field trip to the same town, the issue of the ethics of intervention arose again. By now I was in my late thirties and was armed not only with still vivid memories of Nowai's illness but with a few years of parenthood and other life experiences that fall under Gilligan's rubric of "experiences of irreversible choice and of sustained responsibility for the welfare of others." This time I was in the field for a short summer period of eleven weeks and was accompanied by two students. One was a senior and the other a graduate student who was carrying out a study of the Kpelle treatment of illnesses. The latter, whom I shall call Ted, had as an undergraduate premedical student had some experience working in a hospital emergency room and would thus give townsmen medicine for the more common ailments, especially when the dispensary operator was not in town.

One night after midnight, in the midst of a tropical downpour, Ted was sent for by the head official of the men's secret society, a medicine man who was one of his major informants. The old man's daughter, a young woman in her twenties, was seriously ill. Ted had seen her earlier in the day because she was quite nauseous and not responding to the local healers. Now, the vomiting had become worse and everyone was worried. Ted went to see the woman and came back to our house. His best judgment was that she was indeed seriously ill and needed to go to the hospital, thirty-five miles away, as soon as possible. Our vehicle was awaiting the arrival of a replacement spare tire. The only transportation available was a Volkswagen bug, a "taxi" that had arrived too late to make the return trip to the country seat. We could charter it. The woman's father reluctantly agreed to the hospitalization and to the charter. But he had nowhere near enough money. Who would pay? I would pay for the charter and the hospitalization, I said, casting my money where my feelings were, on the side of intervention. In consideration of the old man's dignity, I said that I would "loan" him the money. In the context of local custom and the immediate situation it was understood but unstated that he would repay the loan if he could, but that he might not be able to.

The sick woman, her father, Ted, and taxi owner squeezed into the Volkswagen for the trip to the hospital. It was midafternoon the next day before the old man and Ted returned with the story of what had happened. By the time they had traversed the thirty–five miles of dirt roads, the young woman was in a state of shock. The doctor, who was roused from his bed at 3.00 A.M., had examined her and determined that she had an ectopic pregnancy, one in which the fetus is carried outside of the uterus, in the abdominal cavity. It was necessary to operate right away. The operation was successful. But, the doctor said, if another four hours had passed, the woman would have died.

Ted's initial feeling was one of elation. He had played a major role in saving a life, largely because he was right as to the seriousness of her condition, even though he could not have known the actual diagnosis. Moreover, he was a hero in the eyes of the woman's father, the most important medicine man in town. The implications for his self–esteem and for the success of his research and his personal standing in the community were obvious.

But by the next night Ted was troubled by consideration of alternative consequences that might have followed our intervention. "How could you let me do it?" he asked. "Suppose she had died? I don't know enough medicine to have assumed so much responsibility." We sat up half the night talking through the pros and cons and the ins and outs of the situation. Space precludes repeating all that was said. Among other things, I pointed out that he knew more about medicine than anyone else in the town, including me, so his expertise was the best we had available. I recounted the story of Nowai and assured him that if the young woman had died, people would not have blamed him but noted that he had tried to help. Moreover, the responsibility was shared since I had supported the decision and backed it with the "loan." Nor should he underestimate the role of the woman's father. Perhaps we were being arrogant in assuming that it was "our" decision. Perhaps the real decision was the old man's and his daughter's.

Being supportive and avuncular during our talk into the wee hours of the morning enabled me to make explicit to Ted what I saw as the critical dimensions in the moral and ethical crisis in which we jointly had participated. The most important of these was commitment in the face of uncertainty (see Perry, 1970, and this volume). Being supportive and avuncular also met my own developmental needs—generative needs characteristic of my own life stage.

In the field situation it becomes clear later if not sooner that humanitarian concern (see White, this volume) is a moral value that prevails over moral relativity. And it may be that, in one form or another, this is a universal or quasi–universal human value.

As a result of the educational changes of the 1960s, many instructors now deem it appropriate to let students become aware of our nonclassroom professional activities and concerns. If we also reveal our personal encounters with ethical and moral issues in the course of those activities and the consequences for our own development, we can advance the moral development of our student (see Kolb's concept, in this volume, of the teacher as "mirror" of facilitator).

The three instances I have recited are among the most instructive experiences of my professional life, and I have recounted them in detail because they can also be instructive for anthropology students. I find it hard to be as self–revelatory as recounting these instances demands. But the gain in doing so is that the chronology of the three events shows so clearly how particular circumstances can wean one away from absolute moral relativity. Because the events are "real," involving the instructor they see three times a week, students to whom they are told can empathize with the dilemma and the pain of the anthropologist's moral growing up and learn vicariously from his experience.

Since I have introduced fieldwork in such graphic terms, let me say something about its place in developmentally oriented teaching of anthropology. Direct experience of culture is the core of fieldwork, the most critical and distinctive part of the anthropological method. Anthropologists take great pride in the fact that they personally immerse themselves in the cultures that they study. Fieldwork is a kind of experiential learning, obviously, and anthropologists feel that through it they learn something that other social scientists do not. What is that? Chickering's (1976) definition of experiential learning helps us to see what that something is: He defines *experiential learning* as "the learning that occurs when changes in judgments, feelings, knowledge, or skills result for a particular person from living through an event or events" (p. 16). In carrying out fieldwork one acquires knowledge about another culture. But one also enhances one's anthropological empathy and insight. Every anthropologist knows that his or her insight into all cultures is enhanced by the fieldwork he or she has done in one or a few of them. In the field it readily becomes apparent that one's own prior personal history and cultural upbringing influence what one perceives and what one understands. Thus, the fieldworker comes to understand at a visceral level the shaping influence of culture and the relativity of truth, to know them in a way that one cannot understand them from textbook knowledge alone. And as the experiences I recounted suggest, one learns not only of the differences among cultures but of the universals.

Obviously, such benefits from fieldwork are not simply cognitive and professional in the intellectual sense. Repeatedly, anthropologists have commented on the fact that fieldwork increased their personal awareness and insight. More than one fieldworker has compared fieldwork to undergoing psychoanalysis. This is partly because fieldwork is like drama. It requires that one play a role and also observe. And like performing in a play, fieldwork "creates an experiential context that supplies rich capital for postplay self–confrontation and self–examination" (Chickering, 1977, p. 70). As my field examples indicate, the postevent self–confrontation may take place while one is still in the field.

Although fieldwork for introductory students is difficult to arrange for logistical, financial, and ethical reasons, it is an extremely valuable experience for developmental education. For the student, as for the professional anthropologists, it can sharpen both anthropological insight and personal awareness. But to be effective, fieldwork requires carefully selected supplemental reading, self–observation, and "working through" by reflection and dialogue with a more experienced person. When all these conditions obtain, fieldwork, more than most learning experiences, can be tailored to the motives, learning style, and developmental stage of the student.

One of the reasons fieldwork is such a good vehicle for developmental education is that as a learning environment it combines attributes of all four "pure" types of learning environment: (1) affective complexity, (2) perceptual complexity, (3) symbolic complexity, and (4) behavioral complexity (see Kolb, this volume). This is one reason why the summer is which I did the fieldwork with two students mentioned earlier turned out to be one of the most satisfying teaching experiences I have had. As the incident recounted earlier indicates fieldwork provides a setting in which the intellectual and developmental relevance of tasks at hand is apparent. And the instructor can capitalize on this in guiding the experience.

Traditionally, developmentally oriented anthropologists have encouraged their students to do minor fieldwork in American ethnic communities or subcultures. This has taken the form of small–scale observation or interviewing or both. It was felt that a class, by learning about minority communities, would become more tolerant of them and minority individuals. The goal was to enhance both ego development and moral development and only secondarily to strengthen intellectual development through some acquisition of field skills. Douvan, in this volume, notes that one goal in developing a capacity for intimacy is avoiding responding to people as members of classes or representatives of roles: First–hand study of one's own group helps the student to see persons more as individuals. Additional first–hand study of another group helps even more.

But student intracommunity studies have become a touchy matter, and for good reason. Anthropology has come more and more and more to recognize that the peoples traditionally studied by anthropologists are also the peoples who, by and large, are powerless and that interviewing them to help develop the interviewers' sense of identity treats them as objects. It is one more form of exploitation or oppression. Hence this form of field experience is no longer utilized except under carefully prescribed conditions.

Students' ethical and moral development is enhanced when fieldwork has a civic orientation, as when students are apprenticed to community agencies in help–giving roles (see Douvan, this volume) or carry out actual volunteer research that otherwise would not be possible for the agencies. This enhances the student's ability to make choices and commitments, which Perry (1970) notes to be the most important outcome of ethical development. Since the 1960s, many anthropologists have increased their students' opportunities to work in this kind of applied setting. At Stanford University this is done through the Action Research Liaison Office (ARLO), which enables students, under faculty supervision, to do research that is useful to community agencies, yet linked to the students' formal course work.

Because it is so difficult to take significant numbers of students to the field, anthropologists increasingly are simulating some aspects of the field experience through the use of ethnographic films. Improved portability of 16mm cameras and synchronous sound recording equipment and changing conceptions of filming have resulted in films that do less processing of the culture being filmed, making it possible for the student to learn more directly about the culture. A noteworthy film of this sort is Rouch and

Morin's (1961) *Chronicle of a Summer.* Other examples include the *Faces of Change series* (miller, 1978) produced by the American Universities Field Staff. Each of these films makes use of the device of interviewing a respondent on camera with synchronous sound, using subtitles (rather than a narrator's voice) for translation of the foreign language. Obviously, this increases the sense of reality, or at least versimilitude, and enlarges the opportunity for the student to learn inductively. Again, the effective use of ethnographic films requires very careful planning and use of supplementary readings as well as written and oral dialogue. With all this in place, the student is drawn into the material in a particularly compelling way, virtually seduced into the experiencing of other cultures and their analysis. Needless to say, learning via the visual mode is particularly compatible with the learning styles of the current generation of tradition–age students and, increasingly, of older students, who have also logged many hours in from of television screens.

Let me return to the matter of how the study of anthropology can enhance a student's moral development. At an early stage of moral development, a student will tend to see the world in terms of moral absolutes, believing that cultures should be consistent in their ideals—for example, not claiming justice for all while treating highly placed persons differently from others in the criminal justice system. Again, externalization and intellectualization may help the student to achieve a more relativistic and realistic moral position. He or she can study another culture in which conflicting polarities are present–equality and inequality, good and evil, cooperation and competition, ascription and achievement, and so on. Consequently, the student may come to accept the inevitability of conflicting tendencies in his or her own culture and no longer perceive their presense as necessarily indicating moral weakness or hypocrisy. Eventually, this should help the student to see the necessity for making moral and ethical choices even in the face of conflicting interpretations (see Perry, 1970). In this effort the student may be aided by exposure to treatises on the question of the universality of values and morals, such as those by Kluckhohn (1952, 1953, 1955), or on the universality of laws (Hoebel, 1954).

Cultural Domination as a Moral Issue: The fact the Western culture, including the American variant, is culturally imperialistic and dominates most cultures with which it comes in contact raises a moral issue of concern to both anthropologists and their students. They may ask questions such as these: What are the sources of cultural domination, cultural imperialism, and oppression of one culture by another? Are there sets of conditions that spawn these phenomena? From the comparative approach of anthropology (and history), students will learn that cultural imperialism has occurred in other times and places, as with the impact of Hindu India on Indonesia centuries ago, that it is not limited to the postexploration West.

The traditional anthropological literature on culture change provides a partial framework for understanding cultural dominance. But the contemporary literature of radical anthropology (see Hymes, 1969) and interdisciplinary dependency theory (for example, Arrighi and Saul, 1973) goes far beyond it in explaining the post–industrial revolution dominance attained by Western capitalistic societies and, less completely, the attempted domination by socialistic societies. These two sets of literature explain phenomena that are salient to socially concerned students of all ages, such as economies dominated by commodity production and extremely sensitive to fluctuating world commodity prices, plantation economies, migrant labor, and the resulting destabilization of family life. The frame of reference of dependency theory provides a means for understanding the mechanisms of oppression and their functions for both the oppressors and the oppressed. The empirical portion of the literature permits students to see the consequences of cultural domination from the point of view of the culture dominated.

Only after grounding in this kind of factual background and analytical frameworks are the students and the instructor ready to tackle the moral issues involved. Is it ever moral for one culture knowingly to dominate another? More narrowly, is it "oppression" when employment on plantations or as migrant miners produces income that can be taxed to build social welfare facilities such as clinics? What does one have to know or take account of to answer the question? Suppose it is elected leaders of the dominated country that arrange for the labor contracts for the miners? Does this make a difference in how we judge the situation? Where multinational corporations are involved, what responsibility do consumers of the corporations' products have for corporate actions in developing countries?

Questions like these speak to the ethical and moral concerns of middle-aged students and call upon their ability to assume a stance of moral relativity (see Gilligan, this volume). The multifold analyses required to answer them demand the integrative and interpretive intellectual skills that characterize the middle stage of life (see Schaie and Parr, this volume). Answering such questions perceptively also requires empathizing with the other, and this ability is more characteristic of the older student (Douvan, this volume). And much of the motivation for making the attempt may be rooted in humanitarian concern (White, this volume). This area is one in which anthropology and our sister social sciences can contribute much to the developmental training of adult students.

Study of the anthropology of cultural domination can play another role in developmental education apart from enhancing the moral development and, simultaneously, ego development of older students. It can help minority students to develop a sense of identity and enhance their self-esteem. Many aspects of ego development of minority persons (for example, capacity for empathy and intimacy) may be impaired by the consequences of racism, such as discrimination. Some coping responses such as self-hate, attempted assimilation, or self-segregation and compartmentalization can cause further complications for ego development, particularly for identity. The literature on the anthropology of cultural domination referred to earlier can be supplemented by the literature on the psychology of oppression (see Fanon, 1965) to help minority students and other students understand the personal consequences for the minority individual of the oppression of a subculture by a dominant culture. Once the minority person understands intellectually the subtle ways in which the dominant culture seduces emulation and rewards it, it may be possible for him or her to assume a stance of principled independence and to be less ambivalent about identifying with his or her own culture. In achieving this goal, the study of other pluralistic societies also is of value.

Minority students and majority group students can benefit from discussing the moral issues implicit in the structure of cultural domination and its psychology–for example, how can one justify either assimilation or pluralism in a society that has a "melting pot" image as part of its ideology? But such discussions are more fruitful when most of the students involved have resolved the more directly personal issue for ego development of the inequality of cultures in a pluralistic society. When successful, moral training of this sort enhances competence as "capacity for action" (see Schaie and Parr, this volume).

Anthropology and Developmental Education

Anthropology has much to contribute to the development of the conceptions that underlie developmental education as well as to the delivery of education in the developmental mode. In recent years cognitive anthropology, psychological anthropology, and cross–cultural psychology all have added to our understanding of cognitive development and problem–solving abilities in other cultures. Especially notable in this regard are the studies of Gay and Cole (1967), Cole and others (1971), Cole and Scribner (1974), Lave (1944), and Bruner, Olver, and Greenfield (1966). Gradually we are increasing our understanding of the cultural factors that influence problem–solving abilities. There are suggestions that the unfolding of the Piagetian stages of cognitive development (Piaget, 1928) are not everywhere the same.

In the literature of psychology there is a significant body of material on individual differences in learning styles (see Kolb, this volume). And there have been several attempts to determine the cross–cultural distribution of learning styles (for example, Witkin, 1967; Wober, 1967). Lesser's (1976) paper summarizing the patterned differences in learning styles that characterize American ethnic groups (and the commentaries on it by Cole and Gordon certainly should be of interest to anyone who proposes to teach the more heterogeneous students of the 1980s. Most of the studies of cultural differences in learning styles have focused on American populations. Work among unspecified "Southern Nigerians" (Wober, 1967), Eskimo, and Temne (Berry, 1966) are notable exceptions. We should sample a larger portion of the world's peoples in testing the validity of our conceptualization of learning styles. Given the anthropological penchant for field-work, anthropologists can be expected to do some of this research. And we certainly can assist with the conceptualization.

How universal are the stages of ego development or their progression as traced by theorists like Buehler (1962), Erikson (1950), Levinson and other (1977), Loevinger (1976)? How about the "developmental tasks" of Chickering and Havighurst (this volume), who are no strangers to anthropology? Mead's (1928) pioneering work on Samoa taught us the adolescence is not necessarily a period of *Sturm und Drang* even though it is in the United States. And even a cursory knowledge of traditional China informs one that old age need not be a period of low community regard. So we have every reason to suspect that all of the proposed stages of ego development may not be universal. And those that are probably unfold in rather different ways in divers cultures. Once again, we can ask: Is the midlife crisis posited for American adults universal? And even among Americans, does it vary in its manifestations across ethnic groups? If we are to design education to promote ego development, we need a much better understanding of cross–cultural and subcultural variations in ego development.

A number of questions relevant to the study of ego development in other cultures are suggested by the cross–cultural farm of reference of anthropology. For example, we know that the life tasks of some periods of adult life are sex–linked (see Chickering and Havighurst, this volume). Under what cultural conditions is the content of the ego stages and their developmental tasks sex–linked? Are the conditions found in some American subcultures? Does the presence of rapid culture change have implications for ego development and therefore for developmental education? One consequence of rapid culture change seems to conflict between the generations. What implications does this have for ego development and for education? Does the presence of cultural heterogeneity have implications for ego development, especially for the tasks that characterize the various ego stages?

Obviously, the list of questions could be extended. Suffice it to say that we should make sure that our conceptions of stages of ego development as an aspect of "human nature" are based on a sufficiently full sampling of the human population. Otherwise, we may overlook some important dimension of the phenomenon. Cross–cultural research can help to resolve the conflict between the approaches of Piaget and Inhelder and Loevinger as to whether ego development involves discrete sequential stages or gradations along a quantitative continuum (see Weathersby, this volume).

The third area where anthropology can make a contribution to the conceptual underpinnings of developmental education is in the study of the cultural of education (see Spindler, 1974). The "ethnography of education" is a relatively new subfield within the subdiscipline of anthropology of education. It asks questions such as these: What are the operating assumptions in an educational institution or portion of it about the role of the student, the teacher, and the nature and purposes of education? Are there latent assumptions as well as manifest ones? How do they affect the operation of the system? Ethnographers of education already are working on issues such as the differential nonverbal treatment by teachers of minority students or students defined as "slow" (McDermott, 1974). We need to know more about every aspect of the culture of educational institutions. For example, in the mode of Levi–Strauss, what are the myths of an institution, and how do they convey important truths about the institution? Are there other truths that are conveyed via other modes of communication, and how do they affect the performance of the various actors in the system? In my view, an important task of the ethnography of education is to inform us as to what really happens in the culture of the education institution so we can begin to judge the extent to which that conforms to what we believe *should* happen in a developmentally oriented educational setting.

In sum anthropological contributions to the conceptual armory of developmental education can address themselves to the questions: Do we know enough about cultural variations in human cognitive, ego, and moral development? And do we know enough about the actual culture of institutions of higher learning? But even as we address these questions, it is clear that the study of anthropology can facilitate the shift from absolute to relative thinking, enhance ego development, and facilitate moral development. Most importantly, perhaps, anthropology can strengthen the concepts underlying education for adult development.

12

Biology Teaching

Many issues in biology have vital significance for society as a whole—for example, the genetics of newly arising mutations, both induced and spontaneous; the relation of carcinogens to induced cancers, especially from cigarette smoking, industrial pollution, and occupational hazards; the use of defoliants, first in the Vietnam war and now in national forests; and the evidence regarding biological determinism of human intelligence and social behavior.

All too often, however, the decision makers who set policy on issues related to the life sciences are biologically illiterate, hostile to the sciences, or willing to follow the advice of a few "expert" witnesses who may not be representative of their scientific disciplines. So far during this century, as a result, biological illiteracy has allowed misguided officers of the Eugenics Record Office to convince Congress of the alleged inferiority of European immigrants, leading to the restrictive immigration laws of the early 1920s. And shoddy research has been used to support compulsory sterilization laws for various categories of the "unfit," including the insane, the chronic pauper, the retarded, and the "habitual" criminal.

As we look at how biological knowledge and principles are applied or ignored by society, it becomes clear that biological education has failed to meet the general public's need for knowledge. Potential leaders benefit little from the standard course for non-science majors, which skeptical professors have dubbed a "tiptoe through the phyla." And the abstract principles of nucleic acid chemistry, Mandelian laws, mitotic divisions, and developmental processes are remote and quickly forgotten by students if they are not directly tied to students' own experience.

How can colleges and universities cure biological illiteracy and make biological valuable liberal arts experience, satisfying students' need for knowledge that can be applied to their personal and public life? It is my belief that this much needed reform of biological education involves two aspects of introductory nonmajors courses—their content and their presentation. Failure to consider both may prevent the successful education of liberal arts students, including those among them who will be tomorrow's leaders.

CONTENT OF INTRODUCTORY COURSES FOR NONMAJORS

Small colleges often offer a single introductory course in biology, but larger colleges and universities offer at least two—one for students planning to major in biology and another for nonscience majors. At these institutions, the content of the course for biology majors is usually departmentally mandated, whereas the content of the course for nonscience majors may be of little concern to the biology department. Moreover, the faculty members who teach the nonmajors course may receive the assignment as a punishment for poor scholarly productivity. The course is usually out of favor with the rest of the faculty, who perceive nonmajors as lacking the capabilities and enthusiasm that biology majors frequently bring to their courses. Yet few biology majors will be among the lawyers, business executives, legislators, ministers, consumer activists, and journalists who will shape and decide the values and laws that govern the applications of biology to the individual and society.

Today many students—both biology majors and nonmajors—enter the college or university with uneven academic skills. Some cannot write effective prose. A considerable number have no idea how to take effective notes during a lecture. Many do not have experience with relational thinking and tend to identify memorization of terms with learning. But despite these shortcomings, most nonmajors who take introductory biology want to learn. They not only want a solid introduction to facts and principles, they want to relate them to an overall view of the world. For them, knowledge of biology is most stimulating when it can be related to other fields such as history, literature, and psychology, to current events, or to different philosophical world views. The degree to which we are aware of that need and the skill with which we can make such connections will often determine the success of our courses.

Basic Principles of Human Biology: Consider five major principles of biology—the cell, the gene, development, molecular biology, and evolution. Taught as abstract principles, they are indistinguishable from those found in any university introductory biology course, and students in their later life are likely to forget the connection between such principles and the reality of their daily existence. But consider how these principles relate to the human condition, and we suddenly see that we and our families are part of this biology:

1. We begin our biological existence as a fertilized egg. But fertility cannot be taken for granted; 20 per cent of all married couples fail in their attempts to achieve a pregnancy for a full year. Sooner or later half of these infertile couples will achieve a pregnancy, but 10 per cent of all marriages will remain sterile.
2. If the fertilized egg begins to develop and an implementation occurs, we expect, some nine months later, to be parents. But one fifth of all pregnant women experience a spontaneous abortion. Nearly 40 per cent of these aborted fetuses contain abnormal chromosome numbers.

3. Even if the fetus does make it to delivery, there is a 5 per cent chance that the baby will have a serious birth defect requiring major medical attention.
4. Some 30 per cent of all pediatric admissions to our municipal hospitals involve genetic disorders and birth defects.
5. The divorce and separation rate of parents who have a child with a serious and long-lasting birth defect or genetic disorder (for example, spina bifida, muscular dystrophy, cystic fibrosis) exceeds 75 per cent.
6. About 20 per cent of adults will die ten years or more before their mean life expectancy because they harbor a higher than average genetic load, which they received at fertilization.

Note that to understand why things go wrong the student needs to know the normal processes by which sperm and eggs are formed. This includes the processes of mitosis, meiosis, and fertilization. It requires a knowledge of nondisjunction and of embryogenesis. To understand birth defects the student needs to know Mendelism, X-linked inheritance, and polygenic inheritance. These, in turn, have to be related to meiosis. But when all this is learned in the context of the student's life and related to the experiences of friends and relatives, the scientific terminology becomes a way of grasping the causes of those age-old human tragedies.

The principles are reinforced in new contexts. Cell division is given new meaning when it is followed after radiation breaks a chromosome. Understanding the cycle of abnormally fused chromosomes and how this prevents normal cell division, eventually killing the dividing cell, provides the basis for understanding radiation stickness and rendering the victims of Hiroshima and Nagasaki as victims of a chromosomal breakage-fusion-bridge cycle. This historical reality and the threat of atomic warfare are thus woven into biology through a simple principle first discovered in corn in the 1930s.

It is precisely this relational aspect of teaching that is usually missing in the nonmajors course. We delude ourselves if we simply teach the principles of mitosis and meiosis and consider that our obligations as teachers end there. Far from it! Unless the nonmajor sees mitosis as part of the human condition and learns why that process is essential for an understanding of certain public controversies, then we have forfeited a basic function of democratic society. We must relate our principles to those realms of life in whch they are critical to responsible decision making. How can legislators decide on regulating nuclear industries if they do not know how to distinguish chromosome breakage from gene mutation? How can good judgment develop from an overreactive fear or a naive denial of any risks from low levels of radiation? Do we not, as citizens, need to know the biology that determines our own health? Why then do we present those principles separated from our human experience? If mitosis is presented in an abstract fashion, with illustrations from the sea urchin or onion root tip, then, of course, neither the nonmajor nor the professional who emerges from our courses will have the vaguest idea of what genetics and biology have to do with human life.

I list below a roster of further topics that lend themselves to the nonmajors course. Not only do they demand the courage to present controversial issues in class, they also demand skill in relating them to the principles of biology and to those biological facts best suited to clarifying and possibly resolving controversies about them. In some debates on these issues, the biology is ignored; in others it is misused. The function of the scholar-teacher in teaching biology to nonmajors is one of clarification—helping students see what biological principles are actually involved, what we really do and do not know, and how the values of contending groups are applied to different aspects of these principles. These dozen topics are only a sample of the current issues related to biology. It would require a textbook to present an analysis of even these twelve issues, and, unfortunately, no such text presently exists for those who wish to teach a biology of the human condition.

Population. The Malthusian doctrine, according to which population growth tends to outstrip the food supply, has been invoked as an argument for population control. But people have values and a technology that affect both sides of the Malthusian equation: reproductive rates and food resources. Is it valid, then, to apply an animal model to humans? Students should be exposed to the values of those advocating zero population growth (ZPG), those advocating no artificial birth control, and those who believe that the problem is self-correcting without misery and catastrophe. Note that evolutionary theory, population ecology, and comparative, reproductive biology are involved in this issue.

Birth Control: There are several reasons why people elect birth control. They may want a small family; they may wish to avoid transmitting hereditary defects; they may be protecting the health of the woman; or they may be concerned about economic, social, or political factors that would influence their ability to be effective parents. The biology involved in this question includes spermatogenesis, oogenesis, fertilization, implantation, hormonal regulation of gametogenesis, anatomy of the reproductive system, and the physiology of spermicides (are they mutagenic? do they break chromosomes?).

Prenatal Diagnosis: Amniocentesis is a diagnostic procedure that can reveal the existence of certain genetic and chromosomal defects in the 14- to 16-week-old fetus. It is used by women who are at risk for birth defects. Involved in the biology of this issue are genetic laws (Mendelian ratios), chromosome karyotyping and banding, and biochemical processes (enzyme assays; how mutant genes work). The election of the procedure involves human values: Should a parent have the right to request a termination of pregnancy for a severely malformed or disordered fetus? Is it psychologically sound for a parent to know in advance that a child will have a birth defect, whether that parent elects to terminate the pregnancy or not? In any such discussion it is important to know the status of the nervous system in the 20- to 24-week-old fetus and also how we relate actual and potential capacity for human functions.

Sexuality: Humans actually have seven sexes: genetic, chromosomal, gonadal, internal genital, external genital, secondary, and psychological. When these come together, a normal male or female exists. But gene mutations, chromosomal defects, hormone therapy during pregnancy, tumors of the pregnant mother or individual, and behavioral models can all alter that congruence. Pseudohermaphroditism, homosexuality, and transvestism are various departures from the anatomical or psychologically traditional identifications of sex gender and function. Our values enter into this when we define what is normal and when we assign social functions (intelligence, talent, occupation, behavior) to sexual gender. Much needed is a clarification of what we know to be a consequence of our chromosomal composition and what we infer, by analogy or by tradition, to be typically male or female traits. Note that the biology includes developmental biology (differentiation of the gonads, wolffian ducts, mullerian ducts, and so on) as well as physiology and genetics.

Carcinogenesis: Why are cancer frequencies ethnically and geographically so variable? Cancers may be induced by habits of food preparation, tobacco smoking, radiation exposure, chemical pollutants from industry, and a variety of additives to our foods. To understand the nature of cancer, we need to know the biology of the cancer cell, the mutational and viral theories of cancer, lysogenic viral life cycles, regulatory genetics, and the developmental differences between cancer cells and normal tissues. To apply this knowledge to social concerns, we need to know the history and economics of industrial waste disposal and the tobacco industry, and the defined role and limitations of the Food and Drug Administration. We also need to know the dietary habits of different societies (for example, the amount of animal fats in the diet; whether food is boiled, fried, or broiled; the temperature of foods when swallowed; the spices and additives used in preparing, storing, or flavoring foods; and so on).

Radiation Hazards: Medicine, industry, and the military are the major sources of radiation hazards. To understand the debates (fallout, nuclear reactor construction, test ban treaties, lead shielding for routine dental and medical examinations) several aspects must be discussed. The distinction must be made between chromosome breakage (which kills dividing cells) and gene mutations, both of which are radiation-induced. Students must learn the breakage-fusion-bridge cycle and its relation to radiation sickness. This includes knowledge of which tissues divide in the adult. It also involves analysis of the risk-benefit assessments by those on both sides of the debate—those focusing on individual risk (which is usually insignificant) and those emphasizing the absolute number affected in a population (which may involve thousands of anonymous victims). Additionally, aspects like biological amplification of trace elements must be understood for participation in debate or arriving at a position.

Mutagenesis: Chemical agents as well as radiation result in gene mutations. Students should learn how chemicals alter purines and pyrimidines. They should identify those products known to be mutagens that are used in households or major industries (for example, formaldehyde, nitrous acid, nitrosoamine, hydrogen peroxide, alkylating agents, and so on). Somatic and germinal mutation should be distinguished. Gene function after mutation can also be discussed (why losses of function are more apt to occur than the very rare changes to new or improved functions).

Racism: Surprisingly, few biology texts cover the genetics and biology of human skin color inheritance. There are several models that give reasonably good analyses of the various miscegenations between whites and blacks and their descendants. Mendel's principle of independent assortment, quantitative inheritance, and the distinctions between dominance, codominance, and intermediate inheritance are applicable. So, too, are the adaptive theories of skin color (for example, the vitamin D theory, protective coloration, ultraviolet filtration and skin cancer, body heat loss, and so on), all of which invoke biological principles. The values involved in racism include notions of inherent superiority, spurious assumptions about the segregation of traits from miscegenation hybrids, and various religious and social attitudes about human potentials and functions.

The IQ Controversy: The measurement of human talent and mental potential for abstract, verbal, or mathematical skills is difficult and flawed with cultural bias. To understand the biology, students need to know the genetics of polygenic and multifactorial traits, the biology of one-egg twins (including the consequences of the MZ fetal-diffusion syndrome on IQ), the environmental and biological factors of mental retardation, and the various models of genius and eminence. The value issues include class prejudice, racism, xenophobia, various types of elitism, and the relation between IQ scores and educational practice.

Eugenics: If gene mutation occurs spontaneously and represents the raw material for evolutionary change, what are its consequences in human populations living in affluent societies where natural selective forces (malnutrition, disease, environmental hazards) are inhibited? Some geneticists claim that an incresing quantity of mutations will gradually occur, resulting in more medical problems for each family. Others claim that other forms of selection (especially assortative mating) will compensate. Those who express concern about the greater number of mutations in the human population often suggest compensatory selection to minimize the number of children born with this risk. Besides the various values (and *Brave New World* fears) students must know the frequency and nature of spontaneous mutation and its consequences in populations (Hardy-Weinberg law, impairment, detrimental genes, and so on) to assess these viewpoints.

Human Aggression: sociobiologists argue that mammals have innate aggressive instincts, which are released by ritualized displays, fighting, or snarling. Such aggression is associated with sexual selection and territoriality. Some biologists extend these animal models to humans. The genetics of behavior is still at an early stage of scientific development. Few Mendelian traits are behavioral, and little is known about the distinction between polygenic and environmental components of such traits. Even less is known about their heritability in humans. Yet many popular books advocate a genetic determinism of behavior, which would have far-reaching implications for criminal justice, warfare, housing, and social justice. Both animal behavior and the genetic analysis of quantitative traits are important for evaluating this controversy.

Germ Warfare: It is now possible to create microbes that are resistant to most antibiotics and novel microbes that combine rapid spread with pathogenicity. If the genes for the toxic effects of diphtheria were inserted deliberately into a bacterium that makes cheese or into a virus that makes cold sores, serious public health problems would result. The techniques of recombinant DNA and many other molecular approaches to miscrobial and cell biology might be discussed. Such social values as those of terrorists could be included in the discussion to how abuses of biology can be prevented. Also needed are realistic appraisals of microbial functions brought about without planning (alleged "superbugs" and other runaway epidemics from naive accidents). Much sensationalism exists, along with complacency among scientists who believe that research per se justifies any risks of abuse.

I have not included in this list the more obvious and much discussed ecological aspects of pollution (DDT, other pesticides, polluted streams and lakes, smog, automobile emissions, industrial smoke) because these have been well documented and brought to public attention. Our internal biology and the hazards of the human condition just identified have not received such public attention, and for this reason I have listed these twelve areas of public debate for those who might wish to construct a biology course that is not limited to ecology.

Students who listen to these controversial topics—racism, the IQ controversy, carcinogenesis from environmental pollutants and additives, mutagensis from radiation and chemicals, eugenics, human sexuality, birth defects and prenatal diagnosis, elective abortion, contraception, human evolution, cloning, and recombinant DNA—soon learn that they cannot escape making decisions on incomplete knowledge. They learn that science does not know all the answers, yet what it does know is an important component for arriving at their own values and decisions.

Concerns of Different Students: Many of the principles of biology developed in this biology course are useful in debating national and international issues. Of course, the response to these issues will reflect the student's age and experience. The chapters in Part One of this volume devote considerable attention to intellectual development, moral judgment, and the life cycle. In all likelihood, younger students (17 to 22 years old) will be particularly interested in population, birth control, prenatal diagnosis, sexuality, and mutagenesis, especially as they approach their personal life decisions to marry and raise a family. Students in middle and late adulthood will be more interested in the problems of carcinogenesis, racism, and radiation hazards. Although their emphases will vary, the concerns of both younger and older students will benefit from the development of humanitarian concern, described by White.

Younger students are more likely to exhibit dualistic thinking and come up with dramatic or radical approaches to solving problems. Older students are most likely to hold opinions that have been shaped by the press, television, and community standards. In both these constituencies, however, there will be conscientious and independent thinkers who will approach these controversies in constructive ways. The reader of the chapters by Weathersby, Perry, and Gilligan will not be surprised to find, in both the essays of a large lecture class and in smaller discussion groups, such differing viewpoints. These will reflect not only genuine beliefs but also developmental stages, with their characteristic moral, ethical, and cognitive strengths and weaknesses.

The application of biological principles to issues of personal and public concern should stimulate the kinds of intellectual development described by Schaie and Parr, turning students from memorization of facts to the integrative use of them in their own living concerns. An example from my own acquaintance was a student at UCLA who had been a theater arts major before he enlisted in the Peace Corps. He was sent to the rural Phillipines to teach English. after a few weeks he complained to his supervisor, "How can I teach English literature to my students when they're dying?" He was taken out of the classroom and sent to a field hospital to learn parasitology. When the student returned to college, his career goals had changed: He wanted to learn tropical medicine so he could help the underdeveloped countries overcome their handicaps of malnutrition, inadequate public health services, and ignorance about waste disposal.

PRESENTATION OF BIOLOGY TO NONMAJORS

It would be an error, I believe, to predicate the teaching of biology to nonmajors on an individualized or even small-group instruction model. Rather, I feel confident that most institutions, and particularly the large state universities and colleges, will require large lecture classes of several hundred students to accommodate the enrollments in lower-division introductory biology courses. The formal lecture has been a college institution for more than 800 years, and it is unlikely to be replaced entirely by tutorials, field projects, independent study, audiovisual self-study, or other modes of instruction. The reason is simple fiscal reality: beginning courses usually enroll the largest number of students, can be taught economically in a large lecture room, and often have the lowest ratio of support in the department's allocation of funds for teaching. The irony, of course, is that the most heterogeneous students, in terms of background and skills, and those at a stage of intellectual development at which they are most in need of individual attention, are likely to experience personal neglect, ineffective teaching, compartmentalized content, and Spartan austerity for much of their first two years of college.

Economical, low-budget lecture courses are often unpopular and are properly criticized by students because they are poorly taught. These is no intrinsic reason, however, why they should be so ineffective in most universities. They can be revitalized, and technology is not the answer. Ideally, the large lecture should be supplemented with special review sessions, a place for optional audio-tutorial cassettes and film loops, and Xerox facilities for copying the instructor's lecture notes. Such aids would not replace a lecture format because a good lecture course serves many purposes that audio-tutorial programs cannot. Lectures can be intellectually exciting and communicate both enthusiasm and the model of a scholarly mind at work. They can provide spontaneity and immediacy through references to current events or sudden flashes of wit or inspiration. They can tie together many ideas and topics that might not come together for students lacking the necessary experience, critical judgment, or mastery of the subject. And they permit hundreds of students to be influenced by the scholar-teacher's values.

Problems must be overcome, however, in large lecture classes—for majors as well as nonmajors. Contrary to general academic belief, majors are not necessarily self-paced and motivated scholars. They are undergraduates, not fantasized images of ourselves as neophyte graduate students. They have considerable difficulty with abstract problem solving and relational thinking. They tend to be more competitive and aggressive than nonmajors and will take up more time arguing over examinations and final grades. They may even panic and resort to theft and vandalism of library reserve materials if they do not have adequate opportunity to learn effectively in class or through properly supervised and helpful supplementary programs of audio-tutorial or other materials.

From every perspective, whether in the actual delivery of lectures or in the administration of courses, large classes are demanding of time, talent, and commitment. Unless department heads, deans, provosts, and college presidents recognize these special needs, both the student and the reputation of the school are likely to suffer. Even some of my faculty colleagues believe that a large class consists of 50 students or that there is little difference in the preparation required for a class of 50 or 500 students. They are wrong.

Consider this analogy: Imagine that you are in a concert hall and a violin soloist comes out with an armful of music, sets up the stand, and announces. "Today, I'll try to cover some Romantic music, starting with Brahms, and if time permits, we'll end the concert with mendelssohn." After this announcement, the violinist selects some music and begins to play, backtracking if an error is made, pausing to turn the pages, and occasionally sounding as if the passages were stitched together rather than part of a continuum. The result would be an outrage. You paid for excellence, mastery, control, preparation, and the unique excitement that a skilled performer can convey to a receptive audience. Instead you got a typical lecture—casual, disorganized, indifferently presented, and lacking in the fire which can ignite receptive minds.

In a room of 15 to 30 or even 50 students, that erratic, informal, somewhat sloppy presentation need not be disturbing. It might even be effective if the teacher knows how to provoke questions and discussions in class. There is an intimacy between teacher and student that is not even disturbed by the invisible line that separates the students' seats from the instructor's desk. But in an auditorium with 500 seats, most of them occupied, that intimacy disappears and a new psychological expectation arises—the teacher is now a performer and the class is an audience. Casual, unrehearsed lecturing will not do in this situation. Rather, the students expect a highly organized, well-delivered, and well-prepared lecture. When they do not get this, they feel cheated.

To be effective in a large class, the instructor must convey a mastery of subject matter, a near flawless delivery in a voice that projects throughout the auditorium, an intensity and enthusiasm that reflect a love for learning, and those special skills that are necessary for reaching large numbers of people. The teacher must be alert to the sounds in the room. Any rustling or murmuring indicates the need for a change of pace or a repetition. But the teacher cannot repeat without using a new context or some of the class will be bored because they did grasp the concept. Thus, when I reach mitosis, I give the chromosomal events first. I repeat the process by showing these events in the entire cell. Then I repeat them a third time by following a broken chromosome in its cycle leading to cell death. The effective teacher learns to organize a lecture as a story. It has a beginning that provides an overview of what the lecture will discuss. It uses extensive relational thinking to bring in history, controversy, the human condition, or current events to enrich the meaning of the subject. It concludes with a summary of the major points and implications of the principles discussed. Throughout the lecture the teacher must be guided by the sounds of silence. Are the students stunned by too complex a presentation, or are they on the edges of their seats with anticipation? The former response is often accompanied by a bewildered look and the movement of heads to a neighbors' notebooks; the communion of an enraptured audience is immediately apparent from the presence of a thousand eyes looking at the teacher.

Achieving mastery of subject matter is easier than achieving mastery of presentation. A scholar may be a master of a body of knowledge but still be unable to share the joy of knowledge with an audience. Stage fright, inexperience, an untrained voice, lack of eye contact, irritating mannerisms, insecurity, and a failure to explore the broader implications of the subject will all defeat the efforts of the ineffective teacher. When students express their boredom or confusion, such a teacher may blame the students' intellectual shortcomings for their failure to grasp the ideas presented.

Lecturing is only part of the organization of a large course. There are problems of testing, grading, and, most important, providing an opportunity for students to discuss the material they are trying to learn. Thus, the large lecture course needs a budget adequate for its functions. It should include provision for a course coordinator, a permanent employee at the B.A. level, who can carry out most of the administrative functions (typing, mimeographing, Xeroxing, filing, recording grades, arranging schedules for discussion sections, calling students or teaching assistants, assigning tutors, scheduling audio-tutorial sessions, and so on). And it should include a modest investment in film loops and supplementary audio-tutorial equipment. If students' study habits or writing skills are to be diagnosed effectively, a special staff should be provided for this purpose.

Over the years I have worked out solutions to some of these problems. First, I recognized that it is both unfair and undesirable to rely on graduate teaching assistants for such a course. There are too many majors courses that have higher priority for these teaching assistants. Furthermore, many graduate students emulate their sponsors' negative attitudes toward the teaching of lower-division courses. So instead, I designed an undergraduate course in college teaching. Students receive credit for being an undergraduate teaching assistant. They apply for the course and look upon their selection as an honor. They are familiar with the students, the instructor, and the institutional facilities. I spend one hour a week with them evaluating teaching by having them prepare ten-minute lectures. They deliver these talks and learn eye contact, blackboard presentation, pacing, elimination of intrusive mannerisms, voice projection, and how to tie points together. By criticizing each other, they learn how to improve their own habits as a student as well as a teaching assistant.

The undergraduate teaching assistants have a one-hour discussion section with twenty or fewer students. They tutor those who receive D or F on the first examination, and they go over the students' notebooks to correct error is. They then invite the students to sit with them to observe an actual model of note-taking. The teaching assistants also grade homework or examination questions. To make sure the teaching assistants are grading properly, I alphabetize the examinations after a test and thus know which teaching assistant is grading any given student. I then provide the students with the same answer keys used by the teaching assistants, and if there is a request for a regarding the student fills out a mimeographed form attached to the examination. I do all such regarding and note what errors the teaching assistant is making. I then call in the teaching assistant and discuss effective ways to improve grading (for example, more marginalia on the students' essays or more careful reading of the students' factual statements). The goal, in working with teaching assistants, is not to exploit cheap labor but to help these students develop effective teaching skills, whether good discussion habits, effective tutoring, accurate and informative grading, or lecturing. Also, the student learns to effectively marshal the facts and arguments in a written request for a regrade. Whether the regrade is granted or not, the student benefits because the error (by the teaching assistant or the student) will be made as clear as possible. My major point in introducing undergraduate teaching assistants to teaching is quite specific: Every function of a course should, as much as possible, be a learning process for the persons participating in it.

Having given both essay examinations and computer-graded examinations in large courses, I have been able to analyze the problems students have in minimizing the gap between what they know and what they actually answer on the test. The computer-graded examinations permit an item analysis that ranks the questions according to their difficulty and shows how the upper, middle, and lower thirds of the class fared on each item. For a majors course in genetics (sophomore-junior level) given to 400 students, I found that almost all students do well on memory questions but about half of the students have difficulty with problem solving or relational thinking (drawing implications or applications from a principle, such as mitosis, Mendelism, or X-linked inheritance). When I have held review sessions or talked with students during office hours, I have learned that students are not given sufficient instruction in problem-solving skills. Most of the students have been called upon to use these skills only in large classes. If they do not grasp the skills, they have few resources available to improve their understanding.

Part of the students' difficulty is developmental and part is just a result of neglect. According to Piagetian learning theory, the capacity for abstract reasoning develops in adolescence. Those students who have not yet developed a facility for problem solving are apt to have difficulties, particularly in their lower-division courses. Regrettably, few colleges and universities attempt to identify those students in need of special instruction to remedy this weakness. Since the students in a biology major's genetics class are a self-selected group of motivated students (mostly pre-med students concerned about their grades), the fact that half of them are in need of such instruction indicates that they are being neglected. It is, I believe, more likely that their interest in the sciences reflects a potential for abstract work that suffers from neglect than that they lack this potential and are in the wrong field. If Piagetian analysis is essentially valid, that abstract skill will be attained by most of them by their senior year.

The nonmajors course, however, most likely has a much higher percentage of students who will be lost if problem-solving skills are demanded to them—for example, mapping genes, computing risk ratios for genetic disorders, or applying the genetic code. For this reason, it is important, in designing the introductory courses, to distinguish between a nonmajors learning environment and that of the majors. The nonmajors would clearly suffer in a course that attempts to reach both majors and nonmajors or that places a heavy emphasis on problem-solving activities.

STAFFING THE INTRODUCTORY COURSE

Staffing the large introductory course is a major problem, which many universities have handled ineffectively. Preferably, the instructor should be tenured because both experience and a major commitment of time are needed for a successful course. One's obligations do not end with lecturing. In a large class there are always special problems that need attention. In a class of 400 to 600 students there are bound to be three or four cases of mononucleosis, a student in a wheelchair, a blind student, two or three foreign students with less than perfect facility for writing essay questions, two or three students with deaths in the family, several instances of missed classes or examinations involving car trouble (if commuters form a significant segment of the student body), and a variety of other unusual situations (for example, suicide attempts, arrests for drug dealing, and students with severe emotional crises) that prevent them from attending lectures or taking an examination. In a class of 30 or 40 students such events are rare and do not require a major amount of time for make-up examinations, assigning tutors, rescheduling appointments, or locating resource persons to help the troubled student. Also, in a large class there will be more A students requesting letters of recommendation for various professional schools.

The problems of examinations are also multiplied for the large class. Alternate seating is impossible in a large lecture room filled to capacity (and that may be the only large room on campus). Thus, duplicate examinations, color coded or numbered, must be used to prevent cheating, and this involves a considerable amount of time for typing and mimeographing. It is much easier for the determined cheater to succeed in such a situation than in a small class where all the students are known by the teacher. This increases the time and energy devoted to prevention of such abuses.

All these activities could easily overwhelm and discourage a young faculty member. But if the course is assigned to an older faculty member who has no real interest in it, many of these factors will be ignored or poorly handled, either because teaching is not that person's forte or because that instructor foresees no personal reward from the job. If effective teaching in such courses has little influence on merit raises, colleague recognition, or further promotion, the person taking on that assignment is not likely to do a good job with it.

What is needed for the reform of introductory courses is an acceptance of the model of the scholar-teacher. Virtually all universities respect the scholar. This has been the prevailing model since Daniel Coit Gilman set up Johns Hopkins University as a graduate, Ph.D.-granting institution over a hundred years ago. But the scholar-teacher is virtually unknown. Instead, a false dichotomy exists: Scholars are intrinsically valuable because they create new knowledge, and teachers are useful to a university only if they remain productive in the creation of new knowledge. The scholar-teacher restores a neglected aspect of Gilman's credo. He sought not only an institution where scholars generated new knowledge but also the dissemination of that knowledge. That transmission has been too narrowly interpreted as technical publications in journals or monographs.

The scholar-teacher publishes reviews, innovative textbooks, and trade book popularizations. The books and essays of T. H. Huxley, Julian Huxley, and such recent scholars as Stephen Gould (1977) and Carl Sagan (1977) are examples of the type of work that scholar-teachers can produce. All these essayists have made their primary contributions not through laboratory research and highly technical journals but through their outstanding ability to think relationally and make apparent to their colleagues and the lay reader the implications of new knowledge. The scholar-teachers know research well but elect not to make it their primary academic activity. They are generalists, not dilettantes, who find pleasure in viewing facts from many perspectives and communicating the excitement of new ideas to numerous audiences, both skilled and uninformed.

If scholar-teachers are as valuable to a university as research scholars, colleges and universities should try to recruit them. They may be identified through carefully screened programs, such as the E. Harris Harbison awards of the Danforth Foundation or the Distinguished Teaching Professorships of the New York State University System. Most universities have faculty-student committees (often from the Academic Senate) that make annual awards for gifted or distinguished teaching.

Annual awards for teaching, however, are not as effective as lifelong recognition. Productive research scholars receive merit raises and promotions, not annual awards. If high-quality teaching is to be encouraged, it must be rewarded by both promotion and merit raises. Scholar-teachers also need grant agency funds for using their summers productively, either for writing or research. Various federal agencies—National Institutes of Health, National Science Foundation (NSF) and others—can provide leadership by mandating a special subvention fund for those universities receiving research grants. The money would be earmarked for the development of improved undergraduate courses and the provision of summer salaries for scholar-teachers. Increased funding to the Fund for the Improvement of Postsecondary Education (FIPSE) would also help scholar-teachers who attempt to make their contributions known to a wider audience.

A major contribution to educational reform could be accomplished by bringing together scholar-teachers at an annual meeting so that they could exchange ideas, techniques, and resources. Funding for such a meeting might be obtained from FIPSE and the NSF, both of which are concerned with science education.

CONCLUSION

Effective undergraduate teaching offers many benefits to a college or university. It stimulates intellect and creates respect for rational approaches to the social applications of knowledge. It makes students aware that knowledge does not exist independently of human values, that the misapplication or failure to apply new knowledge will have serious effects on human life. The well-taught courses attract future majors to the field. They also help students appreciate the relationships between apparently unrelated areas (the arts, sciences, humanities).

The effective teacher also serves those whose work is translated from the technical journals to the working language of the undergraduate. We publish not just for our fellow professionals but for a wider audience because most new knowledge has implications for other areas. Scholar-teachers, who base their lectures and courses on a critical survey of journal articles and reviews, must keep up to date on developments in their own fields and outside them. In all the years that I have taught, I have never used the same set of lecture notes twice. I rewrite an outline for each lecture, adding new material and discarding older, less useful information.

The well-taught course attracts more students. This can be valuable to those departments whose budgets are based on the number of students enrolled in the department's courses. Often the teacher of that course generates additional faculty positions, and thus a department can expand its upper-division and graduate offerings by investing in a first-rate teacher for its introductory course.

The university benefits, too. Students tell their friends and relatives about their pleasures and frustrations with their school experiences. If the quality of instruction is excellent, the brighter students in secondary schools will want to apply. If they hear that the school ignores undergraduates or that its courses are poorly taught, those students in a position to choose will elect to go elsewhere.

Finally, the reforms suggested here for the nonmajors biology course are consistent with the aims of liberal arts education. We want our students to mature intellectually, but we also want them to develop moral and ethical judgment, humanitarian concern, and responsible citizenship. By addressing the principles of biology to the human condition, in a course such as that described in this chapter, we can help achieve these academic and social goals.